Trials of the Earth
The Autobiography of Mary Hamilton

Mary Hamilton, circa 1932

TRIALS OF THE EARTH

THE AUTOBIOGRAPHY OF MARY HAMILTON

Edited by Helen Dick Davis

With a foreword by Ellen Douglas

University Press of Mississippi
Jackson and London

Helen Dick Davis and her family are most grateful to the following people for their generous and valuable assistance in making this publication possible: Ms. JoAnne Prichard, senior editor, University Press of Mississippi, for her swift, decisive action and keen perceptions in guiding us and the manuscript through the publication process; Dr. and Mrs. Taylor Littleton, Dr. and Mrs. Ward Allen, Mrs. Shailah Jones, Mr. and Mrs. Richard Millman, Drs. Fred and Sara Hudson, Mrs. Barbara Beal, and Dr. and Mrs. Cliff Webber for their encouragement, patience, and useful advice.

Maps drawn by Nicholas D. Davis

96 95 94 93 4 3 2 1

The paper in this book meets the guidelines for permanence and durability of the Committee on Production Guidelines for Book Longevity of the Council on Library Resources.

Library of Congress Cataloging-in-Publication Data

Hamilton, Mary, b. 1866.
  Trials of the earth / by Mary Hamilton ; edited by Helen Dick
Davis.
    p.   cm.
    ISBN 0-87805-579-7 (alk. paper).—ISBN 0-87805-671-8 (pbk.: alk. paper)
    1. Hamilton, Mary, b. 1866. 2. Pioneers—Mississippi—Delta
(Region)—Biography.   3. Women pioneers—Mississippi—Delta
(Region)—Biography.   4. Mississippi Delta (Miss. : Region)—
Biography.   I. Davis, Helen Dick.   II. Title.
F347.M6H36   1992
976.2'4061'092—dc20
[B]   92-17772
                                                            CIP

British Library Cataloging-in-Publication data available

To my husband's people
  whoever they are,
    and wherever they may be

Contents

Foreword

"As we had the only livable house in town, we took a few boarders," Mary Hamilton writes, plunging into the story of her life. Her father has died of pneumonia, leaving her mother and six children stranded in a hamlet at the end of the Kansas City and Memphis Railroad, then just building. The year is 1884. At seventeen, while her mother and two older brothers worked at a sawmill, Mary ran the boardinghouse, did all the cooking, and looked after her three younger siblings.

This opening account is already revealing. Mary Hamilton is an extraordinary woman, an indefatigable worker, courageous, articulate, and self-confident: undauntable. Telling this tale of her life forty-eight years later, she remembers vividly that long-ago time and recreates it for us. From the beginning she takes for granted a life of work so demanding and arduous that a twentieth-century American woman can scarcely give it credence, a life that, as the years pass, makes that early adventure ("taking a few boarders") seem like child's play. Sometimes in the timber camps where she later lives with her husband and children, she runs a boardinghouse for eighty or a hundred or more men. In 1887, married now and pregnant with her first child, she writes, "About that time the river or log drivers had come down from Michigan to help get all logs that had been cut during the winter into the river. That meant we had 115 men at the boardinghouse. . . . I have been laughed at for saying we used a barrel of flour a day; but you bake 115 loaves of bread a day, biscuits or flapjacks for breakfast, at least thirty pies for dinner, and always teacakes for supper . . . "

Mary's record of her life is overwhelming in its detailed day-by-day account of a world undescribed, so far as I know, by anyone else. We

have hundreds of slave narratives, both those recorded by the aboli-
tionists and those recorded in the thirties by the WPA. We have
accounts of Reconstruction from southern and northern points of
view. We have journals written by upperclass educated white southerners, male and female, and by visitors to the South. We have vol-
umes of letters. But I know of no account of life in the timber camps
and on small isolated farms before and after the turn of the century,
written by a white woman who lived and worked and raised her family
in the camps and on the farms during the period when the huge tracts
of virgin forest in the American South were being clear cut and the
clear-cut land was just beginning to be farmed.

The story of how Mary Hamilton first decided to write down all she
remembered of her eventful life is a saga in itself. You will read first the
account by Helen Davis of her friendship with Mary Hamilton and of
how the project began in 1931; and then of the rediscovery of the
manuscript in 1991; and finally, as addenda, excerpts from Helen
Davis's journal and from Mary Hamilton's account of her childhood. It
is indeed a miracle that all this rich material has survived.

When Mary and her husband Frank came into the area east of the
Sunflower River in 1897, she writes, "I think I was the very first white
woman to cross Sunflower River coming into this country to live, and
I know I am the first white woman that ever came through what is
now Parchman [eventual site of the Mississippi State Penitentiary],
when we were guided [to the timber cutters' camp deep in the virgin
forest] by the bits of paper Frank dropped along the dim blazed road
through it."

Her life was one not only of hard work and hardship, but of deep
human joy and sorrow. Four of the nine children born to her died and
she writes eloquently of their lives and deaths. She writes of flood and
fire and the deaths of dear friends and good neighbors, of drunkenness
and treachery and the loss of land, of starting over again and again and
yet again. And everything rings with a wonderful resourceful common
sense and resilience and, yes, joy.

Mary Hamilton was necessarily embedded in the time and culture of
the deep South during the years between 1884 and the time of writing
this narrative in 1932. It follows almost inevitably that she did not
question the stereotypical attitudes of white people of the time toward
black people. For us, in the 1990s, there is little to say other than,

"Well, that was the time she lived in." I think, though, of *All God's Dangers,* the autobiography of that extraordinary black man, Nate Shaw, which is comparable in power and authentic detail to Mary Hamilton's story. For Nate, born the year Mary married, the personality and character and behavior of white people were matters of life and death. His fate depended every day on the impulses of white people and on his judgment of their characters and motives. He gives the reader a lively account of all sorts of individuals, good, bad and mixed. To Mary, on the other hand, it is almost as if blacks don't exist as individuals. She gives occasional lip service to white southern attitudes, yes, but in her life she never lived on the labor of blacks. She worked a great deal harder than Nate (as he says himself) would ever have allowed his wife to work, and lived exposed to dangers as great as any he ever faced. In the timber camps, from her own record, from what she doesn't say as well as what she says, you feel that individual blacks—laborers and their women—were like vague, sometimes threatening shadows at the edges of her life. Only occasionally does she give a name to a black—a midwife who helped her through one birth, an old black man with a recalcitrant mule whom she ferried across the Sunflower. (Yes, at one point, along with everything else she did, she ran a ferry.) There is no hint anywhere in these pages of the connections, bathed by most white writers in a sentimental light, with faithful hostlers and cooks and housekeepers and pickaninny playmates. Her own children at five and six and seven were nurses to their younger siblings. And she, of course, was the cook and the seamstress and the housekeeper and the gardener and the hoe hand. She was even known to take one end of a crosscut saw and help cut down a leaning tree that threatened the family tent.

Revealing, too, is her attitude toward raising her children. There was no time in this brutal world for coddling. Time for love, yes, for respect for a child's individuality, for teaching, but not for coddling. I am reminded of something I read once about the plains Indians, whose children were allowed from the earliest age to tumble freely around the unshielded fires and to play with knives and arrows and most of whom were scarred from childhood cuts and burns. They learned to respect fire and to handle tools and weapons—or they died. Of Mary's children, Nina at six is teaching and caring for Frank and Leslie. When there is hoeing and chopping to be done, all the children share in the work. All, male and female, are taught to shoot by the time they are six. Frank at eight is already "almost as good a shot as a man" and is hunting for the family larder. Of his narrow escape from a wild pig she writes, "Some would think we were wrong for letting [the children] run such risks, be in so much danger, but we couldn't see it that way; we thought it not half as dangerous as running around over the country with bad companions, getting into trouble they couldn't get out of by climbing a tree."

Just as she is unquestioning about the place of black people in the world, Mary is unquestioning about her own role as a woman. Again and again, implicitly or explicitly, she takes for granted that her husband's word is law, that her role is to support him without reservation, to support him with all she is and has and can do. "I knelt down by my dead baby," she writes, "and prayed as I had never prayed before for strength to take up my life and my duty to Frank, to be cheerful and kind, stand by him through all trouble." And for all his refusals to confide in her about his mysterious past, for all his dictatorial ways, his trouble with alcohol, his business blunders, one feels finally that if anyone in that difficult and desperate world deserves a good wife and loving children, Frank Hamilton, hard working, faithful, and devoted, is that man.

One of the delights of this book is Mary Hamilton's evocation of the natural world she lives in—of the power of the river and of the wild lonely forests, still resounding with panther screams and the howls of wolves. It seems almost a sin to paraphrase, when her own words serve so well. "We went from Gunnison [to Concordia Island] in a two-horse buggy," she writes. "Frank and Jim on horseback. We drove down the Mississippi River levee about a mile, then turned off the levee into the thickest timber I had ever seen. Oak, gum, ash, hackberry, and poplar stood so thick, with no underbrush, only big blue cane growing rank and tall, almost to the limbs of the trees. . . . When we came out on the Mississippi River, the ground was sandy, but it was black sand, and the woods were thinner; there were fewer trees but larger—big old cottonwoods and sycamores that seemed to me when I looked up like their tops were lost in the sky. . . . The soft black sand was almost hub deep."

One last quote I can't resist: In 1932 she writes, "I have some of my [silver] knives and forks yet [from a time of prosperity], and it does me good to look at them these lean Christmas times and think of the past. When I sit down to write, old memories guide my hand. I am living again. I don't have to think of my husband and Nina and Oswald and almost all of our old neighbors as dead, me old and crippled, but as I lived life then, day by day, young and full of life and fun, trying to make our own home pleasant and home for dozens, yes, hundreds, of men. To me they will all live as long as I do, laughing and joking, sympathizing with each other and us, in sickness and trouble, and working, toiling to blaze a way. . . ."

And not only to Mary Hamilton, long dead now, but to all of us fortunate enough to read her story, they live again.

ELLEN DOUGLAS

Preface

by Helen Dick Davis

I first saw Mary Hamilton on a raw November day. The wheels of our
Ford had mired down to the running board in the black gumbo mud of
the Mississippi Delta and had been dug out twice in the course of the
four miles that lay between our house and that of my friend Edris. The
third time it stuck we abandoned the car, my husband and I, and
walked the remaining half-mile. Clumping across the wide open hall
that extended the full length of the house, our feet still heavy with
gumbo although we had scraped pounds of it off outside, we opened
the door upon a tiny, hunchbacked, white-haired old lady sitting by
the fire. She was patching some hunting pants and at sight of us
gathered them hastily into her arms, as if to protect them, since she
could not protect herself, from our gaze, which clearly embarrassed
her. She spoke a little breathlessly, getting quickly to her feet.

"You must be Helen. Edie never dreamed you'd get here—it's such a
bad day. I'll go tell her."

And with a step surprisingly strong for one who looked so desper-
ately frail, she swung down the hall towards the kitchen. I knew it was
Edris's mother, but I didn't see her again that day. When I knew her
better and saw her run always at the sight of strangers, I knew she did
it because she is as vain as a girl and is embarrassed by the hump on her
back, caused by a bad fall about fifteen years ago. She is afraid she
doesn't look just right, with the hump and with her soft white hair
that will hang in a fringe around her forehead no matter how many
times a day she combs it. I came to know this about her, because when
spring came and the four miles of gumbo between our house and Edris's
dried out from a bottomless loblolly to a surface so hard you couldn't

drive an axe into it, I saw Mary Hamilton often. She began to talk to me of her life nearly half a century ago in this same Mississippi Delta where we live now, and which then was a wilderness of untouched timber and canebrakes, a jungle of briars and vines and undergrowth.

At first she talked to me only in snatches, half apologetically, as if expecting to be interrupted any minute. I realized she had never before talked of those old days to anyone but her children, to whom the events she described must have been harrowing enough at the time. Hearing the stories retold must be difficult, because her children are all still young enough to dream of a future easier than the past. But to me those memories were more fascinating than any tales I had ever heard, and hearing them firsthand added to the enchantment. I would listen to her, spellbound, for hours.

From the beginning, her life has been one of tragedy, violence, and incredible adventure, although it would be hard to imagine anyone seemingly less fitted for that kind of life than Mary Hamilton. But if Henry James is right, and I am inclined to agree with him, that we carry in our own souls or egos or cores of our beings the germs of every event that happens to us, then Mary Hamilton's essence must be tragedy and courage. For as Stephen Crane once wrote of a Canadian gentleman, "Destiny sets an alarm clock so as to be up early and strew banana peels in front of him. If he trusts a friend he is betrayed; if he starts a journey, he breaks an ankle; if he loves, death comes to her without a smile."

Nevertheless, this is not a book of repining; it is a tale simply told of what one woman has lived through in the Mississippi Delta. I say "lived through" because at times this history reads like a record of the extreme limits of human endurance. One of its most amazing qualities is the writer's own unawareness of this fact. At the very end of the book, when she speaks of dying, she is still able to say, innocently and with no thought of irony, that she will soon be going to a better world "if such can be." The italics are mine. In spite of everything, Mrs. Hamilton has found this world good, and so this is a book of much laughter as well as tragedy. For a picture of courage and a spirit that can know no defeat, I do not know its equal. It was always the dream of a home that carried her through the hardships of pioneering, seemingly unbearable tragedies with her children, and a relationship with her husband that was, to the end, filled with mystery. Yet she remains today, as she has been all her life, homeless. In that sense it is a record of defeat, but only in that sense.

When I began to beg her to write down the account of her life, if only as a record for her children and grandchildren, she did it just to please me. She wrote it piecemeal at first, just scattered experiences, ten or fifteen pages at a time written with pencil on cheap tablet paper: stories of terrible flood waters, cyclones, feuds to the death, escaped Negro convicts. I became zealous about letting a larger audience have a chance to read so unique and interesting a record. When I first made the suggestion, Mrs. Hamilton hesitated. It looked like too big an undertaking. She write a book? Why, she'd never written more than a few letters in her life until she began writing those little sketches for me.

But the following fall she had a severe hemorrhage while visiting at her son's home, and on the first day that she was able to write, I got this letter from her:

Dearest Helen,

This is the first day I have sat up and I am going to write you the very first one, my best friend. I am convinced I am a selfish old lady, and it was a dream I had yesterday morning convinced me.

I dreamed I was in a swamp. The ground was covered with black water and black moss, but no mud. On all sides of me rose lilies, white as snow. They grew on large jet black stems. It was a pretty sight, those big white lilies in such clusters and so close to the path they hung over it till I could see nothing but flowers and the rank black bushes, with just a glimpse of the sky above, bright and full of stars. The path was so narrow I couldn't turn around.

There were two children, yours, Helen, laughing and crowding so close behind me. I began breaking off the flowers—the stems were hollow—and handing them back to the children. I had them loaded down with those great white blossoms. I was tired and wanted to rest, but they kept crowding so close and saying, "More, please, more." At last I came to where the path was closed with a tangle of the same lilies only larger, finer. I spoke for the first time. "You get no more, children. This last is mine." As I spoke I reached for the very finest one for myself. But when I broke it off the ugliest black snake head popped out from the hollow stem, bit at my finger, but just grazed it. I screamed and fell back against little Nick, still holding my own broken lily. He

Mary Hamilton with Nick and Louvica Davis, the children of
Helen Dick Davis, 1933

looked at me with a sweet smile on his face, his arms loaded with those beautiful flowers, and said, "It's all right, Hampleton. You all right." Louvica's arms too were filled with flowers, but she only smiled.

I woke with a start. Was I going to die? Was that snake head that just grazed my finger, Death? I woke Edie, sleeping on the side of my bed to take care of me, and told her I was afraid I was fixing to have a hemorrhage, for you know since the fall that crippled me I have so many of them. She jumped up, lit the lamp and said, "Mamma dear, you had that several days ago. You are better now." She bathed my head with cold water, and told me to go back to sleep. Said it was just five o'clock. But I lay awake thinking about my dream, and when the late mail that day brought your letter to Edris I felt sure that my dream meant something and I had been spared for some purpose. Do you remember in your letter you said that Nick woke you at five o'clock calling my name and reaching up his hand to greet me as he always does? I can't help believing that my little friend Nick, himself so lately from the Beyond, by coming to me in my dream and laughing at my selfishness, has given me courage to work on to the end of the trail. I believe that I have been spared to gather for myself that last and largest white lily, the writing down in a book the memories of a lifetime.

So I will write down for you the true happenings of my life, and if I succeed all honor goes to Nick. I can hardly wait till I get home to start work and to see you. I love you.

Your friend
Mary Hamilton

This letter was written in September of 1932. By spring of 1933 Mary Hamilton had given me 150,000 words on this book. I have edited it, worked over it with her, and guided her in her choice of material, but I have in no case added to nor changed what she wrote. My whole work has been to cut down, for once she started remembering there was nowhere to stop. The memories of the busy difficult days of her wifehood and motherhood have been minutely stored in her brain, as bees store honey, so that every smallest event of every day of her life is there: what they had to eat at each Thanksgiving dinner, what became of every neighbor they had in the wilderness of the woods. It has been my task to strain the comb from the honey, removing the less interesting material and leaving in the dramatic and moving events that happened to Mary Hamilton herself, her husband, and her children.

I want to reassure the reader that my presence does not enter the book. I have not touched her style, nor embellished her material. It is a direct and simple autobiography. Deep in her heart I think there remains a wistful, unadmitted hope that the book if published may fall into the hands of someone who will be able to tell her children the full identity of the man who was their father. For that mystery has remained the abiding tragedy of her life and theirs.

Philipp, Mississippi
1933

[Ed. Note: Before her death in February 1992, Helen Davis wrote the following addition to her preface.]

The discovery of the Mary Hamilton manuscript in July 1991, almost sixty years after it was finished, happened as though she had willed it in her final dream. The pages were in a box under my granddaughter Jennifer's bed. She had just married and left home, and my daughter-in-law, Carolyn, found it and called me to say how much she liked it.

What she had discovered was a faded carbon copy, the yellowed pages crumbling, the paper clips marking the chapters so rusted they had merged into the paper in brown blotches. We read carefully, like archeologists examining ancient inscriptions. Once again I was thirty-two years old, hearing the rumble and ring of my old L. C. Smith typewriter and remembering how glad we always were to see Mrs. Hamilton, with her wonderful stories and hand-sewn dolls for the children.

Six years before, I had married Reuben Davis, a Mississippi Delta farmer and writer, and armed with my journalism degree from the University of Wisconsin and his knowledge of the Delta lands and people, we were writing, often as a team. While working with Mrs. Hamilton I learned of a writers' competition sponsored by Little, Brown & Co., and we decided to enter her autobiography.

We were living in a small white house beside a boardwalk on the main dirt street of the sawmill town of Philipp, Mississippi. An entry in my journal dated January 28, 1931, reads: "Conditions here in the delta are very bad. An old Negro man came to the back door yesterday and said he and his wife have had nothing to eat but one rabbit in two weeks. They have made shoes of inner tubes . . . This year, with banks breaking everywhere, most of the big delta land owners have no way of getting 'furnish money' to feed their labor, and the road is full of Negroes and whites looking for homes."

The autobiography was submitted to Little, Brown in 1933 but did not win the competition. We were told by our agent that publishers were at the time primarily interested in literature about southern Negroes. Little, Brown in fact confirmed this by publishing our first novel, *Butcher Bird*, in 1935.

By 1936, we had lost our own property, and we rented a cottage in Hendersonville, North Carolina, hoping to energize our minds with fresh scenery, while escaping the gloom of the depression. During our three-year stay in North Carolina, we were saddened to learn that Mrs. Hamilton had died.

It was also in North Carolina that we learned just how deeply our roots had grown into the soft Delta soil, and so in 1939 we returned, settling in the little cotton town of Carter, Mississippi, in Yazoo County, where Mary Hamilton had spent her last years in a comfortable little home of her own and where her daughter, Edris, and her husband were living. In this ideal setting, so close to people and so close to nature, we published several short stories and a novel, *Shim*, in 1953.

In 1957 we moved to nearby Yazoo City, another friendly, peaceful town. My very dear husband, Reuben, died there in 1966, continuing to write until his last day. In 1973 my daughter, Vica, and I moved to Auburn, Alabama, where my son, Nick, teaches architecture. All this time the Mary Hamilton manuscript somehow escaped being thrown out, and sometime in the early 1980s I must have lent it to Jennifer, who is herself interested in writing. She must have stored it under the bed, where it was found.

There are in the manuscript several troubling references to racial and ethnic minorities, and these have been left in as authentic indicators of attitudes at the time. There are also many stories illustrative of the human community at its best: generous, hard-working, and eternally hopeful.

I am profoundly delighted that after its long, long winter, Mary

Hamilton's finest snow-white lily has escaped from her dream and blooms for all of us.

Auburn, Alabama
January 1992

PART ONE

THE WILD COUNTRY OF ARKANSAS

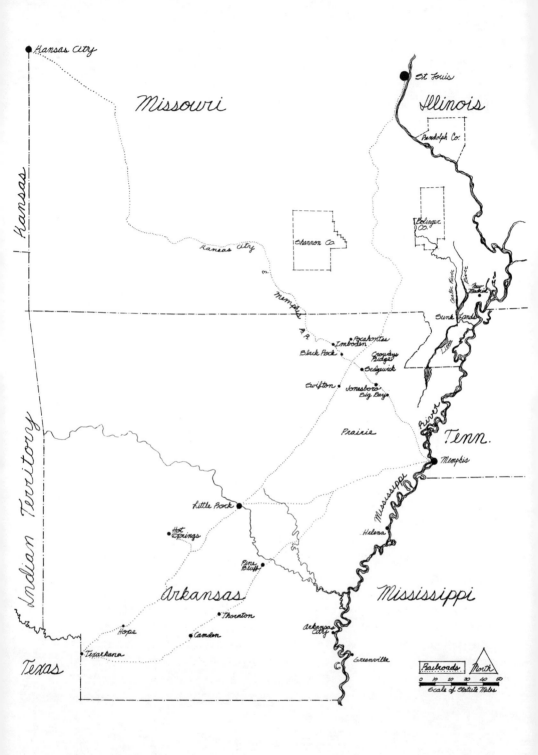

The Binding

I N THE EARLY 1880S MY FATHER BROUGHT HIS FAMILY from Missouri down into the wild country of Arkansas that was just beginning to settle up. The Kansas City and Memphis Railroad was just being graded through, and trains were running only as far as the little sawmill town of Sedgwick, so there we stopped to wait until the road was completed into the prairie country near Jonesboro, where my father expected to buy a home. Within a week he took pneumonia and three days later died, leaving my mother and six children stranded and helpless in a strange country.

Sam and Billie, my older brothers, went to work at the sawmill, and as we had the only livable house in town, we took a few boarders. I was seventeen, and with the help of my sister Lucy, thirteen, and a Negro woman, I did all the cooking. Jane, the sister between Lucy and me, had been a cripple for five years, and had never walked a step without the aid of a crutch. At the age of nine she had been thrown against an elm tree that had been twisted off in a storm, and a sliver ran almost through her ankle and broke off. The bone was affected and the leaders drawn, and we thought her a cripple for life. But she was lots of help and comfort to us all.

I was timid and bashful, getting just the right age to be thinking about boys, or rather to be teased about them, and my brothers and younger sisters never missed a chance. One day just a few weeks after Father died, Jane opened the living room door and called me from the kitchen. I thought something was wrong and so never stopped to take off my apron. My sleeves were rolled up and flour was on my hands. I went rushing like a whirlwind into the front room, where I almost ran over a man standing in the middle of the room, his hat in his hand. He bowed, amused at my embarrassment. Jane said, "Mary, this gentleman wants to board with us two or three weeks, and as you are the cook, can we keep him?"

The man laughed, introduced himself as Frank Hamilton, and said, "You seem to be the boss as well as the cook. I have three men with me. We only want meals, for two weeks. We have our own camping outfit."

Just then my mother came in and I turned to her and said, "Yes, we can manage their meals," and with my face burning with embarrassment, I flew back to the kitchen. I knew I looked a sight on earth, and to make it worse I could hear him and Jane laughing and talking, for they were good friends from the start.

I didn't think I could ever face him again, but as I had to wait on table I couldn't help it. He was about thirty years old, of medium height and build, with a light complexion, brown hair, and piercing steel-gray eyes. He carried himself as straight as a soldier or athlete. We knew from the way he talked he was an Englishman.

The more I saw of him the more I disliked him, but I don't know why and didn't know then, for, although he held himself aloof, he was friendly enough with all of us and took the greatest interest in little Jane. He gave her books to read, helped her with her lessons, and was always doing kind things for her.

Before his two weeks were up he took down with rheumatism, and the superintendent of the mill, Mr. Gray, persuaded him to throw up timber work for the railroad and go to bookkeeping for the mill company. Frank told me years afterwards his object in staying was me. Yet up to that time I had never spoken to him except when I had to, although he had won my respect and gratitude and all the family's for what he did for Jane. He persuaded my mother and brothers to get a doctor of his choice to come and operate on her at home. Hospitals weren't so plentiful in those days. He said the doctor would operate for twenty-five dollars and if he didn't cure her, he wouldn't charge anything. Jane begged so hard Mother gave her consent.

The day the plaster cast was taken off, she took her first step in five years and walked straight to Frank, her eyes full of tears. "I will always think of you as the best man on earth. I have you to thank for my life."

Frank said, "No, it is the doctor you have to thank, not me."

All the family but me crowded around Frank and the doctor. I slipped out to keep from thanking him, for something about him made me know he held himself above us, didn't want or need our thanks, for all his kindness. I respected him more than ever but disliked him more, for now we were all under obligation to him, as I knew that operation had cost more than any twenty-five dollars. When I saw him slipping out a few minutes later—he was sick and looked so pale and lonely, but self-sufficient—was the feeling that stirred in me for him hate, or was it love? Oh no, not love; I was sure I didn't love him, yet something seemed to say, "It is fate, and it will bind your life to his to the end of the trail." I wonder if that was love and have wondered hundreds of times since.

About that time the mill was being enlarged, work was pushing farther out into the woods, and Frank was taken on as assistant superintendent, in addition to his other work as bookkeeper. He was never very popular with the men. They thought him a big-headed dude, a man of mystery, for the simple reason that he stood for no interference and tended to his own business. He was polite to everyone but claimed no friends.

My oldest brother Billie held a good job and made good money; Sam, my next brother, had a better job than Billie's and made more money but wasn't steady, didn't work regular. He had a small crop of wild oats to sow and never let his work interfere with his oat sowing, so we couldn't depend on him for much. But we were able to live now without keeping boarders, and as that left me very little to do, Mother sent me back to her old home in Illinois to go to school. When I got there and saw how far behind others my age I was, I wouldn't go to school but went to work instead for a cousin of mine in her dressmaking and tailoring shop to learn the trade.

Up to the time I left, Frank and I had been cool and polite to each other, but we were not friends. So I was surprised when I got a letter from him soon after I got to Illinois. Just a nice friendly letter telling me all the news about his work and how they all missed me, especially my baby brother Johnny, who was just six. In it, Frank said how sorry he was that I wasn't going to school. Important as it made me feel to think that proud Frank Hamilton would write to me, that part about my not going to school made me mad. He was no friend of mine and it was none of his business. When I answered his letter I didn't mention

school. As the months went by, I got a letter from him every week. I
never wanted to see or talk to him again, but I was glad to get his
letters.

Three months from the time I left Arkansas, I got a telegram saying
my mother and Billie were dying of pneumonia and to come home at
once. My brother died two days after I got there, and my mother
followed him in just one week. But before they died, they each begged
a promise from me. When I first went in the room to see Billie, dying
quietly so Mother in the next room wouldn't know it, he sent the
others out and said to me straight out, "Mary, I am dying and my
death will kill our mother. If Sam was a steady boy you could keep the
family together, but he isn't. Mary, do you like Hamilton enough to
marry him? If you do he will give the children a home until they get
homes of their own."

It was a terrible shock to me. I told Billie that Hamilton couldn't
care for me, and if he did it was asking too much of him. But Billie
said, "Frank does care for you. We talked this over yesterday and he
himself proposed doing this for the children. He asked Mother and me
for you long ago. He is a man of too much honor to speak to you
without having got our consent first."

I had the strangest feeling that I had known all along, since the first
day I saw him, that something like this would happen, but that didn't
keep me from resenting it. Why was Frank Hamilton always trying to
put us under obligation to him? How could I promise to marry him,
disliking him as I did? But Billie was dying, and I promised. That
evening my mother begged me for the same promise. Twice in one day
I promised to marry Frank Hamilton, and he had never asked me.

A week later we sold all our worldly goods to pay the funeral
expenses and doctor bills. We children were heartbroken and alone,
not knowing which way to turn. Sam was nineteen years old, but he
wasn't steady. Neighbors came and gave their advice and sympathy,
but that didn't solve our problem.

Frank said nothing to me about marriage, and I hoped and prayed
he wouldn't. I wanted to forget the promise I had made my mother
and brother. If Frank had asked them for me I felt it was because I was
healthy and strong, a good cook and nurse, and yes, I was not bad-
looking. He had as much as told me I was good-looking in a letter he

wrote me urging me to go to school. "You will marry some day," he wrote, "and all men want an educated wife, not a tailor."

Two weeks after Mother died, he came to me and asked me to marry him. I told him, "No, you want an educated wife, not a tailor."

He said, "I would prefer your having more schooling, but I can teach you, and very few girls in this country have the common sense you have. You must use it now for the good of both of us, Mary. I talked to your mother, told her how tired I was of boarding around from pillar to post, with nowhere I could call home. You can make a home for me and for your sisters and brothers."

I tried to understand my feelings for him. To be honest, I admired him more than any man I had ever seen, but I did not love him, and I couldn't believe he loved me. Lucy said I did love him but just didn't have sense enough to know it.

I said, "But he thinks he is so far above us."

Jane said, "He is above us. He can't help knowing it, but he has never mentioned it or acted like it. He knows we are honest and straight. You had better marry and settle down, take Johnny and Lucy. Sam has promised to work and send me to school in Kansas."

Everything and everybody was trying to crowd me into a marriage I didn't want. As I look back, I believe I loved him even then; but I was young and had a will and dreams of my own. I was eighteen that May, and one afternoon in July Frank came to me with a marriage license. Said we would wait no longer. There was no word of love on either side. I remembered my promise to my mother and determined to do my best to make the home Frank had talked to my mother about wanting as near perfect as I could. We were married that day.

He had built rooms onto his office, and we were to live there. Lucy and Johnny were to live with us. Sam was working steady and had sent Jane to school in Kansas. The rooms were nicely furnished, and the kitchen and pantry were stocked with everything to eat. I was glad. I was a good cook and never happier than when cooking. After the first meal I cooked, Frank came into the kitchen and said, "Mary, I want you to cook my way for me, but don't let that stop you cooking for yourself Yankee style. I can't stand anything fried in lard nor boiled with fat meat. I have had fat meat and bacon shoved at me so much the five years I've been in this country I can't meet a hog in the road without shedding tears of grease. Use butter in my food instead of lard."

I was glad to try and suit him. He liked a cup of coffee when he got up of a morning, then a breakfast of toast, coffee, and eggs at eight; dinner at twelve, of beef in some form, soup, and vegetables seasoned with butter. At four o'clock he wanted a bit of cheese, bread and butter, and a glass of beer; then supper. It took me a long time to get used to his way of cooking, but I tried hard to learn and he took great pains showing me. I knew I pleased him, but he never praised me in one thing, and he gave me to understand that he picked our friends. When a gossipy man or woman came to see us, he would be so cool they never came again. Then he would say to me, "It is better to treat them so. They are just trying to pry into my business and the company's."

He even chose the books I read, books I had never heard of before: Kipling, Charles Lamb, Dumas, Robert Burns. To me he seemed like a man that had taken a silly child to raise rather than a wife. I didn't even know what salary he was getting for a year after we were married. As time went on I found there were plenty other things I didn't know, too.

The first thing I found out was that he drank. It was funny the way I found it out. I had heard he drank but didn't believe it, and as I had never seen a drunk man, I wasn't hard to fool. Frank had one man he called his friend then, Jim Thompson from Michigan. Jim was a machinist working for the mill company. He took supper with us one night in September, and he and Frank went out together after supper. Frank told me they had some business to attend to and he would be late, so Lucy and I went on to bed. Business often kept him out late, but I had thought nothing of it.

About eleven o'clock someone knocked on the door, and I called, "Is that you, Frank?"

Jim Thompson answered, "Yes, Mrs. Hamilton, Frank is bad sick."

I opened the door so quick. There was Frank leaning on Jim and groaning terribly. Jim said, "He has had a hard chill and must get to bed quick," and he started to take him to his bedroom. But I happened to know something about chills so I took charge.

"You put him right down on that sofa, and you go for a doctor quick as you can."

Jim helped him onto the sofa and rushed off, I thought for a doctor, but found out afterwards it was to keep from bursting out laughing, for he saw what Frank was in for. I covered Frank up good and warm, wheeled him up to the stove, threw in wood and kindling, poured coal oil over it and set it afire. He stood it about fifteen minutes, then threw off the cover, jumped up and started for the door, me right after him begging him to come back. I thought he was delirious and almost dead. Lucy was helping me try to get him back on the sofa, but he fought us off and got to the edge of the gallery. Then I saw why he'd been in such a hurry. Between spasms he yelled at us to let him alone, he wasn't sick, but "drunk, just plain drunk," and all he wanted was to be let strictly alone.

Well, he was let strictly alone. I shoved the sofa back from the fire, put the fire out, raised the windows and went to bed. I thought the shock of seeing him like that would kill me.

Next morning I got up at five o'clock as usual to make him coffee and get our breakfast. I took him his coffee and asked him how he felt.

"All right," he said. "Why shouldn't I feel all right?"

"Don't your conscience hurt you, deceiving me like you did?" I began.

But he waved me away, saying, "I know I acted dirty, damn dirty, but I must tell you right now preaching won't do any good. I don't believe in lady preachers. I came to America because it's a free country, and because I couldn't stand petticoat government any longer."

I said, "Wait, I don't believe in women preachers either, but I want to say one thing. I am not asking you to quit drinking if you can't. But I do ask you to bring your liquor home. I won't nag you, and when you get too helpless to get up and get it, I'll bring it to you. Just don't let anyone else see you as I saw you last night."

He looked at me so hard, and said, "That is a bargain. You live up to your part and I will do mine."

From then on I began to see he needed me far more than I needed him. He had rheumatism and would take spells that would last for days. Sometimes it was in his limbs and again it would strike in his chest, or the blood would rush to his head. His suffering at those times was terrible, and I tried so hard to do all I could for him. The only relief he got was from drawing the blood from his head by what was called in those days "dry cupping."

I will never forget the first time I used the dry cups on him. He showed me and told me how to do it, but it looked so cruel. I was nervous. The glasses used were made much like jelly glasses but were thin as watch crystal. I was to take a little soft brush, dip it in alcohol, wet the inside of the glass with it and set the glass afire. When it got to burning good I was to press it down on the shoulder near the spine. It would draw the blood and flesh up into the glass till the glass was full; then I was to take a little ivory knife, slip it under one side of the glass to let air in and the glass would come off easy. But that first time I lost my head, and when the cup filled with flesh, I threw the knife down, grabbed a cloth and wrapped it around that glass and began to pull. I was strong, and fear lent me extra strength, so in spite of Frank's groans and struggles I got the glass off but left a blister as big around as a saucer on Frank's back. It made a scar he took to his grave. He didn't scold, but a few days later when I told him I thought his head got better quicker that day than it had before and that was the way the glasses were meant to be used, he looked at me so straight and said, "You know jolly well no doctor expected me to have my back barbecued."

That was the only time I had any trouble, and I soon got to be a good nurse. And I had lots of it to do for the next fourteen years.

Meantime Frank had charge of the boardinghouse and was having lots of trouble. He had to have men cooks and helpers, and they were always quarreling among themselves, or the boarders were raising a roughhouse with them. It would end in the cook or assistant cook quitting and no one to cook the next meal for eighty hungry men. It went on from bad to worse till Christmas. We had been married six months. Frank's crew at the boardinghouse promised Frank they would stay sober until dinner was over, but he was a little uneasy, knowing all timber men celebrate Christmas by getting drunk. Sure enough we were just sitting down to our own Christmas dinner when the Negro helper from the boardinghouse came running by and hollered to Frank that men were fighting there. Frank tried to stop him as he hit the railroad track like he was running for his life, but he called back, "Don't stop me, white folks. I'se on my way to Kansas City." At the rate he was going he must have got there soon. We never saw him again.

Frank got Jim Thompson and went over to the boardinghouse,

where the boarders—a French head cook, an Irish second cook, and a southern white boy helper—were having a free-for-all fight, with knives, clubs, anything they could lay their hands on. Frank and Jim got the room cleared and closed the boardinghouse for that day. Of course our dinner at home was spoiled, too.

Next morning Frank, Lucy, and I and three neighbor women went over and cleaned up and got breakfast. Frank met the men and told them there were ladies in the house and the first man that couldn't behave could go to the office and get his time. They all looked so ashamed, and they all behaved themselves. It worked so well that I told Frank we had better try running it ourselves, and if he would get me a pastry cook I would do the general cooking with Lucy to help me. We had a boy and girl to wait on tables, but even with that help, the cooking for eighty men was hard and the hours long. After working all day I would go home at night to rest, and more often than not, be up half the night with Frank. He had been in this country long enough to be full of malaria and that made his rheumatism worse; also, he was drinking more.

The latter part of January the pastry cook left suddenly, and that threw the whole job of cooking on me. There was a man boarding with us named Charlie Flynn, one of these "handy Andys" that could do anything. He offered to help out until we could get a cook but said he could only do general cooking, not pastry cooking. At the time I didn't guess what the scoundrel was driving at, but it all came out soon enough. You see, my sister Lucy helped with the general cooking, and that would throw him to work with her. Lucy was not quite fourteen years old and was large for her age, but a child in ways. She was good-looking and very sensitive. We found out later that Charlie had caused our pastry cook to quit by lying to him. Well, Charlie went to work. I disliked him but could find no fault with his work; it was a hard cold winter and cooks were hard to get. He was good-looking and a great talker, but Lucy never had much to say to him and I thought she shared my dislike of him. He was old enough to be her father.

About that time something happened that set me to worrying and wondering about Frank. Around the first of February Frank went off on business, and while he was gone two new men came to work and to board. They were fine-looking, tall men, who carried themselves like Frank did, straight and soldierly. One was, I think, the handsomest man I ever saw, with a dark complexion and black eyes; the other had a light complexion and dark gray eyes. They had been there two or three days when Frank got back one morning while the men were at breakfast. He stepped into the dining room and stood facing the door talking to Mr. Gray, the superintendent, when those two new men walked into the dining room a little late. They saw Frank, stopped dead still, jerked their shoulders back, and saluted. Frank started and lifted his hand as if he was going to return the salute, but instead he dropped it with the palm down as if signalling them for silence. A little ripple of astonishment ran over the whole dining room as the two men walked to their places and sat down. Frank drank his coffee and went outside. Those two men followed him out to where he was saddling his horse. They shook hands, talked a moment, and walked down towards the mill together. The two men went away that day.

Naturally I was curious, and tried to quiz Frank about it, but all he told me was that he went to a military school in England for four years before going to India in the English army. Who the men were and why they left so suddenly, he didn't tell me; he just laughed and called me "Eve" for my curiosity. I couldn't help being hurt to feel he was keeping something from me, and I felt sure he had sent those men on their way, and that he knew them. But I was too busy with the boardinghouse to have much time to worry.

On February 16, 1886, it commenced snowing about three o'clock in the afternoon. It came down in sheets and by the next day drifts were so deep that we were all wet to our necks floundering through the snow to get to the boardinghouse. By night Frank was suffering terribly with rheumatism. It settled in his chest, lungs, and heart, so he couldn't move nor speak. Soon in the morning I got a doctor. He said the only hope Frank had was to get to Hot Springs at once.

Mr. Gray came over to the house and arrangements were made for the doctor to take Frank the next day. The doctor left, and Mr. Gray told me to go get some rest as I had been up all night. I thought he wanted to talk to Frank about business so I went to my room, separated from the one they were in by a thin partition. I lay down on my bed. I was so sorry for Frank, and back of that I was scared wondering what would become of me and my baby coming in July. I didn't know whether we had any money or not. I had been saving and hadn't spent one penny on myself. I knew we were making money since I had taken over the boardinghouse, but whether we had saved any or not I didn't know. I didn't know anything about Frank's business, nor about him either, I soon learned. For just as I began to doze, I heard Mr. Gray say, "Frank, do you realize your condition, and that you ought to make things plainer for your wife? I like you; anybody can see you are a gentleman; but from things you have dropped when drinking, along with what you told me the day those two men gave you away in the dining room, I can't help feeling you are being unfair to your wife. She is a fine girl, a perfect slave for you, and she has a right to know."

Frank said, "Friend, you are the only man on earth that could talk to me like this. I have never done anything dishonest nor dirty in my life, but my past before I came to the United States concerns no one. When I landed in New York I closed that life forever."

Mr. Gray said, "It concerns your wife. And what about the child you told me you are expecting?"

"I never thought of that," Frank said in a changed voice.

Sleep was out of the question for me now. I went in and told Mr. Gray I would sit with Frank now. I did not want to eavesdrop any longer. If my devotion to Frank had not brought me Frank's confidence and trust, then I wanted to hear no more of confusion and mystery. I was sure now that my feeling before we were married was right. He had married me not for love but for a nurse and housekeeper. I felt glad he knew, as I was sure he did, that I had married him through gratitude. But as I sat beside him thinking these things, believing him asleep, he spoke quietly. "Mary, do you think I have ever deceived you?"

"I know you have, for I heard you and Mr. Gray talking."

"If you heard that," Frank said, "then you know already how I feel about it. Can you forget it? You married Frank Hamilton, and there is no law in England or America to change that. My past concerns no one."

"Frank," I said, "am I your wife?"

He took my hand. "Mary, I will swear to this. I am pretty sick, and I may not get back from Hot Springs. You are my lawful wife, my first and only one. I come of a good old family in England and for more than 600 years there has never been a real stain on our name. But I choose to be dead to that family. I have my own private reasons, and life nor death nor anything else will ever change me."

I knew he was telling the truth. I tried to be satisfied, but I knew he didn't look on me as his equal even if I was his wife.

The next morning when the doctor came for him, he took a large sealed envelope from under his pillow and handed it to Mr. Gray. "Keep it locked in your safe. If I live, I will get it sometime. If I don't and our child is a boy, then open it and do what I ask you. Remember I trust you, my one American friend. But if the baby is a girl, burn it unopened."

That was our good-bye, though he took me in his arms, held me tight, and told me he loved me better than anything on earth. But I couldn't believe him. He told me to go ahead and manage everything while he was away, but after he left I couldn't feel much like going ahead. I was only nineteen years old, expecting every minute to get a message my husband was dead, and wishing it was me. I felt sure he had married me just because it was safer to marry than to hire help. How foolish and bitter of me, but that was the way it looked to me then, and it wasn't a light heart to carry on my work with, doing all the pastry cooking and managing the general cooking for eighty men. It was years and years before I could see Frank's marrying me any different.

The day after Frank left, this handyman Flynn, who had been doing the general cooking, gave notice he was quitting in a week's time, so that left me to take his place too, as it was impossible to get another cook. I didn't care, for I wanted to work until I couldn't think. The same day Flynn left, Lucy asked me to let her go to town with one of our neighbors, as she had often done before. I was glad to let her go as she worked hard and was so good. She had just turned her fourteenth year. Everyone said afterwards she had been acting queer for a couple of weeks, but I had been too worried about Frank to notice it. That morning I gave her fifteen dollars, kissed her, and told her to have a good time. I worked hard all day, doing Flynn's work, Lucy's, and my own.

When the four o'clock train came in that afternoon I was still in the boardinghouse kitchen. I looked up and saw Flynn and Lucy standing together in the doorway. They told me they were married. I thought they were joking at first; then I stormed and cried, telling them she shouldn't live with him one minute. That child, a mere baby. Poor Lucy looked so bewildered. She looked at Flynn, then at me, then came and put her arms around me and said, "Mary, I can't understand why you are taking it so hard, when both you and Frank have told Flynn again and again you wanted to get rid of me as I was too much expense. God knows I didn't want to marry and leave you."

For the first time in my life I found I had a temper. I could have killed Charlie Flynn where he stood.

He looked at Lucy and said to me, "I didn't tell Lucy you had anything to say about it. It was Hamilton. He told me repeatedly he wanted me to marry her. He is her guardian, and when I told him I might have trouble over her age, he gave me this written statement giving his consent."

He handed me their marriage license and with it a paper giving a guardian's consent to Lucy's marriage.

"You forged it," I told him. "It isn't Frank's handwriting." But some of the other men looked at it and agreed that it was Frank's handwriting. They hinted to each other that they had always looked for something like this from Frank. He was too closemouthed and distant not to be dirty.

I felt like my heart would break. I couldn't believe Frank had done such a thing, but the rest of them did. Frank was at the point of death and couldn't be bothered. So Flynn gained his point and took little Lucy away with him. Hard work was all that kept me from going crazy those weeks that followed.

I wrote Frank about Lucy's runaway marriage, and when he wrote back blaming me for it, man-fashion, I was glad, for I knew then he was innocent. In about a month he was able to come home. He looked so much better; his skin was white, and he was twenty-five pounds lighter. I told him he looked as if he had been put in a kettle and boiled until he shrunk to half his size. He said the doctors told him he must leave the country and go to a dryer climate, but when I asked him if he was going, he said, "No. I have traveled as long as I had any money. From Canada where I had my first bad spell straight to old Mexico, and I am as well here as any place. But I am going to give up all indoor work and am going to work on my own. Mr. Gray and I are partners from now on, running the boardinghouses that are going to have to be built further out in the woods, and hauling ties and having them made."

About that time the river or log drivers had come down from

Michigan to help get all logs that had been cut during the winter into the river. That meant we had 115 men at the boardinghouse, besides the six helpers and Frank and me. I have been laughed at for saying we used a barrel of flour a day; but you bake 115 loaves of bread a day, biscuits or flapjacks for breakfast, at least thirty pies for dinner, and always tea cakes for supper, as I did, and you will see. Then we had to make our own yeast, and that took lots of flour. We made a five-gallon churn full every two days. The only leftovers of anything we could use were bits of beef roast or soup meat and boiled ham, run through the food chopper. To this we would add cold potatoes and onions, mix well, thin with soup stock, season with pepper, sage and salt, press in a pan, and bake brown. We served this hot for supper. It is boarding-house hash, older I think than boardinghouses themselves. I don't believe there is a timber man in America that hasn't eaten it. But bread, cakes, or pieces of pie we would never put on the table a second time. It didn't make any difference how much we had left over, but God help us if we didn't have enough.

Sometimes for days I would forget the shadow that Frank's past threw over my thoughts, and then a little thing would come up and remind me. One day Frank and Mr. Gray were in the office when a man came in talking some kind of gibberish I couldn't understand and neither could Mr. Gray. Frank told him what the man was saying, and after he went out I heard Frank laugh and say, "A regular frog-eating Frenchman."

Mr. Gray said, "Frank, how many languages can you speak, and where did you learn them?"

Frank turned it off, saying only, "Five or six. Some I learned at school, but most of them in the army in Bengal, where a man is liable to learn anything. Learning languages is just associating with different nationalities, and I've been around with several."

I worked so hard I didn't have much time to think and didn't want to think, but it was always there, the feeling that he didn't belong to me at all, but to that past.

Lying Aloud

THAT SPRING FLYNN CAME BACK and went to work for Frank. Poor little Lucy begged so hard to come back; Flynn owned to Frank that he forged the permit to their marriage, but pled his love for her was true and all was fair in love and war. He was good to her in his way—waited on her, wouldn't allow her to do even her own housework, spent every cent he made on her, kept all kinds of novels for her to read—in fact, spoiled her like a little child. She soon got lazy and selfish, and her head was filled with romantic nonsense; but through it all she always loved Frank and me like a father and mother and would do anything for us. Even offered to leave Flynn after finding how he had deceived her into marrying him. But bad as we felt about the marriage, we thought now that she had got into it, she ought to work out her own salvation, so we gave him work and did all we could for them.

Our business was running smooth enough, and we were making money, but as always I had no idea whether we were saving any. Young as I was, I could see where Frank would make so much more if he drank less. Nobody could drive a harder bargain than Frank when he was sober, but when he was drinking, he threw his money away like water, saying, "What is it good for if not to spend on my friends?" Yet when he was sober he claimed no friends, or very few.

I was expecting to be confined in July but was still running the boardinghouse, doing almost half the work myself for eighty men. I knew I needed some little clothes for my baby, but didn't know what to get. I had no one to go to for advice. I had never asked Frank for one penny for myself. But one day I determined I would. He was at home sick. I had been running over from the cookhouse every chance I got to see how he was and to do for him.

So in the afternoon when work was over for me for an hour, I thought it a good time to slip over and have a talk with him and ask for money to get what I needed. I slipped in, walking easy so as not to wake him if he was asleep. I went in through my bedroom; he was sitting just inside the living room with his back to me. He had a newspaper in his hand, reading, or had been. Just as I stepped in, he crumpled the paper up, threw it down with a moan, more like a sob, and said, "Go ahead, spend, spend. Spend all the money you have looking for me. Damn the lot of you. I am dead, dead to all of you."

I cried out, "My God, Frank, what do you mean?"

He jumped like he had been shot, snatched up the paper, went to the stove, stuck it in, took a match, and set it afire, burning it all up. Of course he was all that time getting hold of himself. Then he turned to me and said, "Why do you look so frightened, Mary? I must have been reading aloud."

I said, "And now you are lying aloud. I came over to help you, thinking you bad sick, and I find you sobbing and crying about your past. If you are dead to your people on my account you can just come to life again. Forget me and my child. I can get along."

"Now, now, Mary, you are tired and overwrought. You are over-worked, and you are going to stop and rest up. I have made arrange-ments with the old lady Green of Jonesboro to board you through your confinement. You will be right by a good doctor and I have spoken to him to wait on you. Mrs. Green is a good nurse and a good friend of yours. She wants you to go a month before your time, rest up, and prepare your things. She will be good to you, and God knows you deserve a rest. Now come, kiss me, and forget this. Next time I will be more careful about reading aloud."

I said, "Frank, don't you think I can see you are just plain lying? A smart man like you don't get down, grovel and cry like a nigger at the mourners' bench just over reading an advertisement in a newspaper."

"You're right," Frank said. "But as I told you once before, it doesn't concern you in any way, so why worry your head about my trouble? It can never come between us unless you let it. If I choose to cut loose from my family, why should you care? My wife and child come first and with that you must try to be satisfied, and if you care for me you will say nothing about this miserable secret between us."

I said no more. Two weeks later Frank took me to Mrs. Green's. The first thing we did after Frank left was go shopping. Such an outfit as we got. What joy I took in making the little clothes, or rather big clothes, for every little dress measured fifty inches long. Fine tucks, then inserting, then more tucks, and so on to the bottom of the dresses, and there they were finished with a wide ruffle of embroidery. White linen underskirt was made the same way but finished at the top with a broad band five inches wide; white flannel underskirt made as long and finished with the same kind of band, then the usual muslin band to wear next the little body. We made several suits and bought a ready-made cloak and cap of white cashmere, silk-lined; that, with forty yards of heavy white cotton flannel for diapers, was the whole outfit. It cost forty dollars. That was the first money I got out of my year's work. It kept me busy sewing up to the twenty-fifth of July when my first baby, a fine eight-pound boy, was born. Frank didn't get there until after the baby was born. I wouldn't let them wire him till it was almost over as I couldn't bear to have him see me suffer. But, oh, the joy I felt when he came and saw his boy! When the doctor asked me what I was going to name him, Frank spoke up so quick and said, "She doesn't have to name him. He has been named quite a while."

I said, "We are going to call him Frank."

Frank said, "My dear, you have nothing to do with it. His name is Jim Hamilton."

He had had a drink or two, just enough to loosen his tongue. Mrs. Green looked at him and said, "What is the idea of 'Jim'? You mean James."

"I mean for Sir Jim Hamilton, the greatest friend I ever had, madam," Frank said.

Again that past! I changed the subject. My baby was mine anyway.

Mrs. Green brought me a bowl of weak toddy, smoking hot, with crackers broken up in it, and Frank left. He came back for me when the baby was just two weeks old.

I had just one week's rest after I got home when our Negro cook took sick. The German cook they had got to take my place had gone a few days before with some of the men, laid off for a month on account of repairs at the mill. That left us thirty-five men at our home house with no one to cook for them, so there was nothing for me to do except go to work and do the cooking with the help of my dishwasher and one boy.

I had to get a nurse, one of our neighbor women, to take my baby and take care of him. When she brought him to me every three hours to nurse, I would be hot and tired and I was afraid my milk would be bad for him. She would bring him home at nine o'clock at night when I was through at the boardinghouse, and I could have my baby until four in the morning when I had to go back. It was hard on him and on me. In September, when our men all came back, we still couldn't get but one cook, so I had to go ahead with the baking and pastry work for eighty men, which was harder than all the cooking for thirty-five.

How I had looked forward to the love and care of my little baby. How I longed to do the thousand little things that no one but a mother knows how to do. I could hardly wait for the time when he would know me and understand I was his mother. Instead I was a stranger to him. Even while he was nursing, his eyes would follow his nurse. In November his nurse got sick and I had to bring him home. We still hadn't got a cook to take my place, so I had to have his little crib in the kitchen, as it was too cold in the dining room. The kitchen was hot and steamy, and when I would take him home with me every night after my work was done, no matter how well I wrapped him up he took cold. In the latter part of November he took a bad cold and croup. That same night he took sick our old cook came back, but too late to save my baby. We had the best doctor that could be got in that part of the country, but nothing did any good. My baby choked to death before morning.

I knew he died because of neglect, because I had not been able to care for him as I should. I blamed Frank, myself, life. I thought my heart was dead, but when I saw how Frank was suffering I had to turn to him for he wasn't as able to stand it as I was. I couldn't feel as bitter as I thought I could. I knelt down by my dead baby and prayed as I had never prayed before for strength to take up my life and my duty to Frank, to be cheerful and kind, stand by him through all trouble. And I tried during the long busy days to remember that my baby was with Jesus where he would be cared for as I could never have cared for him on earth.

In spite of all I could do, Frank lost all grip on himself. He drank harder and had longer spells of rheumatism; he was almost always sick. His business began to fail, but he carried on for another year before he failed entirely. That was a long winter, but the summer that followed was a happy one.

Jim Thompson had married my sister Jane, and they were living with us. Jim was a good friend of Frank's, and both Jim and Jane were so fun-loving, full of life, and so happy with each other, that nobody could be blue around them. I would look forward all day to the pleasant evenings Frank, Jim, Jane, and I would have when the work was done; that is, if Frank wasn't sick or drinking, and as Jim wouldn't drink, Frank drank less now he was there. And if Frank did slip over to the house during the day and drown his pain with drink, he would be rich that evening, and laugh at trouble, full of fun, trying to convince us he hadn't had a drink but this was just his natural disposition. He would tell us stories of his war days in India or cowboy stories of Texas and old Mexico. When he first came to this country he got lead poisoning in Nebraska lead mines and took down there with rheumatism. He got to Canada before he had to go to a hospital. As soon as he could travel he went straight to old Mexico.

One hot evening in September we were sitting talking of one thing and another, when Frank said suddenly, "That reminds me, Jim, I will soon be hunting a new job. The railroad has shut down on taking any more ties for three months and God only knows how much longer."

"But your contract," Jim said. "You can sue."

Frank smiled. "What good will that do? The law is the only thing about this country I don't like, Jim, and won't get mixed up in. You Yankees have too much law and too little justice. Start a lawsuit and it would take a year, and in the meantime the ties will be wormy and worthless. It won't hurt Gray so bad, but it will take every cent I have to finish paying off. You see, we've gone to a big expense making seven miles of corduroy road and a bridge through that swamp. If they hadn't shut down on us we'd have come out with good money, but bad luck seems camping on my trail."

This was the first I knew we were broke. Now I understood why Frank was so often blue, and where all the money we had been making on the boardinghouse had been going. I couldn't think it was as bad as he said, but it was. In the late fall, a little more than two years after we married, Frank straightened up everything, and all we had left was our stock and the home boardinghouse. I wanted Frank to stay on, get rid of all the stock but the cows and what horses and hogs we would need, go over to Crowley's Ridge—a fertile strip of ridge land beginning within a mile of our home and running up into Missouri, one of the finest fruit countries in the world—and buy a place, build a house, and start an orchard. I would stay on and run the boardinghouse, and we could easily pay for the land that way, as land was cheap. That country was home to me. My father, mother, brother, and our baby were all buried there on Crowley's Ridge. Even a little eighty acres there would be home. But Frank would not do that. He said he would never be satisfied there any more.

Jim and Jane had gone to Michigan to Jim's people, for Jane was going to have a baby in December and was not well. Our baby brother Johnny went to Michigan with them to go to school. That left Frank and me alone for the first time since we were married.

About this time I got a letter from my brother Sam. He was married and doing well up in Missouri and begged me to come and see them. Frank thought it would be a fine idea, as he didn't have so much to do but what he could look after the house, and I needed a rest, as I was pregnant again. So I went, to stay a month. The first week I got a letter from Frank saying they were getting along fine, and for me to have a good time, as there was nothing to worry about. Well, I was having a good time. Sam was sawyer and filer at the mill and was making good money and taking care of it, and Ida, my new sister-in-law, was a fine girl of a good family.

Ida's family lived away up in the hills of Bolinger County. We went up to spend the week-end. Her mother wasn't very well so Sam went home alone, and we stayed a week longer. I enjoyed every minute I was there. They lived in a broad valley between two hills, almost mountains. The valley was a half-mile wide and a mile long, with a creek running through it just in front of their yard. It wasn't wide nor deep, just a clear, rock-bottomed brook. On still nights, you could hear it from the porch. The hills were alive with birds and full of honeysuckle, great pink patches of blooms against the solid background of green pine. I was half-sorry when Sam came for us on Sunday in a buggy, but we had a glorious twenty-five-mile drive through the hills to the bottom country where they lived.

There was a letter from Frank with the same good news as the last. Then a blank two weeks when I didn't hear, but in my letter to him I begged him to let me come home, as I felt so rested and good I wanted to go to work. I was sure I was needed. At the end of three weeks, I got a letter from him saying he had sold out, lock, stock, and barrel, all but teams and wagons and what household goods he thought we would need, and was going by land to Shannon County, Missouri, where he had a contract at logging. As soon as he got settled he would send for me.

There was no use my telling what a blow that was to me and my dreams of a little home on Crowley's Ridge. My heart had been set on it, and now I felt I would never have a home of my own. I didn't even have the satisfaction of writing to Frank, as he was traveling all the time. He wrote me every other day along the way. I could see Sam was out of patience with him. He said it was whiskey causing him to go to pieces like he was.

"I can't see," he said, "how a man as smart as Frank is can let drink down him. He is the smartest man in this country. Has the best education by far, is honest and straight and did so well while working for the company. But as soon as he goes to work for himself, he gets reckless, makes foolish trades, wastes his money."

I stopped him. We had quite a row. I told him he knew Frank was sick all the time and had just had a streak of bad luck that no one could help. I knew it was no use to talk to Sam, as there were only three people who understood: Jim, Jane, and Mr. Gray. They had all seen him when the pain was so bad, especially in his right leg, in the knee he said had been crushed in a steeplechase. We had seen that knee twist out of place, and Jim had set it many times. I felt I was beginning to understand Frank the more others got out of patience with him. It was his condition caused him to drink; that, and his past life, and of this no one knew anything but Mr. Gray and me, and we knew very little. My brother was ashamed of letting his feelings get the best of him and did everything he could to make up for it. I think Ida wrote to her parents to make some excuse to come for us, for they came to spend the week-end and begged us to go back with them. I was so glad to go.

When we got there I found my beautiful hills were all brown and gold except the green pines. They made a far more beautiful picture than when I was there before, and the little brook babbled and sang sweeter, maybe because my own dream of a little home had gone up in smoke. How I loved it all.

Evenings we would sit around the fire listening to old man Serrett, Ida's father, spin yarns of old days in California. Old man Serrett was hale and hearty, didn't look over fifty-five, but he was seventy-three and an old "forty-niner." When he got his pipe going and got started talking of old times, nothing disturbed him but the coughing and grunting that came from his little wife sitting by him knitting. Now and then when she thought he was exaggerating, she would say gently, "Now, Cal dear, stick to the truth."

He would look at her so cunning and say, "Cinthy, who is telling this story? If it is you, then take the pipe and give me your knitting."

"Oh no, not that awful pipe. Anything but the pipe, Cal."

So the stories would go on. But one evening when everything was peaceful, someone knocked on the door and called, "Mr. Serrett, the fire is out, headed for this valley."

We all rushed out, and, calling to us to watch the house and out-buildings, he left. I wish I could paint the beautiful picture we watched. The mountains were covered with pine and dead grass, and as the fire curled along it set fire to pine knots that looked like great stars twinkling in the sky. It was grand to see that fiery mountain top trying to burn a hole in the sky, but it was sad as well, as it was destroying much valuable timber.

By four o'clock in the morning when they had it in check, Mr. Serrett came in and seemed to be more worried over his deer lick than anything else. He said he thought he had cleared a wide path around it and hoped that would stop the fire, as "I want to get a deer for Mary before she leaves." He did get one, the very next day, which was Sunday. Bright and early he was up moulding bullets, Cinthy scolding about his not going to church with us.

"You know the preacher is coming home with us for dinner, Cal."

"Yes, I know," he said. "You and the girls are enough to bring him home, and I'll have a deer for his dinner. It will save your chickens. That damned Methodist circuit rider can eat more chickens than any man I ever saw. He must be fed up on them. You see I am thinking more about your preacher's welfare than you are."

"Oh, Cal, you will do anything to keep from going to church."

We went, all but old man Serrett, with one of their neighbors, so the man could drive. We rode in a two-horse wagon with two spring seats and a board across the back of it, with a quilt over it to make it sittable.

The sermon seemed to impress the congregation the right way, for both men and women got to shouting. When the preacher got them all shouting he had nothing to do but jump up and down and clap his hands and holler. Tears were running down his cheeks, but we couldn't hear one word he said after the shouting started. That went on until the women gave out. The men had given out long before. That was one time I was glad men are weaker than women. Women can stand more work, more trouble, and more religion than men.

We went home, the preacher riding alongside us horseback. Just as we drove up to the house, old man Serrett came around the corner taking a dressed deer to the smokehouse. Poor little Mrs. Serrett was so embarrassed, but Mr. Serrett didn't care at all. When the preacher asked for a second helping of venison steak at the dinner table, Mr. Serrett said, "The fire ran the deer out of the back country, and this one came by my lick and I got him."

"Brother Serrett," said the preacher, "that was a case of the ox falling into the ditch on the Sabbath Day and you pulled him out."

"No, by gum, I shot him out." He looked straight at the preacher and winked. "Does it hurt the taste of it?"

"No, indeed. It's fine, and you were committing no sin up there alone. So please pass the venison."

Dinner passed off as merrily as you please. That night as we were sitting around the fire talking over the day's happenings, Ida told her father of the sermon on sin that morning, and that the greatest sin was breaking the Sabbath Day, and of the men and women who had got religion and gone to shouting. He said, "No, by gum, they haven't got religion no more than I have. Just excited and imagine it's religion."

The old lady spoke up at that and said, "Cal, they were really serious. Maybe you think it was imagination that took me in the church."

He said, "If you had got up and made a show of yourself, cut the buck like some of them do, I'd believe it was. Besides, you have got lots of silly imagination, Cinthy."

Cinthy gathered up her knitting, saying, "Calvin, you make me tired, and I'm going to bed."

"I'm glad of it, for I've had all the religion I can stand for one day, so you go to bed, and I'll light up and talk about something more interesting."

The old people slept in the living room. They would put the lamp out and sit by the firelight. So while she was getting in bed, he whispered, "I'm going to fool her."

Every time he "lit up" as he called his smoking, she would start coughing and quarreling. So he put his pipe down by Ida's side but began to puff and talk and draw as if he was smoking. The old lady began to cough and grunt, and the more she coughed, the louder he puffed. At last she begged, "Oh, Cal, please put that awful pipe out. It is strangling me to death."

He said, "Don't be silly, Cinthy, that pipe is not bothering you."

Of course we girls had to giggle, and that finished her. She got out of bed and said, "I am going into Ida's room till you put out that pipe."

As she came by the fire, the old man said, "Look, Cinthy, at my pipe over by Ida where I put it as you were getting in bed. Confess, old girl, that you have a fair share of imagination as well as everyone else, and toddle back to bed. Just where I am going, as I am tired."

We all laughed, even the old lady.

About a week after that, it commenced snowing in the evening, snowed till about midnight, and then cleared off. When we got up in the morning, the sun was shining on a blanket of snow about four inches deep. That day I got a letter from Frank telling me to come to him and giving me directions. I was to start in a week. It would be a long trip and cold, but I was so anxious to see him it seemed I could not wait the week.

Sam came for us in his horse and buggy. We bid those dear old people good-bye and started soon in the morning.

"Let's go the near way round the mountain, Sam," Ida said. "I want Mary to see the big waterfall at the old water mill."

The horse was fresh and wild, and we were all young and full of life, but when we got to the mountain road that wound around the side of the mountain for over a mile, the mountain two hundred feet straight up above us and fifty to a hundred feet down, it was so narrow I looked every minute for the horse to get scared and all of us to go tumbling down to the bottom and be drowned, if not killed before we got there, in the big creek that wound round the bottom of the hill and fed the mill.

At last we came out on almost level ground, and there stood the old mill, all grown over with vines and ground ivy, and the mill dam with the water still turning the big wheel, water and foam playing around. It was a clear bright morning, snow all over the dead vines, and icicles clung and sparkled like diamonds; along the edge of the water the green ivy made a thick carpet. I carried that picture away in my mind to remember always. Next morning I started on my trip to Frank.

Calamity Ann

FRANK MET ME AT THE LITTLE BOXCAR DEPOT of a new town on a branch road of the Iron Mountain Railroad that ran through to get the oak and pine timber, which was fine and plentiful. He told me I I would get some more rest, as there was no house we could get, and we would have to board. Frank was logging. We stayed there only a few months, for in February Frank got a letter from his old friend Mr. Gray, telling him if he would come to Kansas City he had a good place for him, as he was opening up a new lumber business there. He told Frank not to bring but one good team. So in March Frank wound up his business, paid off, and didn't have much left. He sold off all stock but one team of big fine horses, a Norman mare, one wagon, and camping outfit. He was going to drive through the country to Kansas City; I was to go to my sister Lucy's at Black Rock, Arkansas, and stay there until he got settled and sent for me. I didn't want him to go without me, but I had no choice. I had always done what he thought best, so I packed my trunk.

Frank took me to the depot, bought my ticket, checked my trunk, and kissed me good-bye. He saw I was about to break down, and he took me in his arms.

"Little Calamity Ann," he laughed. "Always looking for trouble. I am acting for the best. In your condition you will be better off with Lucy. I promise to send for you before your time. Now cheer up."

My first thirty miles was on a local freight, as there had never been a passenger train on that road. The seats in the caboose were hard and the road rough. I had to change cars at Sedalia to go to Black Rock. Frank had wired them I was coming and Flynn met me at the depot in

Black Rock. We had to walk about two hundred yards to their house. I don't know how I made it. I was, and had been, in awful pain for about two hours. Lucy had a good supper for me, but I told her I was awful sick and must get to bed. I got steadily worse. Charlie went for a doctor. I didn't know anything more till morning. When I came to myself, my baby was four hours old, but dying. Born a month too soon. The rough road caused it.

My husband was somewhere on the road to Kansas City. He started the same day I did. No use trying to find him. I got a letter from him the next day and the next, from wherever he was able to mail them as he traveled on. What was I to do? My baby son to bury, my doctor to pay, and only fifteen dollars over my railroad fare Frank had given me. The doctor said if I worried and caused fever I would soon follow the baby, as I was in bad condition. Little Lucy was so good and kind to me and Flynn seemed to be. He told me not to worry about money, he would lend me all I needed. I had all kinds of nice clothes for my baby to be buried in, and it cost twenty-five dollars to bury him.

Two days after my baby was buried I got a telegram that Frank was in a hospital in Kansas City bad hurt. His team got frightened and ran away and down off the pike. He was found unconscious almost at his journey's end and taken to Kansas City. Flynn came in and blurted it all out, but instead of killing me as the doctor said it would, it saved me, because Flynn added, "Of course, Frank was drunk."

How could I die after that? I knew it was not true, and that I must get well, as he needed me. And I began right straight to mend and get well. In ten days I was up. Can't a woman stand a lot when she feels she is needed to take care of someone she has grown attached to, or was it love? I wondered.

While Frank was still in the hospital, the news came to him that Mr. Gray, who had sent for him to come to Kansas City, had gone on a business trip, taken pneumonia, and died there. The first letter I got from Frank said that he was almost ready to leave the hospital and was about broke but was sure he could get a job, although both his horses had been killed. Not until his letter came did I write him of my trouble and the loss of our child.

About that time Flynn began hinting he needed his money that I owed him, so I sold first my watch, then my feather beds, pillows, quilts (one fine silk quilt), scarfs, rugs, a Brussels carpet (a wedding present), silverware, everything I had, even down to my trunk and all my best clothes. It took nearly all to pay Flynn what I owed him after I paid the doctor. After I settled up I put everything on earth I owned in one suitcase.

I saw an advertisement in the paper for a good cook at a hotel in Imboden, Arkansas. I went to see about it as it was not far from Black Rock. It was owned and run by a Mr. and Mrs. Childress, fine people. He wasn't at home, but his wife was. She said, "You are so little and look so frail you can't stand the work long, but I will help you and maybe between us we can do until William can get a man cook."

I asked her whether I could hold the job if I could do as well as a man cook, and she said, "Yes, indeed, but this is a hard job even for a man. We have three drummers' families besides twelve regular boarders and always from fifteen to twenty transients to feed, mostly short-order meals."

But while we were talking we were working and got along fine. Supper was the first meal. I soon caught on to the work. The next morning while I was getting breakfast (Mrs. Childress hadn't got in yet), here came Mr. Childress, a great big, loud-voiced man, puffing and blowing.

"Where is Clara's new cook? She swears she is the finest cook we ever had." Just then he stepped inside the kitchen, stopped short, looked at me, and said, "My Lord, you poor little thing, do you mean to tell me you can take a man's place as cook? I expected to see a strapping big Irish woman, and instead I find a little delicate girl about the size of a washing of soap."

I told him all I asked was a chance, and he said, "All right, Lady Grit, I almost believe you'll do. We'll give you every chance."

And they did. That night I wrote to Lucy to send my suitcase, and I wrote Frank telling him all and sent him all the money I had left. I gave the letter to Mr. Childress to mail and to register. He looked at it, then at me, and said, "You are Frank Hamilton's wife? What the devil are you working out for?"

I said, "For a good honest cause. We are broke, and Frank is in Kansas City just getting out of the hospital and has no money to start over with. But that won't affect my work."

"I should say not," he said, more gently than I had ever heard him speak. Then he said to his wife, "Clara, this little lady is Mrs. Frank Hamilton, known as the best woman cook in this country."

I made two friends right there and with their four children I was treated more like a daughter than a servant, only I got a man's wages. I went to work there in April and worked till the 28th of December, before I ever saw Frank. By that time I had got well and strong. Didn't look much like the little, frail girl I was when I went to work in April. This is one chapter in my life I have tried to forget. Not that I am ashamed of it, I only did what any true wife would do, but just the same it is a part of my life not one of my children knows of, nor will unless they read of it here.

Frank had got work when he left the hospital, but he had a big debt to pay even with my help. Once in debt it is so hard to get out, and living in the city was expensive, and every time he would get about straight, he got sick again. He couldn't stand the smoke and dust and confinement of the city. The doctor told him his lungs were badly affected, and he must go to the country at once if he wanted to avoid consumption. He came by to get me and we stayed with Lucy a week. He had saved some money and so had I. He talked over his plans with me, so that was one big victory I had gained by being patient.

He had a job of millwright which would last a couple of months at Camden, Arkansas, and a job at Thornton, Arkansas, after that. Flynn was moving to Big Bay just two miles from Thornton. We were happy as two children, planning how we would keep house and start life over again. We had each other and all life before us, but I almost choked over that word "us," for Frank didn't look like he had longer than two years before him. But getting out of the city would help him.

At the end of a week, he went on to his work, and I went back to mine. Lucy and Frank both begged me not to go back, but I told them Mrs. Childress had been too good to me for me to leave her without giving her a chance to get another cook. So I went back for a month, and when I left them in February after almost a year, it was like leaving home. I loved every one of them.

I went to Frank to start my new home. We had money enough to start housekeeping and a little ahead for a rainy day. Thornton was a nice little town; two or three big sawmills, several stores, churches, and a good school. The country was just rolling enough to be pretty and was covered with heavy pine timber, what is called longleaf pine, I think. It was valuable, for there were sawmills and planing mills every two or three miles from Pine Bluff to Camden on that railroad. Frank was out in the timber all the time.

We made a fine little garden, late, but we could get all the fresh vegetables we needed, and we had fine water. Frank's health was soon much better except for spells of rheumatism and headaches. He didn't drink any that summer and got to be jolly; I was happier than I had been in all my married life. We were living just close enough to Lucy so that we could visit each other. Some way we were drawn closer together since Jane's death. Poor sweet little Jane. Her baby was born while I was in Shannon County, Missouri. She never got over it and died just one month later, two days after my baby died. I can't think of her even yet as dead. Her death made some difference in us all. She gave her baby to Jim's mother, and our baby brother Johnny and Jim stayed on there in Michigan.

Summer that year drew to a glorious close, and fall came in bringing my third baby boy. He was born the second of October. Of course, he was the sweetest living child on earth. We both knew it and had no trouble proving it by Lucy and Flynn. They had rented a house next door so Lucy could be near me, and both of them were as silly as Frank and I were about the baby. As usual, I tried to name him after Frank, but as usual Frank said, "No, I have him named. His name is Oswald Hamilton."

I said, "Why do you always tack on 'Hamilton'? What else could it be? And why will you never have but one name before the 'Hamilton'?"

It seemed strange to me in those days when most children had three or four names. But Frank just laughed and said, "An old habit of mine, but it won't be changed."

I had to make the best of it, but it became a part of the cloud of his past that was always dropping between us. One day not long after our first baby had been born, I told Frank I wanted the baby christened in my church, the Presbyterian. But Frank said, "My children will be christened in the Church of England or in none."

He had been drinking a little and when I went on to say I would like the baby to have more than one name, he looked at me so hard, and said, "When he is christened in my church he will have another name, but not until then."

Then he got up and went out, and when I asked him about it when he was sober, he put me off as always. And I wondered and worried. Was Frank's name really Hamilton, and if it wasn't, was I legally married to him? I studied about it, but it was all darkness, and I had his promise, so I tried to forget it.

Before the baby was a week old, Frank got a letter from a friend of his, an engineer at a big band sawmill not far away, and also one from the superintendent, asking him to come and take the engineer's place for a week. He would get good wages and be doing them a great favor. We knew the engineer had lost his wife, and had a little two-year-old girl that he wanted to take to his mother in Missouri. I told Frank he must go, that I could get along. Lucy told him she and Flynn would stay with me, and the baby and I were both doing fine.

Frank was to go down on the four o'clock train that same evening. He got ready to start, and Flynn came in. He said, "Frank, I want to show you my new clothes."

Flynn was close, stingy with himself—he spent everything he made on Lucy—but this time he had ordered himself a new suit of clothes, hat, shoes, and all, and they had just come in that day. He ran home and brought them all over. Frank said, "I believe I will try them on."

He began putting them on. He was quick in all his movements. He got them on, strutted around over the room. Flynn began to get uneasy. "Hurry up and get my clothes off. You'll be late for the train."

Frank looked at his watch and said, "You're right. I won't have time to change. Don't worry, Flynn, for they look almost as well as my own, and you can wear mine if you need to dress up before I get back."

Flynn looked like he was about to cry. "You even have my hat and shoes on. Please take them off."

Frank picked up his satchel, kissed the baby and me, and said, "So long, Flynn. Just one short week till we meet again, and nothing but death will separate me from your new clothes."

He left. Flynn grumbled around for a while, but Lucy and I laughed at him, and he soon got over it. I got along all right, except I had an uneasy feeling about Frank. Lucy laughed at it and said, "You're just remembering the last time he went away to be gone a few days, and it being when your last child was born. You are all right and so is Frank, and there's nothing to worry about."

Still I worried but didn't let her know.

The next day about eleven o'clock Flynn came by the house. He had been uptown. We could tell he was excited and asked him what was wrong. "Nothing," he said, but he stooped down and kissed the baby. Lucy was nursing it, and I saw him whisper something to her. In a minute she got up, laid the baby down on the bed beside me, and said she had to go over home for a few minutes. In about half an hour, Flynn came back in, sat down beside me, and began trying to talk.

"Mary, I—I—you see—oh, damn it, I can't tell you. I'll go home and make Lucy come."

I said, "Flynn, are you still grieving about those clothes?"

"No, no, I wish it was the clothes," and he was gone, leaving me to think what I pleased.

It must have been another half hour before Lucy came back, and when she came in I could see she had been crying. She picked the baby up, knelt down by me, hugged us both in her arms, and began to sob and cry. But before she could speak, Flynn came rushing to the door, and said, "Never mind, Lucy. Here he comes."

She jumped up and went tearing out the door, and in about five minutes here came Frank into the room. He walked, or staggered, up to me and said, "Well, thank God, home again."

I wish I could describe how he looked, for you would understand why I was so angry and so humiliated. He was dirty and had one eye bandaged. He had on a suit of black serge clothes about three sizes too large for him and a straw hat. Frank was a neat, well-dressed man at all times, and this was the first time I had ever seen him look slouchy. It was somewhat comical, but I was too mad to laugh. He could see out of one eye, but there was no sober intelligence in it. I said, "This is the first time I have ever been sorry to see you come home. You have been drinking and fighting after promising me you never would drink enough away from home to get drunk. You got your just dues this time, as I see you got whipped."

He looked so astonished and so hurt and said in such a queer voice, "Yes, my dear, but not as bad as the other two. I am the only one that came out alive. And I didn't know I was alive until a couple of hours ago, so I borrowed this suit of clothes, as I was naked, and hired a man to bring me home on a speeder to keep you from being scared to death, and now this is the thanks I get."

Lucy burst out laughing. "If you could see yourself as you are, you wouldn't blame her. Go look in the mirror while I explain. Mary, two hours ago we got a telegram that the mill Frank was to run blew up two of its boilers and killed the engineer, fireman, and Frank, all three. That is what Charlie and I were trying to tell you, but thank goodness Frank got here, or his ghost, just in time to spare you."

Of course I was so sorry and begged him to forgive me. He patted my head and said, "Since looking in the glass, I'll have to. Yes, poor Taylor is dead, and someone else will have to take his little baby girl home to his mother. He was to work with me until noon, then I was to take charge. I was with him, stooping down to look at a new piece in the engine he was explaining to me when we heard a hissing noise. He raised up. I didn't. Then steam, brick, wood were whirling around us so fast I couldn't see him, but I felt him knocked against me. I knew he was dead and I soon would be if I got driven into that engine. I crawled as far away from it as I could, kept crawling till I saw daylight. How I ever got clear of that wreck only God knows. I managed to get back to the hotel and was trying to get up on the porch, when a bunch of women came out of the hotel, and when they saw me began screaming. That was the first I knew I was naked. I didn't have a stitch of clothes on and was covered with mud, sand, and gravel. I was a pretty sight. I must have fainted, for when I came to, a doctor and bunch of men and boys were standing around, but no ladies. Mary, that show was for men only. I told the doctor to clear the bunch out and lend me a shirt and pair of pants as I was going home.

" 'Not yet, young fellow, till we get some of this mud off to see how bad you're hurt,' he said.

"About that time the superintendent came up. He said, 'It's Frank Hamilton of Thornton. We've been looking for your body for an hour.'

"I told him I must get home as you would be frightened to death, so he lent me these clothes. While I was bathing and dressing, he told me poor Taylor was killed outright, a large iron rod drove through his head, and he was scalded all over, but none of his clothes were torn off. The fireman was found a hundred feet from the boiler shed and lived just long enough to tell them he had let water into dry red-hot boilers. I got partly washed and dressed, and the superintendent had a speeder and a Negro ready to bring me home."

Frank had left word for the doctor from town to come out, and just then he walked in. How he did laugh when he saw Frank. "You are the dirtiest-looking customer I ever saw, but no offense, for I don't want to have to fight a man that has gone through what you did and then got on a speeder an hour later and rode twenty-five miles home. That takes grit."

When he took the bandage off Frank's head, he saw that one eyelid was cut almost off. He had to take three stitches, but the eye wasn't even scratched. The only burn he had was a blister on the top of his head about the size of a saucer. Except for that, there wasn't a scratch on him. Where the gravel was forced under the skin, it didn't bring a drop of blood. While picking the gravel out of his scalp, the doctor said, "Hamilton, this is not the first wreck you've been in, from the look of the back of your head."

Frank said, "Those are leech pits. I was sunstruck twice, and they used leeches to draw the blood from my head."

The doctor said, "You must have been in a hot country to get sunstruck twice."

"Would it ease your curiosity any and make you go a little easier if I told you I spent a few years in India? Twice I tried going bareheaded from my office to another about thirty feet away. The sun got me both times, but it wasn't half as hot as you trying to dig that gravel out back there with a grubbing hoe."

Frank got word from the superintendent to come back as soon as he got able and help set the new machinery, but Frank said it would be a long time before he'd trust himself around machinery again, that he'd stick to timber work. Flynn and Lucy were moving to Pine Bluff.

"Why don't we go to Missouri, Frank?" I said. I had had a letter from Sam asking us to come and spend the winter with them, saying he needed Frank to keep books and could give him good wages. I wanted to go. If I couldn't be near Lucy, it would be next best to be near Sam and Ida, for I was afraid the shake-up Frank got in the mill was going to be worse than he expected. The work up in Missouri wouldn't take up more than half Frank's time, and he could get out in that mountain air, drink good pure water, and when spring opened up could hunt squirrels and fish for trout and bass in the mountain streams. Sam had a sawmill on the edge of the Castor River and would furnish us a nice little house on its bank, free of rent.

We couldn't see much money in it, but there would be a year's pleasure and maybe good health for Frank. So we sold out the most of our things again, packed our trunks with what was left, clothes and bedding, took our boy Ozzie, and started.

For Better and Worse

WHEN WE GOT THERE, SAM WAS AT THE DEPOT with a sleigh to meet us. Our trip to Sam's house was a treat. There was just enough snow on the ground to make sleighing good, and when we got there a good warm supper and a warm welcome awaited us. We were all young; they had two children, we had one. We stayed with them a week until Frank could get to town to get a stove and what few things we needed, and then we went to housekeeping.

The cold weather bothered me some, but I soon got used to it. Frank enjoyed it. He had a good warm mackinaw and other heavy clothes. Our baby was growing fast, and fine, and was so good. To me who had lost two boys he was the sweetest child on earth. Frank made a desk and worked on Sam's books at home. I believe it was the first time in my married life I was really happy, all my worries forgotten. Someway Frank and I seemed nearer each other. We both loved this outdoor life, this being away alone from boardinghouses and the thousand little worries that go with them.

We could hardly wait till spring came to get out in the woods, and all at once it came. A few warm days melted the snow and left no mud, as it was a gravelly, rocky soil, heavy yellow-and-gray clay, but good, for where they farmed they made good corn, wheat, and oats and had fine gardens and fruit orchards. It was a wonderful fruit country.

The Castor River was so pretty, water clear as crystal, and the bank, as spring opened, was covered with groundvine and grass to the very edge of the water. No cane, briars, or underbrush, but big tall straight pines made a shade all along the river bank and ran back on the hills clear to the tops, looking like they almost reached the sky. I had never fished in my life, but the water was so clear we could see the fish three and four feet under water, and I was anxious to try my luck. Frank rigged up trout hooks that winter for himself and me and told me so much about trout and bass fishing I felt like an old hand at it and could hardly wait for my first day's try. My hardest lesson was learning to bait my hook. I could manage the crawfish at last, and as they used crawfish for trout and bass fishing, that was all I needed.

So the great day came. I took my baby, who was beginning to walk and talk some, and went fishing. When I dropped my hook in the water, something jerked and started running and thrashing, but at last I landed it. A big black bass. I was so excited, and I caught four more in just a little while. As they weighed from one to three pounds apiece, I had a good mess for us all. I smothered them and basted them with lemon, and Sam and Ida took dinner with us.

After that Frank rigged some set hooks, showed me how to set them out just before dark, and told me they must be looked at about daylight or the fish would get off the hook. He told me he would look at them the first morning, but I slipped out of bed, got my fire going and water on to boil for coffee, and went down to the river. I couldn't wait for Frank to go. I wanted all the honors. And sure enough, something had my hook. The pole was bent down to the water. I took hold of it and began to pull. It was so heavy I thought sure I had a whale. I gave a big heave and jerked it out of the water—it was a terrible big black snake, wriggling and squirming. One look was enough. I screamed and started running, screaming every jump, but scared so bad I didn't have sense enough to drop the pole.

Frank and my brother and his wife all came running in their night-clothes, but I was headed for home and never stopped nor dropped my pole till I ran against the steps. When the two men saw the eel, they howled with laughter. But not me. I shook like a leaf. When Frank could speak for laughing, he said, "Little Eve, I had another hook up the river. Run and get that."

"Why don't you kill that, or put it back in the river?" I said, still shaking with fright, not daring to take my eyes off that black, writhing snake.

"Not much," Frank said. "That is the finest fish I have seen in the river. We will have it for dinner." And we did. But he cooked it, not me. He killed it by chopping off its tail instead of its head.

The next morning he caught a white salmon. Just like the saltwater salmon except that it was snow-white. There were very few of them in that river. The four years we were there we never saw but two.

That year was almost too happy to be true. Sam and Ida were jolly good company; Frank had a few spells of rheumatism, but not many, and he didn't drink. Sam didn't drink, and Frank didn't seem to care about it. He was out in the timber a good deal, scaling logs. He kept all the books for Sam, but almost every evening would take his gun, go around a cornfield and kill three or four squirrels. He or I caught fish almost every day, just any time we wanted them.

Almost every Saturday in that country there would be a shooting match. The men shot at a mark with a rifle at a hundred yards; every man got two shots, and the one hitting the closest to the bull's-eye got a prize—a turkey, ham, or quarter of beef. Each contestant had to pay ten cents to enter. A man called Jim George was the best rifle shot in the country and carried off the prize every time. One day Sam said to him, "Jim George, I have a dollar to bet that Hamilton can take your own gun and beat you shooting."

Between them they talked Frank into going to the match that Saturday. The prize that day was a turkey. They had to go horseback five miles through the hills.

Frank said there were about twenty-five men and boys gathered there to shoot. When George got his two shots, he came within an inch of the bull's-eye. He said, "Sam, you as well give me that dollar."

Sam said, "Wait till Hamilton shoots. He is good, and if he beats you, you carry the turkey home for him."

Frank took George's rifle and hit the bull's-eye both times. They all cheered him and guyed George about having to carry the turkey. We invited Jim George and his wife and Sam and Ida over for dinner to eat the turkey next day. After that Frank went every Saturday and if he didn't carry off the prize, George did, and as we always shared everything, it didn't make much difference. Frank got to be popular with those good, old-timey hillbillies. One old man walked up to him one day and said, "Mr. Hamilton, how long was you in this country afore you could talk our language?"

Frank, just as solemn, said, "I have been here, sir, ten years, and can't speak it yet."

So the sweetest, happiest year of my whole life began to come to a close, and in a still, beautiful fall day in October my little Nina was born. I had been so happy all year I knew she would be sweet-natured and good. At a week old her little short golden curls shone like a halo around her head. She had dark lashes and dark gray eyes like her father's. Now that is just a mother's view. As she was my first girl, I could easily be excused for thinking her an angel; but I must say that her hair was an unusual color in everyone's opinion. It was pure yellow gold, and it never changed color from her birth to her death. Another thing: across the bridge of her little nose was the same faint bluish line her father had there, and that I had often asked him about. It was such a mark as might have been made by wearing glasses, but he had never worn glasses since I knew him, nothing but a single eyeglass or monocle. But when I would ask him about it, he would tell me first one thing and then another. He was always teasing me about my curiosity, telling me things just to get me to worry over them. Sometimes I think he told me silly tales to confuse me, to keep me from studying over things about his past life that in spite of his hugging so close, every now and then bobbed to the surface. But one night when he had had a drink or two, he said, "Well, little Eve, that mark on my nose is a birthmark." I thought he was trying to put me off and didn't believe it any more than the half-dozen other things he had told me it was, but when Nina was born with the same little faint mark, I began to think maybe it was a birthmark.

That second winter Frank had a spell of pneumonia in February that left him with a cough two different doctors told him was consumption. It fretted him and made him so mad to have them say that, but the first time he got out in the cool dry air, he took a coughing spell and had a hemorrhage. But as the weather got warmer, he got better and went about his work cheerful as ever. My brother said he was the grittiest man he ever saw, so determined to get well, to try to make something. We both loved the country and the people, so we went through another summer, with sickness, joy, and trouble, mixed. Little Oswald had a few chills, but not enough to make him stop playing with his little sister. I would take them for long walks all over the woods. We would fish in the river and gather wild flowers. Ozzie knew almost every bird and flower by name. He was full of joy and the love of living, but every time he got a little sick we had a doctor and gave him so much medicine I think we made him nervous. I can see that now, but we had lost two baby boys, and we loved him so, enough for all of them.

Late that fall the mill shut down, Sam moved to his home in the country, and Frank got a job as bookkeeper in a nearby town. It was a beautiful little village on the same river, but my outdoor life was at an end. One thing, we were in a country village, and those days a woman was supposed to stay indoors; another thing, I got all the sewing I could do and we needed the money. Part of my work I couldn't get money for, but took butter, eggs, fresh meat, vegetables, or fruits, so Frank could save almost all he made.

Not long after we made this move, Lucy came to us to stay. She wrote us a heartbroken letter that Flynn had got in trouble, and although Sam despised Flynn, for Lucy's sake he went to see about him. When Flynn and Lucy moved to Pine Bluff, Flynn went to work as watchman for a man who owned a big mill and store, an old friend of Flynn's years before. Flynn was trusted with all the keys and knew the combination of the store safe. They began missing money and goods of all kinds from the store. This went on for several months, and when they checked up they found they were short almost $3,000. They arrested Flynn. Sam hired a lawyer when he got there and paid the biggest part himself, and we paid fifty dollars of it, which drained our little savings.

When the trial came up, Flynn's lawyer got him to plead guilty. Lucy was in the courtroom. She was a good-looking girl, always dressed nice and neat. Her clothes were not fine, but she had a weakness for jewelry and wore two or three gold rings at once, her watch and chain, and bracelets. Had had them all for years, as Flynn gave her jewelry every Christmas. She believed in his innocence, as Frank and I did, but when he pled guilty in court (I could just see her big blue eyes open in wonder and surprise), she walked over to where he sat and asked him if he meant that. He hung his head and nodded yes. She stripped off all her jewelry, flung it at him, and walked out of the courtroom. She never saw him again. Of course that cooked Flynn's goose. Whether he was guilty or not, the court all thought the jewelry had been bought with the stolen money, and Flynn was sent to the penitentiary for six years.

Lucy went home, packed all the clothes she could in one trunk, sold everything they had, kept out train fare to us, and sent Flynn the rest of the money. We knew now she had never cared for him, or she would have stood by him. Married at fourteen to a man twenty years older than herself, who made it a business to spoil her, she was lazy and no wonder. She had never had to work and wouldn't work, but she was so good to my children. Loved them as her own. I could trust them with her, and I sewed almost day and night after she came. The doctor told me I was sewing too much, that it was against me and the baby I was expecting the coming December, but we did need the little I could make that way so bad.

Oswald was going on five years old, Nina soon would be two. She was playful and healthy, had been all her life. One day Oswald was teaching her to play marbles. He shot his marble; then instead of her shooting it, she picked it up and started to run. He ran after her to get his marble away from her, and she threw it in her mouth. She was running, laughing and it slipped down her throat. For a minute I thought she would choke to death, then it went on down. We had a doctor there in a few minutes. He did all he could to pass it off, and I kept her close for more than a week trying to get it, but never did. There were no X-ray machines that we knew of those days, and the doctor said, "It may never hurt her, and again it may kill her years from now." We worried a good deal and watched her so close for months afterward, but there was nothing we could do, and she showed no ill effects from it.

As cold weather was coming on, Frank gave up his bookkeeping and got work nearby in a factory as foreman. We were doing well, making big preparations for Christmas and the children. Oswald could talk of nothing else, and for Nina, it was "Santa Claus, Santa Claus," laughing and playing all day long in the house, as it was cold.

On the sixteenth of December my baby was born, a little girl. Frank named her Leslie. Two days later Oswald had a chill. Just a light chill, and not very high fever, but he mustn't be sick for Christmas. The doctor was coming to see me again that day, so Frank, who was going into the country and wouldn't be back till late that night, met the doctor and told him to fix up some medicine for the boy. "I think he has a touch of malaria," he said, "but if you give him calomel, put Dovers powders or something in it to keep it from making him so sick."

When the doctor came, my house was full of callers, ladies who had come in to see the baby, who was small and frail, not much like Nina. The doctor found I wasn't doing so well and scolded me about the baby. Said I'd almost killed the baby and myself by sewing so much the past year. This doctor and his wife were our very closest friends in that country, and their little boy was Oswald's constant companion. He was in the yard playing with Oswald then. They were just of an age. After fixing my medicine, the doctor called Oswald in to start taking his. He looked at the boy's tongue and eyes, thumped his chest and side, and said, "Old man, your spleen is a little enlarged. I'm going to give you just a little calomel, for you want to have a big Christmas."

The boy began begging off. "Oh no, no, it makes me so sick."

The doctor said, "Yes, but I've put something in it so it won't make you so sick," and he took an orange from his pocket and gave it to him. "Every time you take a dose you can have a piece of that orange."

The doctor left. Everyone left, and the woman who was staying with us came in to give me my medicine and get Oswald to bed. She gave me a dose of my medicine while Oswald got his clothes off and got ready for bed. Then she gave him one dose, and he climbed into his little bed across the room from me. The woman took Nina with her and went back to the kitchen to get supper.

I fell asleep almost as soon as she was out of the room. I have no idea how long I slept nor what woke me with a start. Then I heard a strange sound from across the room. It was Oswald. He was choking, struggling in his bed. I called to him. He didn't answer. I slipped out of bed to see what was wrong, and how can I write it, even now? He was dying, struggling in a hard convulsion. I grabbed him up in my arms and ran screaming through three rooms to the woman in the kitchen. She tried to take him from me, but I was wild, crazy. My boy dying, who less than half an hour before was laughing and playing. His poor little twisted face, and his hands, jerking, struggling, were almost as black as a Negro's. At last she got him away from me, laid him on the bed, and ran for a doctor. But before going she gathered up all that medicine and burned it. She said afterwards she thought he was having a spasm and the medicine was too strong for him, and she was afraid we would give him more unless she destroyed it. But I never thought of the medicine then. God knows, I never thought at all.

Our doctor, the one who gave him the medicine, was gone, but we got in another doctor, a German, and the minute he laid eyes on the child, he said in a voice I'll never forget, "Strychnine poison." Hour after hour they worked with him, but his suffering grew more and more terrible. Late that night Frank came, saw there was no chance for the child, and asked the doctor to give him something to let him go easy. On my knees I begged him to have mercy and let the child die, but they kept trying to save him even when there was no hope. He died at three o'clock that morning.

He died of strychnine given to him through a terrible mistake by our best friend. Frank and I couldn't bring ourselves to consent to an autopsy, and the medicine had been burned; but the German doctor said there could be no doubt. Our boy was gone; nothing we could do would call him back. The lives of that doctor and his wife were wrecked, too, and they were dear friends of ours. That very day he gave up the practice of medicine. We knew it was an awful mistake he would gladly have given his own life to undo.

It never made any difference between his wife and me; if anything, she was nearer and dearer to me than before, but I could not stand to see their little boy. I had always loved him as my own; he and Ozzie had been like brothers, in and out of our house all day long, and now every time I saw their boy I would go wild with grief. I sent him all of Ozzie's Christmas toys but told his mother I couldn't ever see him again. In about a month they moved away.

For weeks after Ozzie was gone I would wake in the night, screaming "Oswald." I would run out in the yard looking for him, and they would have to bring me back. What little milk I had was hurting my baby. It took Lucy to bring me back to my senses and get me to take care of poor little Leslie. She had a bad start in life and has always been little and delicate, but she is the grittiest one of all my children.

Frank, like me, felt life in Missouri had gone stale, and he was just waiting for any chance to leave. It came early that spring. We had one churchhouse in our village, owned by the Methodists and Christians. The hardshell Baptists met there every third Sunday. One third Sunday, a good old hardshell brother came along and said he was there to preach in that church till he got every man, woman, and child in the town in his church. He preached all through the week and started on Sunday, the Methodists' day. They tried to reason with him, but it ended in a row and there was no preaching that day. Monday morning he started preaching again. Lots of the mill hands and the second foreman under Frank had joined the church, and the mill work was suffering. They were trying to run double time on a rush order for strawberry crates and boxes. The next Sunday when the Christians began to gather for their services, there came the Baptists, too. They had some scrappers on both sides, and this time it ended in a free-for-all fight. When the Christians won, the second foreman of the mill hollered out, "Come on Baptists, we'll go to the mill and have preaching."

Frank was at the mill tinkering at the boiler when the crowd of Baptists got there. He tried to reason with the preacher but couldn't do anything with him, so when the preacher took his stand near the boiler and began ranting, Frank pulled off his shirt, slipped on a jumper, picked up a big hammer and crawled inside the boiler. He began hammering and swearing so you couldn't hear the preacher for him. When he crawled out of the boiler, he heard the preacher announce they would hold services in the mill all week.

"Like hell you will," Frank said. "This mill starts tomorrow and every hardshell Baptist in the county can't stop it."

But he was mistaken. The second foreman sent a wire to headquarters in St. Louis, saying the head foreman was drunk and trying to tear down the mill and kill all hands. So on Monday morning Frank got a wire suspending him as foreman till they could investigate. This was all he wanted. He wired back: "To hell with the mill. I am through. Am starting south tomorrow." Then he came home and told me he was going.

We had talked over going south many times, for he could never be well here any more. He had talked of trying Texas but now decided he would go by and see my brother-in-law Jim Thompson on his way. Jane's baby had died six months after Jane's death, and Jim had come south again and was in Arkansas City. Johnny was with me. How I hated to see Frank go so soon after losing Ozzie, but that was the way he always did things, all in a minute, asking advice of no one. It took all of our money for Frank, but I could easily get along by taking a few boarders, along with my sewing. Lucy and Johnny were with me to help. So Frank left the next morning, promising to send for us as soon as he could.

It was so lonely after he left. In a week I heard from him. He was with Jim in Arkansas City and was feeling fine. Jim, he said, was fixing to move to Gunnison, Mississippi, and had a settlement to make that covered eight years. Frank had agreed to straighten his books over there which were in a hopeless tangle. It would take him a month to do the work and he would send money in his next letter. The next letter said he was well and was going to stay in Gunnison as long as he stayed well. He seemed in good spirits.

Almost a year from the time he left us, he decided Mississippi was at last the climate that suited him, and he sent for us.

PART TWO

The Mississippi Delta

Memphis
Tenn.

Arkansas

Prairie

Mississippi River

Delta

Y. & M. V. R. R.

Y. & M. V. R. R.

Ill. Cen. R. R.

Concordia
Island

Dublin

Tutwiler

Charleston

Convict
Farm

Rome

Sumner

Shelby

Gunnison

Tombarland

Sumter River

Mund

Webb

Parchman

Mound Bayou

Lomaston

Potts

Merigold

Drew

Line

Ruleville

Phillip

Mississippi

Mississippi River

Southern

Yellow

R. R.

Greenwood

Grenville

Moorhead

Railroads

North

0 5 10   20   30
Scale of Statute Miles

Carter

Yazoo City

Concordia Island

IT WAS A COLD GLOOMY MORNING IN JANUARY 1896 when I started with my two little girls, my sister Lucy, and my brother Johnny, to what was to us a new world, the Mississippi Delta. Frank sent us directions how to go to Memphis, but no further, as he was to meet us there, and we were to go on by boat, the *Kate Adams,* to our new home on the Concordia Island, five miles from Gunnison, Mississippi. Through a mistake, we missed Frank and had to take a train to Gunnison. Frank got to Memphis and came tearing across town just in time to see our train pulling out. He knew we wouldn't get to Gunnison until the next day, as we had to lay over night in Delta, Mississippi. So he came right back by boat and met us the next day at Gunnison.

Oh, I was so glad to see him again. He was tanned, the white chalky color all gone, and was fifteen pounds heavier than when he left Missouri. Nina knew him, but baby Leslie wouldn't have a thing to do with him. He hadn't seen her since she was a few weeks old, and now she was running everywhere and talking some.

Frank and Jim Thompson were working together. Jim was there to meet us, with Frank.

"Wait till you see your beautiful new homes," Jim said, and I could see my good jolly brother as of old was a little uneasy for fear I would be disappointed, as this was going to be my first experience of camp life.

We went from Gunnison in a two-horse buggy, Frank and Jim on horseback. We drove down the Mississippi River levee about a mile, then turned off the levee down into the thickest timber I had ever seen. Oak, gum, ash, hackberry, and poplar stood so thick, with no underbrush, only big blue cane growing rank and tall, almost to the limbs of the trees. It looked so odd, but what looked odder still to me was the black mud, "gumbo," Frank said it was. When we came out on the Mississippi River, the ground was sandy, but it was black sand, and the woods were thinner; there were fewer trees but larger—big old cottonwoods and sycamores that seemed to me when I looked up like their tops were lost in the sky. It was a pretty sight, except the road. The soft black sand was almost hub deep, but at last we came in sight of our future home, and what a sight!

Jim's office and commissary and bedrooms were built of clapboards, his cook shanty the same, with a small dining room for the white men, who were never more than four, as he worked Negroes altogether. Then there were the Negroes' cooking shanties and a few cabins; it was altogether like a little town. Jim rode alongside the buggy and asked me what I thought of "Clapboard City." I choked back a sob, I don't know whether of relief or disappointment. I didn't know then. But I managed to say, "Fine. I have always wanted to try camp life."

Frank had stopped at the roadway to see about some teams, and Jim went on with us. He explained to us that at Gunnison the river began a forty-mile bend, coming back almost to Gunnison again, and that was why the land lying between the river and the levee was called Concordia Island, although it was really a long neck of land sur-rounded by water—all but a little strip at Gunnison. Beyond Jim's place we saw a big white tent, the largest I ever saw. Nina pointed to it and said, "Pretty white house." Nothing would satisfy her but to drive right on down there. It was a big tent thirty by twenty feet, floored and boxed in four feet high; there was a nice big cookstove in the front end and a big Kind heater in the middle. The back was curtained off into bedrooms, small but large enough. This was to be our home, as Frank had to live and sleep out of doors. I had left Lucy at the hotel in Gunnison until our things came, and I was glad I had known better than to let her come out in camp before we got fixed up.

We stayed that first night with Jim. Nina took up with him, and he said it was like finding his own little girl. Nina, like me, had never got over her brother's death, but the change to this new country, and being with her father, was helping us both already. She had always seemed to love Frank so much, and he worshipped her.

The next day our things came, and I sent after Lucy. She was, as I knew she would be, disgusted with everything, but I kept her so busy she couldn't say much. We put down carpet in the back of our tent house. It reached from the back of the tent to the heater, and I had rugs for the other side of it. We put up our beds, two bedsteads and a child's bed. I had four big feather beds besides the child's feather bed and eight big feather pillows. That sounds silly now, but those days the more feather beds you had the better off you were supposed to be. And I had plenty of nice bedclothes. So when we got all our things in, our dining table, little cook table, cupboard for dishes, cupboard for clothes, trunks, and small, splintbottom homemade chairs, we were all fixed up nice. We had plenty to cook, and, oh, how you can eat in camp. Jim took his meals with us. He had a big commissary and wouldn't let Frank charge hardly anything to himself. He never went to town without bringing us all kinds of choice cuts of meat, and fruit, and he never forgot the children. Would bring them toys, clothes, anything he could see that he thought they would like.

One time when he was in Greenville he got Nina a beautiful white silk dress and six yards of white ribbon with pale blue and yellow violets "to trim it in," he said. I told him I would lay it away until she got older or until we got in a house. He said, "Make it now. She looks just like a fairy or an angel. I can't understand how a child as hand-some as Nina could be the child of you and Frank. I guess you want to save it for her wedding dress."

Nina spoke up so serious. "Uncle Jim, I don't want a wedding dress. Mamma is going to make it now and I am going to wear it and wear it for you, and I am going to wear it when I go to heaven."

Then she ran out to play, and Jim said, "Why does she talk so much of going to heaven? It isn't right to put such stuff in a child's head, Mary."

I told him I had not, and I couldn't understand it either, unless it was her brother Oswald. Ozzie had always talked that way, and they were so devoted to each other. When he died, and they told her he had gone to heaven, she ran to him and clung to him, crying, "Wait, Ozzie, wait. I go with you. I want to go. I want to go." They couldn't console her. Lucy tried to get her to notice the baby, Leslie, but she would only say, "It is sweet, but I want to go to heaven with Ozzie." She was in bed several days with fever after he died.

When I got hold of myself a little, I told them they must ignore her talk of going to heaven, but it did little good. In time she talked less of Oswald and heaven, but when something like this would come up and she would talk so natural about going to heaven, I sometimes thought it was never out of her mind. How little we can know what is in the mind of a child.

Jim said, "I have heard her mention heaven several times. She is so happy and contented, full of fun and mischief, yet she has the saddest look at times. You make that dress, Mary, and I will see she wears it out, and I will never get her another white dress." He kept his word and got her every other kind, but never white.

Once settled, I had time to look around me, see more of the strange country and people, and adopt them as my own, for why shouldn't I love a country that gave Frank back his health, his very life? It was a mild winter, and almost every day I took my children and Lucy and went to the river bank to watch the men build their raft. It was fine to go up there well-wrapped and build us a fire; the children and I never tired watching the stream of boats and the waves rolling behind them. But Lucy, not her! She didn't like anything about camp life.

Either Frank or Jim was at the raft all the time, the other one in the woods. They had from six to eight log wagons going all the time; eight-wheeled wagons, the wheels boxed in to keep them from bogging up in the mud, and from eight to ten oxen to a wagon. Many of the logs were so large they couldn't get but one on a wagon. I have seen Frank stand on the ground beside the butt cut of a tree, and he could just lay his hand on top of it. They hauled the logs to the river bank and rolled them off in the river; then the men would float them up against the raft and fasten them together with poles. Gum and oak they called "sinkers"; these they would pin between cottonwoods, ash, and cypress, "floaters," to keep them from sinking. A large rope was tied every fifty feet with wire cables to trees along the bank or to posts driven in the ground. When they got enough logs rafted together to send to Greenville, they would send for tugboats, bunch the rafts together, and float them there to be sold.

I was happy and contented and so were the children. Every day brought a new adventure. Soon winter was over, and spring came with warm rains. Violets were everywhere, and green grass, and the trees putting out new leaves. Spring was in the air, in our blood, in the frogs, too, for they held a concert every night. Bees were flying around gathering honey from the holly blooms, and the holly trees were shedding their old leaves and putting on new. Every day in falling timber they would find a bee tree, and Frank would bring in three or four gallons of fine white honey.

We were all happy but Lucy. She was gloomy, blue, discontented. Said she couldn't stand this godforsaken place any longer. The lady that ran the hotel in Gunnison had visited us several times, and she and Lucy took a liking to each other. Lucy's romantic dreams weren't coming true, camping and living like Indians as we did, and I wasn't surprised when she came to me one day and said, "I'm going to Gunnison to stay at the hotel with Mrs. Huse. I will help her enough to pay my board, until you get out of this hole."

I was sorry, but she was twenty-four years old and knew her own business. She had taken her life in her own hands ten years before. So Johnny took her out to Gunnison, and she left the island to return only on short visits. I am afraid we all felt relieved when she left, for she was so dissatisfied she took lots of the brightness out of our lives. But she was so good to my children I missed her lots.

Frank and Jim had sold their first big raft and were starting another, which would clean up all the timber on the island. One morning at the breakfast table Jim Thompson could think of nothing else to get up a laugh, so he told a dream he had the night before. We all knew he made it up, but that made me wish I could ever have a dream to tell. Next morning Jim spun a yarn that lasted all through breakfast and then asked, "Who's next?"

I said, "I had a dream last night, a real dream. I dreamed Frank cut his foot with an axe and bled almost to death."

"Mary," Jim said, "that's fine for a beginner. I couldn't spin a bigger fib myself; if you keep on, you'll beat the prophets of old."

We all laughed, but Frank had not been in the woods that morning two hours till he went to show a new man how to hew a stave and stuck the corner of the axe in the side of his foot to the bone. He said that just for fun that morning he had put a white cloth in his pocket for a bandage, and as he went to hewing, the cloth fell out of his pocket and made him remember my dream; he laughed, and that made him whack his foot. He told me to leave the dream-telling to Jim from now on. I laughed, but from that night on I dreamed every night. You can't work so hard that your mind is not busy too, and I had no other women to talk to, no time to read. I gave myself up so to dreaming at night, and studying about it the next day, that I believe I must have marked the baby I was carrying, though I never thought of such a thing at the time nor until long afterwards.

For a week I dreamed every night, and it seemed as if always some little thing I dreamed came true the next day. But I didn't tell any more dreams, until about a week after Frank hurt his foot, I had another bad dream about him. This time it was his hand he cut. I told it at the breakfast table, and the men had lots of fun over it, urging him to take an emergency kit to the woods with him. He asked me why I always picked on him to get hurt, and I told him I didn't know whether it was because I knew he was careless, or whether it was because he was always in my mind.

However it was, that day just before quitting time, he picked up a small axe to trim a stick of timber. He was in a hurry, holding the stick upright on a log, and made a mislick that split his hand between his thumb and forefinger, almost severing his thumb from his hand. That stopped his working for several days, and it stopped my telling my dreams for several weeks. Then again I had one that was so real to me I couldn't keep from telling it to Frank while we were getting breakfast. I wouldn't have told it to the men or to Mr. Cavenaugh for anything.

Mr. Cavenaugh was a very fine man who had been boarding with us ever since we arrived. He told me one morning to make out his board bill as he was leaving for a while. Might be back in a month but couldn't say, as he was taking a crew to cut some cypress timber about five miles away. That night as he came to supper he brought me a set of five books by Charles Lamb and gave them to me.

It was that night I dreamed I saw him working on a scaffold with three other men, sawing down a big cypress tree. The tree started to fall, and they all jumped off the scaffold and started to run. He jumped last and fell. The tree was coming back on them. I saw him scrambling around trying to get out of the way, but it caught him. Frank said, when I told him the dream, "This is one time you've made a mistake,

Calamity Ann, with your dreaming. That man can come nearer throwing a tree where he wants it than any man I ever saw."

I said nothing to anybody else about it, but when Mr. Cavenaugh came to bid us good-bye an hour later, I felt sure it was the last time we would ever see him. Three days later word came that he had been killed exactly as I had seen it in my dream. I never told another dream until the dream that was set down in the preface of this book. But I dreamed every single night until the following January, when my baby boy Frank was born. I can't account for my dreaming like that, as I never had done it before, and with the birth of my baby, it stopped, except just now and then. Whether it was the dreaming did it or not, that baby was the worst child to sleepwalk that I ever heard of. From the time he was three years old, we had to guard him every hour of the night.

My brother Johnny was a great big boy now, and like all boys of sixteen thought he could do everything anyone else could, but was so full of mischief they were afraid to trust him around the raft or on the loading or dumping ground. So he spent lots of time helping me. There was one thing he could do better than anyone except Frank, and that was shoot. He was a fine sharpshooter but had never hunted much, so Frank began taking him along to get him used to the woods. It was quite a while before he would get too far away in that thick timber to hear the sound of the axes and falling trees, but even then he brought in lots of game—big jet-black squirrels and fox squirrels, but no gray ones. As he learned the woods better, he killed wild turkeys and deer.

One day he was hunting and heard something in a felled treetop. He thought it was a deer and went slipping along with his gun, ready to shoot. He stepped up on the tree, peeped over, and looked straight into the face of a great big bear playing with her cubs, not five feet from him. As he saw her, she saw him. He dropped his gun right down among them, turned and ran yelling for Frank every step of the way.

"Frank, oh Frank, there are a dozen lions after me."

Frank had to make him go back with him after his gun. When they got there they found the gun where he had dropped it and could see where the bears tore up the brush and cane getting away. Game was scarce at the house for awhile after that, as Johnny wouldn't get out far enough to get anything but squirrels. They tormented him so much about his "lions" that he said he would try fishing awhile.

He was as lucky fishing as hunting but insisted on fishing from the raft. Frank rigged him up a shrimp sack out of a towsack, put weights on it, and helped him sink it. Told him to raise the sack carefully every morning when he looked at his hooks, and he would have some fine shrimp. Every morning we would ask him if he had any, and it was always "no." But he brought in plenty of fine fish. One morning Frank and Jim were at the raft, and Johnny came to them carrying the empty sack, threw it down by them, and said, "There is your old shrimp trap. You fellows have just been joshing me. There isn't a shrimp in this river, or if I get any, those old big white crawfish eat them up. The sack is full of them every morning." How they laughed at him, telling him that was shrimp he'd been throwing away!

He was hopping mad by that time, and just then a big tall Negro working on the edge of the raft straightened up, laughed, and said, "Haw-haw, little boy, you sho' is green 'bout dis heah country." Quick as lightning Johnny whirled, hit him on the jaw and knocked him off in the river. They had a time saving him, as he couldn't swim and they were afraid he would get under the raft before they could get him. That stopped their tormenting Johnny so much.

One day he came home, got a big bucket, and told me to get one and come with him. I went, and all along the river bank there were the biggest dewberries I ever saw. They were as large as guinea eggs and made such fine pies for dinner. After dinner we went again and were no time getting five gallons. We went every afternoon until I got enough for all the jam and jelly I wanted.

I must tell you of one more little blunder of Johnny's. Mr. Donalson, whose place was about a mile away, had a big bull that would break in our corral almost every night and fight the oxen. It had gored several of them pretty bad. Jim tried to buy the bull from Donalson just to save his cattle from being crippled up so bad, but he wouldn't sell it, and they couldn't fix a fence he couldn't break through. One morning Jim said, "Frank, are we to be outwitted by Donalson's bull? I was up four or five times last night. Maybe we could hire Johnny to guard the corral nights. If he just wasn't so afraid of lions."

Johnny spoke up, "If you'll pay me in advance I'll risk the lions. I'm older and wiser now." They laughed.

That day Frank brought Jim's double-barreled shotgun down home, put two shells in it and set it down. In a couple of hours Johnny came running to the house and said, "I see a deer just across the bayou."

He grabbed the gun up and broke it down. "Birdshot," he said, taking them out and putting in two buckshells. He was gone about half an hour, came back and said the deer was gone, and set the gun down where he got it. I thought no more about it. That night Jim stayed on after supper. He and Frank were working on the books. About nine o'clock we heard the bull bellering. They both got up. Jim yawned and said, "I'm sleepy. I'm going home." He reached and got his gun. "I'll take my gun home, in case I need it."

Frank went out with him. The noise at the corral was getting worse, and all at once I heard a shot like a cannon. Then everything was quiet. In a little while Frank came in looking so queer. He said, "Who changed shells in that gun?"

I told him Johnny thought he could kill a deer.

"The damn gun almost kicked my lights out. Johnny's great thoughts are going to cause trouble some day," and then he burst out laughing.

In a few minutes Jim came in laughing and asked, "How's the arm?" But they wouldn't tell me anything more, except Jim said, "If Donalson comes around asking about that old baby, Mary, tell him you haven't seen it."

Weeks later Frank told me they got out there that night just as the bull had the gate partly torn down and was jumping over it into the corral. Frank let drive with both barrels of what he thought was birdshot and killed that bull stone dead. They hired a couple of Negroes to haul it to the river, tie a rope around its horns, and tow it downstream a couple of miles.

There was but one drawback to life on the island, and that was water. We had to haul it from the Donalson place or from the river and filter it. They kept saying they were going to drive me a pump, but as their contract called for a certain time to finish their timber, and what they couldn't get out in that time they lost, they kept putting me off about the pump. They were trying to get some timber from Donalson and he was to let them know before they got through, and then they would drive my pump.

When they finally began to draw their work on the island to a close and were sure of Donalson's timber, they drove a pump for me about two hundred yards back from the river. They drove sixty feet and got fine water, clear and cold. It was a treat, but it didn't last long.

The raft they were making now was a mile and a quarter long, fastened securely, tied back on the bank with oiled ropes and wire cables to big trees, some of them a hundred feet back from the bank of the river. The next day after they drove my pump, the wind got up. Not so high, but we heard a roar like thunder, then another. All the men in sight began running to the river. My brother came back, ran to the corral, and caught Jim's horse. He told me the river banks were sloughing off, and they were afraid the raft would go before they could get tugboats enough to handle it. Jim went to Gunnison to telegraph to Greenville for boats. Everything was hurry, confusion, excitement. Frank came to the tent and told me to stay away from the river and keep the children away.

"And if you see it is getting too close, take the children and go back half a mile from the river. Never mind taking anything else. It looks serious, and there's no telling where the banks will stop sloughing." Then he hurried back and left me.

Johnny got all the buckets he could and he and the cook began carrying water from the pump. They hauled the cook a barrel and us one. That roaring, "boom, boom," came every few minutes, and I could see tree after tree slipping into the river and out of sight. Woman's curiosity is so far ahead of her fear that in spite of Frank's warning I had to see. I took the children up the road a piece, fixed them a playhouse and left them to play while I went closer where I could see. What a sight I saw! The big muddy Mississippi River waves were rolling and lashing the banks, and the banks were crumbling away, maybe fifty feet at a time slipping into the river. The roadway was gone, and my dear pump stood out in the river at least a hundred feet from the bank. The raft was swinging around but hadn't broken apart yet, and the end was securely fastened to one tugboat they had managed to pick up. The men were working like mad, unfastening the ropes from the raft where it was swinging away from the bank and reenforcing it further down, almost half a mile.

Johnny was busy as a bee, on the run all the time. As he went by me on some errand, he hollered and asked me if I could swim. I said, "No," and he called back, "Well, you better get a life preserver then, for this place where you're standing will be in the river before I get back. I'm going after the cook now to help me take down our tent and haul it further back."

I went with him, and as we got close to the men's tent, Johnny winked at me, started to run fast, and yelled, "The tent is going in the river. Run for your life." Out of the tent, in his nightshirt, his shirt and pants in one hand, his suitcase in the other, came a man who had been in bed sick for three or four days. Talk about running, he was almost out of sight, when Johnny looked at me and laughed and said, "One outfit less for me to move." Things never got so dangerous but what some of us could find something funny in them.

About three o'clock three more tugboats came and the work of launching the raft started. When they got it all ready it looked like a big island in the middle of the river with four tugboats pushing it. But they weren't pushing it; they were holding it back, and even then they lost more than a hundred big fine logs—big trees breaking the raft, whole sections of it breaking up and scattering. Of course their names were stamped in the end of every log, but there were people living on the Mississippi River then who made their living stealing timber like that, towing the logs to the bank, sawing the ends off and stamping their own names instead.

Well, that dreadful day drew to a close. The responsibility for that raft was over, or our part was. Of course Jim and Frank went along to Greenville with it. They cautioned us to be very careful as there was no telling when the banks would stop caving. The men were to take turns in watching all night. I got a good supper for the white men and made them a big pot of strong coffee to drink through the night. The roaring now was steady, but further away, sounding like distant thunder. I got the children to sleep but didn't undress them. Johnny stayed with us, and neither he nor I slept a wink all night.

By next morning everything was quiet. The trouble seemed over, but the river was running within two hundred feet of Jim's cookhouse, and a steamboat could have passed easily between my pump and the bank. As much as I loved the island I was afraid after that, and the fall rains were still to come. I lived in dread all the time.

The company Jim was working for wanted him to go to Louisiana, and Frank too, but the doctor at Hot Springs had told Frank if he ever found a climate that agreed with him to stay there. Jim argued the climate was the same in Louisiana, but I told him it was too much risk to take. He hadn't had one minute of his old trouble since coming to Mississippi. There was a big stave works opening up not far to the east of us, across the Sunflower River, where he could get work. It was a perfect wilderness over there, and Jim and Johnny were afraid for the children and me to go into it. They, and Frank too, wanted us to stay in Gunnison. I told them I would not live in Gunnison; if Frank could stand the wilderness I could. This time I had my way. Frank and Johnny moved our things across the Sunflower River; Jim moved by steamboat to Louisiana; I took the children and stayed at the hotel in Gunnison for a week to give Frank time to get a camp built.

The saddest part of all was telling Jim Thompson good-bye. There never was a dearer, better brother than he had always been to me as well as to Frank, and something seemed to warn me it was good-bye forever. Poor little Nina clung to him crying like her heart would break, and big strong man as he was, he shed tears, too.

Water

WHEN THE WEEK WAS UP FRANK CAME. He had to go back the same day but made arrangements for a rig from the livery stable to take us out the next day. The driver knew the way to Shelby and on to the Sunflower River. Frank told him to start early so we would have daylight to travel by. Said on the other side of the river he would tear off pieces of paper and drop them in our road so we couldn't get lost after we crossed the river. He gave us plain directions and told us unless we followed them we would be lost and lost bad.

It was fall—clear, sunshiny weather, and the wind was blowing, leaves were falling. When we came to the river, there was a small ferryboat, a public boat built by the stave company. It was on the opposite side, but by pulling on the rope we got it over to us and pulled across. Then our trouble commenced. Standing there on the boat and looking at the bank, I could see everything but a road. Timber of all kinds stood so close together as almost to shut out all daylight; tall cane, blackberry vines, and a tangled mass of all kinds of vines wove around and over it all. I could see the driver, a boy, was nervous and ready to turn back. I felt scared but didn't let on. I laughed at him and told him to come on, I would beat him finding our trail. We found three dim trails spreading out fanwise from the river: cane cut off about a foot from the ground and blazes on the trees about six feet from the ground. We followed all three to the top of the bank, to where they spread out enough so we could pick ours, the middle one. The papers Frank had dropped had all blown away, but at the top of the bank he had pinned a large piece down with a stick, and a few feet further the same. We went back, got in the buggy, and started on, rejoicing. Every little while we would lose our way, have to stop and hunt our paper. We had driven miles, it seemed to me, when we saw ahead a board tacked to a tree, and when we got close enough to read it, saw a hand pointing up a crosstrail and the words "200 yards to F. Hamilton camp."

Thank God. Home at last. We could hear hammering and see smoke rising above the treetops. I was weak with relief and joy. I want to say right here that the baby I was expecting in a few months I was dead sure would be a boy and a regular woodsman, and he was. At three years of age, he could find his way through the woods better than most men. I don't believe he could have been lost.

Frank heard us, came to meet us, and took us into camp. About the first thing I noticed was that Frank and Johnny both were all speckled with a kind of rash. I looked closer and saw it was sand gnat bites, or mosquito bites, and wanted to know why they hadn't unpacked the mosquito nets for the beds. Then, woman fashion, before they could answer, I went on, "Why haven't you moved into the house and put up the beds and the cookstove, instead of living here by a camp fire, and why put the house over there instead of here where your camp fire is?"

Johnny waved his hand and said, "Wait till I catch up before you ask any more. We haven't moved into the house because it isn't finished, and in this pretty weather we like sleeping under the stars. I am cook, and I don't propose having carpenters dropping sawdust and shingles and nails in my cooking. And we put the house here where it is instead of by the fire, because that big range was unloaded there and it was easier to build the house around it than to move it. So you quit asking questions and come and eat a lunch and feed the children, and you will feel better."

My, what a lunch! Good hot coffee, bacon, potatoes, flapjacks, honey, and butter. After we washed the dishes, we looked around. They had cleared off a place for the house. Had felled a big oak tree near, sawed off a cut the length for rafters and framing work, put up the frame thirty feet long and sixteen wide, then rived out boards five feet long to use as boxing, put on like boxing, only in two layers, overlapping, and covered with three-foot boards. We had no floor but the ground. The roof was rived boards. They cut a small ditch all around the house and banked the dirt up against the wall. Left a few windows, made clapboard shutters. Doors were board, like the windows, and hung with hinges. In changing camp so often we always took our doors. In all my camp life I never had a leaky roof. It was snug and warm in winter, cool in summer. We never had many flies, and mosquitoes didn't worry us much as we always slept under mosquito bars.

That first night we had smokes all over the place but couldn't sleep. We covered up heads and all with sheets, but the sand gnats would get under the sheets. In the morning as soon as the sun got up and the wind blew, they were gone, and by that night I was ready for them, our beds up and mosquito bars on each of them. I got everything ready for housekeeping, and everything was clean and nice. You would think we couldn't keep a dirt floor clean, but it was smooth and hard as brick. And they had driven a pump almost at the door.

As soon as we got everything fixed nice I sent for Lucy, as she told me in Gunnison she would come and stay with me, and I needed her to help me with the work and to take care of the children. Johnny went back to Michigan. He was only staying until we got settled.

Frank was making staves. He bought the timber and paid so much a tree for all he used. If they split one and ruined it, they had to pay just the same. Their staves were inspected and taken up and paid for in the woods once a month. It was a pretty particular piece of work. They were hewed smooth as marble; the men got so much apiece and had to pay four dollars a week for board. Frank soon had a pretty big crew of men working for him, and we had our hands full. Our work wasn't so hard, but steady. We bought all our groceries wholesale and were making money boarding the men.

We soon found that the country was full of all kinds of wild animals. We could hear wolves howling, see bear tracks, and hear raccoons fighting over the cans we threw out. For months and months I didn't see a single woman. But time passed off quickly.

Winter was coming all too fast, and the winter rains set in. The woods were full of water. Men were beginning to leave the woods, and the work was pushing out farther from our camp. The men that stayed through the winter built camps and cooked for themselves, about two miles from us, as I wasn't in condition to cook for so many. We had a good warm camp that winter—had built a large fireplace and had plenty of wood. There was but one thing bothered us. We lived so far from a doctor and trading place. We were about a mile from where Tutwiler is now, but then it was all just a wilderness of woods and canebrakes. It was about fifteen miles to a ferry where we could cross the Sunflower River, and eighteen miles from there to our nearest trading place, Shelby, where we got our mail, when we got it. Nearly two years after Johnny left us, I got my first letter from him. It was eight months old, and in it he told us he had joined up in the Spanish-American War. It was fifteen years afterwards before I found out that when I got that letter Johnny was already dead. He died of dysentery in the war.

It was raining almost all the time, but we could get freight across the river in spite of its being swollen. Christmas came. We had a good dinner—wild turkey, plenty of venison, and even a Christmas plum pudding. The children were happy, for Santa Claus had filled their stockings. We were all happy; Frank real happy as he got a Christmas jug. I didn't care, for as he said, "I have worn the temperance blue ribbon all year." We didn't have a cloud in our sky that winter. Even Lucy was contented. She loved my children better than anything on earth, and she had nothing to do but romp and play all day long with them. I had my sewing machine and was as particular about making our clothes as if we were in town. My children and Lucy were always neat and clean. We all were, after we found out how to break the hard water.

When we first came to this country, to get water we had to drive iron pipes in the ground, thirty to sixty feet. If the water threw white sand, it was soft; but if it threw black sand and mud, it was alkali and iron. Then it had to be broken for washing clothes or dishes. To break it we pumped it into a barrel and put in it about three tablespoonfuls of concentrated lye or about two pounds of sifted ashes. We filtered it to drink, to cook rice, potatoes, or make coffee. It turned potatoes black, rice almost red; coffee made of it without first being boiled or filtered was black as ink and tasted flat. When lye was used to soften it, it would, after standing overnight, be clear and ready to use, but there would be about three inches of feathery yellow settlings in the bottom of the vessel.

The fifteenth of January, 1897, dawned clear and bright, but the woods were full of water and mud. About noon the sky was overcast.

During the afternoon it began to cloud up and thunder, and lightning flashed. It looked as if a terrible storm was coming. It broke about six o'clock, but about five o'clock I was wandering around outside. I went up on a small Indian mound with Nina. I was feeling badly, restless and uneasy. I didn't know what about, except that my time was near. I was sure it would be within a week and was afraid the coming storm meant so much more water in the already-full streams that it would mean serious trouble about getting the doctor we had made arrangements with, as it took almost a day to go after him and as long to get back. I sat down and began to cry. Nina put her arms around me and asked me what I was crying about, if I was afraid of the storm. I said, "Yes, dear. I think that is it."

I got up. As I did I saw something bright on the ground, just an edge. I scratched away the soft earth and picked up what at first I thought was a dime, but when we scraped all the dirt off and washed and rubbed it bright it was a silver piece, English, Frank said, worn so smooth and thin he couldn't make out what, but the date was 1717. I took it as a token of good luck and it helped me.

Just as we got to the house the storm broke, almost a hurricane. We had all the dangerous trees around the house down, but there was one Frank hadn't had cut. It stood within six feet of the house, and a few minutes after we got inside it crashed down, straight away from the house. My luckpiece was working already, I thought. We could hear trees falling and thunder crashing, and the lightning lit up the whole house. The storm lasted till daylight, but about midnight I lost all fear of the storm as I found I had a greater one to face than the one raging outside. I slipped out of bed, went into the children's room, dropped down on my knees and prayed as I had never prayed before. I got up from my prayers without a fear, but not Frank. When I woke Frank and told him, he was wild. I never saw him so excited. He blamed me for not telling him in time to get the doctor. He broke down and cried like a child, "My God, what can I do?"

I had never seen him cry. I said, "You can brace up. Wake Lucy. I am not afraid." And strange as it was, I wasn't afraid. Lucy proved a bigger goose than Frank. So with the help of God alone I pulled through that night. When I held my fine nine-pound boy in my arms, I heard Frank pray for the first time. He fell down by the bed, gathered the baby and me in his arms, and thanked God over and over. He whispered, "Isn't little Frank sweet. I know you want to call him Frank."

And Frank he is. My oldest boy living, a big strong man, married and with children of his own, but I can never forget him as he was the night his father gave him his name, how he kicked, screwed up his face and cried. He was as proud of his name as his mother was, and I felt like God had sent my boy to replace the one He took from us a little more than two years before. I prayed God to make me worthy of the gift and to help me to raise him right, to do my duty by him.

After the storm of the fifteenth and sixteenth, it cleared up. Frank was pushing the stave work but found time to get a man to help him rive out palings so he could build us a garden fence. Every minute he had he was spading it up to make a garden. We had made up our minds to stay at that camp through the most of the summer, and Frank would get a horse to ride to his work, which was pushing further away from the camp. It was warm and sunshiny and we were sure of an early spring, so the first of March Frank went to Shelby to get a load of groceries that he had ordered from Memphis for us and for the other camps, and garden seed to plant our new garden, and a man to come and take up the staves that were ready. They came back with just a small supply of groceries they thought we could make out on till the roads got better to haul the rest. The Sunflower River was bank full, and the Mississippi was high but not yet dangerous. They got their staves taken up; we made a garden, and in a week everything was up. Work was being pushed, the baby was growing fast, and sweet, and good. The spring frogs kept croaking "more rain, more rain" and the hoot owls were hooting their warnings every night. Groceries began to run low, but we had over five hundred dollars in the trunk and didn't owe one cent. We laughed at fear of anything, starvation least of all. We had no newspapers, no mail of any kind, except about once a month when someone went to Shelby.

By the twenty-eighth of March, everything was getting so low that Frank and one of the men started to Shelby to get more groceries. They would always walk to the river and get teams from the Lemasters,* a family living just across the river, to do their hauling. This time they liked never to have got to the river at all. Every bayou

*This is probably the LaMastus family, who were among the earliest residents of the area.

and slough was full of water, and when they reached the river it was all out of its banks, and there was no ferryboat. Not even a rowboat or a dugout. They began to yell and holler across the river, and at last a man came down to the bank and hollered back to them that there was no way to get across the river. "The ferryboat broke loose and is gone, and we've got all the other boats trying to gather up our stock."

There were about five families of those Lemasters, and they had lots of stock. The man that hollered to Frank that morning was Bob Lemaster, years afterwards one of our best neighbors. He advised Frank to hurry home, warn all the men to make boats, make one himself, build scaffolds to put everything above the high-water mark, and be prepared to live in the loft of our house.

They had nothing to do but come back home. How were they to build boats with not over a pound of nails in all the camps put together and not a stick of lumber in any of them? There wasn't a sawmill in fifty miles of us. But the old saying "There is nothing so bad but there is some good in it" proved true. From the big tree that fell so near the house the night little Frankie was born, an ash tree it was, Frank sawed off a sixteen-foot cut, split it, and after hewing it off on the outside, turned it over and began chopping it out inside with a chopping axe. He sent word to the men in the camps to do the same. I helped Frank with ours. It took two days to make it by working at night by firelight. We were all on half rations, and in three days more we would have none at all, except for the children.

The men from the camps divided everything they had with us. One of the men came and helped put scaffolds up. Sawed off trees seven feet from the ground and put poles across from the top of one stump to another. They were for the cookstove, the sewing machine, for everything that wouldn't float. But the stove was so big and heavy they couldn't get it up after all and so had to leave it alone, but dishes and all vessels were put up. All bedding, clothes, trunks, books, and everything like that was put up in the loft except what we had to use. Then the men helped throw up a three-foot-high levee all around our house about six feet away. Frank took a hatchet, put a five-foot handle in it, took a compass and blazed a road with the hatchet as high as he could reach. It went through a great tangled mat of cane, vines, and timber over to what is now No. 2 Camp on the state farm at Parchman (the penitentiary). Part of our men were camped there on some Indian mounds in tents above the high-water marks on the trees around there, but they were afraid and making their way to the hills. They turned over all their outfit and tents to the rest of us, so we had some place to go, but we had to wait until the water got high enough over all the land between us to go by boat.

I just couldn't believe the water would get as high as Frank said, in spite of high-water marks he showed me which would put it over the top of our six-foot garden fence. But I went about preparing as though I did believe it to please him and to forget how hungry I was. Lucy helped me wash and iron and pack. We packed as carefully as if we were making a long move. She said she hated to work so hard but it was work or starve, and we were doing both. We were almost down to our last bite the day before the water came in on us. Two loaves, and some of the boys brought us two squirrels and a little coffee. I boiled the squirrels for supper. We had one piece and one slice of bread each and carefully divided the gravy. I had two cans of milk left. I gave the children one that night and saved one for morning. I made half the coffee, saved the other half for breakfast, and packed everything that was left in a bucket with a tight lid. We pulled up all our onion sets, cabbage plants, and tomato plants and put them in a box in the loft.

But all this we did after Frank got back from the camp two miles from us. The water was coming in on them, and he told them to be ready to pull out in the morning to the mounds and come back and help us in the evening. In the meantime I had been down to a little bayou with Nina, and we wanted Frank to come and look, for it was full of big fish. We told him they were wallowing like hogs, for there were muddy streaks all through the water where they had been swimming. Frank turned pale, said, "My God," and was off down there. He came back, called me off, and said, "Mary, that muddy water is the Mississippi River water filling up the bayou. No need to alarm the rest. With that storm coming up, it looks bad. We will put everything up in the loft except two bedsteads and two mattresses. Get your lunch fixed for morning and get a few things packed for the children. I am going back to camp for help."

But the storm broke too quick, and he didn't go back. There was nothing the men could do anyway. We must just wait for the water to come up enough to use the boat. We tried to be cheerful and believe there was no danger till morning, but the storm was raging, the rain coming down in sheets, the wind blowing so hard. I was so scared that at times my heart seemed to be in my throat, at other times to have sunk below my ribs. And I had to be cheerful. You see, no one but Frank and me knew the real danger we were in.

About ten o'clock that night the storm seemed to be over, only a steady rain kept up. Frank went outside, looked around and saw how everything looked. His boat was safe; the bayou was bank full but not out of its banks. When he came in he said, "We had better go to bed, get some rest."

The children were all asleep. We went to bed and soon to sleep as we were all tired, but about three that morning something woke me up. I listened and heard a kind of hissing noise. I woke Frank and asked him what it was. He jumped out of bed and into water about two inches deep. The sound of hissing I had heard was the water running into the fireplace and putting out the fire. He said, "Mary, get Lucy and the children up quick. The water is pouring in the house like a funnel."

It didn't take me two minutes to get dressed, and while I was dressing the children, he and Lucy were getting the rest of our things up a pole ladder into the loft.

That levee around our house was three feet high and the water was pouring over it, and in places had washed it out. In half an hour water was two feet deep in the house. I had put the children, our extra clothes, and the lunch on the large dining table. They were high and dry, but the rest of us were wading around in water above our knees. We didn't get out because there was still a steady downpour of rain, and I didn't want to take the children out in it as long as I could keep them dry inside. The water was whirling around and around and was so swift we could hardly stand up. Lucy said, "Let's get on the table." We both jumped up on the same side and the table turned over, spilling the children out in the water. I grabbed the baby, Lucy grabbed Leslie, Frank picked up the lunch basket, suitcase, and Nina, and said, "Go to the stove."

It was a big range. We put everything on it, and I made Lucy get up and hold the children. Leslie was crying, "I am drownded in Mississippi water."

Frank said, "I am going for the boat and get us out while we can. The children are wet anyway."

Lucy said, "Go, and shut up, before we are all drowned." I felt like her. He was gone it seemed to me like an hour, when he stuck his head in the door and said, "The boat is gone."

There are times in every woman's life when it is a greater relief to swear than to pray. Well, I did both then. He went back. It seemed another hour but was really only a few minutes before he came back with the boat he had found at last. The water was waist-deep in the house by that time. The rain was letting up a bit. Frank brought the boat up to the door and put the little girls in it with all the things. I told him I would walk and carry the baby. He was walking and pulling the boat.

When they built the house they left quite a low place in front, so when Lucy and I stepped down out of the door, the water came up to my chin. I had to hold the baby up over my head. Lucy was taller than I was, but I wouldn't risk Frankie with anyone but myself in that water. When I got to the little levee though, I put Frankie in Nina's lap until we got out of the water.

We went slowly up by the garden. The water was only three feet high there, as the land was higher. We went up the ridge a hundred yards or more to dry land. Frank fastened the boat. He had some dry matches in his hat, found a hollow log, got some dry pieces out of it, and started a big fire. We began to dry and wait for daylight, and Frank got ready to make coffee and get out lunch. But when he opened the bucket, there were thousands of black bugs in it. They had eaten their way through and through the bread. We didn't know how hungry we were until we saw our ruined lunch—bread and squirrel that we had done without the night before. How those bugs got in the bucket I don't know unless Frank loosened the lid when the table turned over. Either that or the lid didn't fit as tight as I thought. The coffee was tied up in a cloth and the milk hadn't been opened, so I knocked the bugs out of the bucket, and Frank went to the edge of the water, washed it out, and filled it with water. We boiled the water and made some weak but hot coffee. We drank it almost scalding hot. We opened the milk, took some coffee, and made it half milk for the little girls; then I washed out the pot, heated some more water, mixed the rest of their milk, and gave it to them to drink.

We tried to laugh it off and be thankful we were alive and that the worst of our dreadful experience was over. We were soon to find out it had only started. The rain had settled down to a steady drizzle. By a good fire we didn't mind it so much, but how we did look and wish for daylight. It seemed it would never come, but at last it got light enough to see, and what a sight! Just the top of our house was showing; water lapped the edge of the roof. I couldn't see any sign of a garden fence. During the darkness Frank had pulled his boat up every little while as the water spread, till it was within a few feet of us, but now it seemed rising a little more slowly. Frank said it was because it had so much territory to spread over.

"It may not rise much more," he said, "but according to the high-water marks I am afraid." He got in the boat. He went down to the house, knocked some boards off the roof with his hatchet, and got out a chair and a dry blanket. He worked his way around in the water till he got in the path of the blazes and tied up the boat, looking around for the highest place he could see. It was a stump, six feet high or more and about four feet across. He lifted the chair up on it, and the chair was a pretty close fit. Then he came to us, picked up Leslie and said, "Come on. Let's get this job over the quickest way we can. We'll have to make two trips. Mary, you and I and the baby and Leslie will go first, and I will come back for Nina and Lucy. They can sit on that stump. There's a chair to sit on and a nice dry blanket."

You see, it was turning cooler as that was only the first day of April and the wind was getting around into the north. But I told him, "No, you take Lucy and Leslie, and I will wait here with Nina and the baby. It's nine miles to camp, and the water is not high enough on some of the ridges to run a boat. Lucy is big and strong and can help you, for you will have to fight through brush, cane, treetops, and all kinds of drifts every foot of the way, and what kind of help would I be? I will make a big fire, and Nina and Frankie and me will have a big time. If the water gets over this place, we'll get up on the stump."

It looked so silly, that chair way up on that high stump. I couldn't believe Frank really thought the water would go that high. Frank said, "We can't tell. The water may not rise much more, but the levee breaking near Rosedale straight across from us has thrown a terrible body of water in here. It seems like it is coming in from the other way too. There is a ridge surrounding us here a little higher than this place, but I can't find a stump on it that I could put a chair on. When it starts the water may come with a rush and you couldn't put Nina up, nor get up there yourself after I'm gone; but Lucy and Nina would be safe till I could get back with help."

I said, "Frank, if that is the case, I will stay. Lucy is too nervous and too easy excited. I am not afraid, so help me up, for I will never go and leave any of my children here."

Nina came over to me and said, "Father, I am going to stay with Mama and baby Frank. You go on and hurry back. We aren't afraid."

So Frank helped me up onto the stump and gave me the baby, after kissing him, saying, "Young man, you have a terrible day ahead of you. I don't see much chance for you to live through it, but who knows? The English are hard to kill." He kissed Nina, told her to be brave, and helped her up. Then he got up, put the blanket around us, got down, put all the things in the boat, and Leslie and Lucy got in with him. Leslie waved her little hand to us, and they were gone.

It was seven o'clock when they started. I can't describe my feelings when the boat passed out of sight and hearing. Not till then did I have time to look around me. The rain had never let up for one moment, and it was getting colder all the time. Nina, standing close beside my chair, was shivering with cold, and so was I. I could keep the baby warm for a while yet though with the blanket.

We could hear trees falling all out in the water. I wondered what could be causing it, as there wasn't enough wind to blow them down. Then I thought of the water-soaked ground. There was a big dead tree standing close enough to us so that if it fell towards us it would kill us. I was so afraid it would, and as we were having all kinds of bad luck I couldn't see how it could miss us when it did fall.

In less than an hour the water had crept up to our stump. We couldn't see a speck of dry land anywhere. Water was everywhere in all directions and rising fast. It was at least eight inches deep around us now. I could see Nina was tired, as she had no room to move around and could just stand close against my chair. She was so brave and patient that I made her get up on my lap with Frankie. That got the blanket so tangled up I threw it off, as it was soaked with rain anyway. But I hugged Frankie close between us, and we kept him dry and warm. He never cried all day. I wondered why. Nina said it was because he was so sweet and good, but years after I would think about it and be sure he was just too lazy.

You could never believe there were so many mice, rabbits, and snakes as were swimming past us trying to get out of the water. The strangest part was they were all going the same direction. I wondered if it was their natural instinct telling them which way to go, but if it was, why didn't they go before the water got up? Bugs there were too, of every kind, but more of those old big thousand-legged bugs, the terriblest-looking worm that crawls.

We heard something come lunging through the water. At first I thought it was a horse or cow. It passed within twenty feet of us, a big bear. Nina clutched me so tight and began to cry, "Oh, Mama, Mama. What is that?" I told her it was a bear, but it wouldn't hurt us as it was only trying to get out of the water. It swam on past us, out of sight, never turned its head to look at us, but poor little Nina was so shaken and frightened I began trying to tell her stories. You can just imagine how good they were in our surroundings. She wanted me to tell her of Noah and the ark. I tried it but failed. I was watching that old dead tree so close to us, and how the water whirled around it, climbing higher and higher on its trunk. Nina said, "I wish Father had made an ark instead of that little boat, so we could all have got out together."

I told her, "But you see, dear, it took Noah over 100 years to build the ark, and Father only had three days to make our boat."

Then I tried playing a game with her to while away the time and make us forget the water. I would point out a limb or twig on a nearby tree, and we would see how far we could count before it went out of sight under the water rising so fast, so fast. Things were getting serious, I was numb, tired, discouraged, and we were so hungry and cold. I knew it must be about noon. The rain had stopped, but the sun couldn't get through the heavy clouds, and the water was halfway to the top of the stump. I had about given up all hope of ever seeing Frank, Lucy, and Leslie, for I could hear what seemed to me a child crying. I had been listening to it for some time and was sure it was Leslie. In my imagination I could see her floating around in the water, or in the boat maybe with Lucy, Frank dead, them hopelessly lost. Lucy was so excitable. I was frantic, but what could I do? No condemned man ever waited for the hangman with more fear and dread than I was waiting for the sure death so near us. I didn't care for anything now, just to see the baby and Nina die first, for to feel I might die first and leave them alone was horrible.

It was midafternoon, and the water was up over the stump, lapping my feet. The old tree that I had been so afraid of in the morning was still standing. Now I prayed it would fall on us, kill all three of us at once and end this suspense. About that time I saw the top kind of quiver. I shut my eyes, clutched my children tight, and to myself said, "Thank God." It came down with a crash; cold water poured over us. I opened my eyes. It had missed us by a few feet but almost finished drowning us with the water it had thrown over us. Of course I was glad it had missed us but disappointed to be facing again this slow sure death. I could see no possible hope.

I had hopes as long as I was sure Frank was alive, but now, since hearing Leslie's cries which were getting further away and fainter, I knew there was no more hope, nothing to do but wait for the end. One child floating around maybe half a mile away from me, dying; two in my lap sure to die in less than an hour, and the only prayer I could think of to ask God was to let them die first so I could take care of them to the end. I felt I must prepare Nina. I was sure she understood our danger, so I said, "Nina, do you know, darling, that we are soon going to die. Father can't come back. I am sure he and Lucy are dead. I have heard Leslie crying for hours. She will soon be gone. So will we."

"Is that the reason you think Father is dead? I have heard that crying too, but I thought that was some little animal. Father isn't dead. I know he isn't."

But I saw her look down at her little feet in the water and turn pale. The water was now within four inches of the chair bottom.

"Mama," she said, "why don't you pray? Ask God to send Father back quick. You always tell me if we are good God will give us whatever we ask."

I said, "I can't, Nina. God has forgotten us." But to comfort her I added, "But maybe if you would pray . . ."

She folded her little hands and began, "Dear God, Mama thinks you have forgotten us because she is so scared. Please send my father quick to take Mama, little brother and me off this awful stump. I know you will."

Already her prayer was doing good. It cleared my brain, for since she mentioned it, that didn't sound like Leslie's voice, and I could think more clearly. Frank had said it was nine miles to those mounds, and it would take until four that afternoon to get back. I could last another hour by standing on the stump and letting Nina stand on the chair. But she interrupted my thoughts, clapping her hands and laughing and saying, "Father is coming. Listen, Mama."

Yes, I could hear them, paddles splashing the water and men talking. We could hardly sit still and wait just the moment it took for them to come into sight. Frank and three more boats. When they saw us, all talk stopped. Frank ran his boat right by my chair, picked Nina up, set her in the boat, gave her the baby, and took my hand to help me. When I tried to step in the boat, my feet and legs were so numb I couldn't stand. I fell. I didn't think I would ever be able to walk a step again. But I was so happy.

Up to that minute there hadn't been a word spoken, but when I looked at Frank I knew the reason. Tears were running down his cheeks. Like me, his heart was too full for words. When we were safe in the boat he turned to the men and said, "Boys, I will go on back. You go to the house, get everything you can carry out through the roof." Then he turned to me and said, "Mary, this is awful. I can't trust myself to think what would have happened if I had been twenty-five minutes later. Thank God I was in time."

He picked up a paddle and we started back through the woods. He told me what a time they had going. Some places where the land was high, they had to drag the boat for a hundred yards at a stretch; but when they got there some of the boys had a good fire going and hot coffee ready. As soon as he could swallow some and get the boys ready, they started back. He said he had showed Lucy our tent, told her to have some supper ready for us if she could scrape up anything, and have our clothes dry as we ought to get there by dark. Then, for the first time that day, the baby began to cry. Frank said, "Poor little fellow. He can't get over this, can he, Mary? Has he cried all day?"

I said, "No, he wouldn't be crying now, but he knows the danger is over."

Then Nina told Frank about my thinking I heard Leslie crying, and he said, "The boys found a couple of little drowned calves on our way back."

All this time we were following the blazes, some of them still above us, but in many places already hid under the water. We came right through where Tutwiler is now over the top of canebrakes and underbrush. Between there and where we were going it was low, and we rode over the tops of saplings. At last we got to what is now No. 2 Camp on the state convict farm at Parchman, on the Indian mounds. Here there were about six acres above high water. I want to tell you that on that six acres of dry land there were at least twenty rattlesnakes killed within the next month—all sizes, and not one snake of any other kind.

The next day after we got out of the water was clear and bright. Several boats had gone for groceries. I spread our wet clothes to dry on the tent ropes and on the bushes and cane near the tent. You see, tall blue cane twenty feet high had been cut off and just shoved back enough to clear a space to build their camps and put up their tents. The sun was shining bright and the wind was blowing almost a hurricane, so it soon dried the cane and dead leaves. By noon everything was dry.

We had one crank of a man in camp who had two big dogs, and about noon he started hunting on that few acres of dry land. The wind was blowing from the south; so he took the dogs and went out after a deer. The deer got in a thicket where the dogs couldn't get it out, so that silly man set the thicket afire. We were getting dinner when we heard the roaring and ran out to see what it was. We saw that wall of fire coming down on us. I hollered to Lucy to try to save the children. We were within twelve feet of the high water on one side and that wall of fire sweeping down on us from the other. I caught up a bucket and began throwing water on the tent. Two or three men came running with cane axes, trying to cut the cane back away from our tent village. The top of our tent was catching afire, and I was too busy throwing water to think about Lucy, for I thought she and the children were safe, but as the flames began shooting up over the top of our tent, and a tent less than a hundred yards away was burning down, I heard one of the children scream. Some of the boys had brought a kitten and a pup out of the water and given them to the children, and the kitten was mewing and the dog howling, so I took a minute and looked.

My sister had them all huddled up in the middle of the little clearing like a hen hovering her chicks, fire falling all around them. But before I could get to them, the puppy darted to a big hollow log a few feet away and disappeared inside it. The kitten went next, then Lucy put Leslie inside it, and Nina got in and took the baby. Lucy ran to help me, and the fire swept on by. The rest of the camp was on the far side of the mounds, away from us, and there were men enough to save it. The man that set the fire was the only one whose tent was burned down. That fire burned the cane right down to the water for a hundred yards out in the water. But all things end sometime, and after it was over it was funny to think over the silly things we had all done and said. I had stood and thrown water on the tent the whole time and let all our clothes hung out on the tent ropes burn up. Lucy hadn't had as much sense as a little puppy in the face of danger.

About three o'clock that afternoon Frank and the men got in with the groceries, and such groceries! We had a real feast that evening. Troubles were all forgotten, all but one. All day long it seemed to me I could hear someone hollering. I spoke about it several times that day, but every man I asked would say, "It must be some animal," but they all acted so funny, I couldn't be satisfied and the hollering kept up. So when Frank got home I asked him. I knew by the way he looked, so guilty, that it was someone, and he knew all about it. I kept quizzing him till he told me.

I've told how Frank and another man started to Shelby a few days before the water came in on us to get groceries and how he came back by those boys camped on the Indian mounds to warn them. Well, there was an old Swede, a bachelor, hard-headed and contrary, camping alone and working alone, about a mile from the mounds. Frank went a mile out of his way to warn him and to try and buy a few groceries from him to last till we could get to Shelby. Frank showed him how high the water would come on his house and told him to build a boat. The old Swede told them to keep their damned advice, and he'd keep his grub. The man with Frank told the old Swede the water would get over his house and he damn well hoped he'd be in it.

It turned out he was. The next the men knew of him was when they passed his house the morning of the same day the water came in our house. There sat old Swede John on his mattress on the comb of his roof, his feet in the water, hollering and begging and praying. When he saw them and hollered at them to come get him off, they just laughed at him. It was sundown of the next day when I got to asking Frank about him and finally persuaded him to go after the old man.

"Them boys wouldn't come by for me, so I had to set there another night. *Ach, mein Gott,* I thought I would die," the Swede said, telling me about it afterwards. "When morning came the wind was blowing so hard I could hardly hold on, and I didn't dare fall off for I can't swim. I must have dozed off about noon, for I woke up and the whole world was on fire. I thought to myself, 'Old John, you didn't go to sleep. You died and just woke up in hell. Too bad Frank nor none of the boys is here.'"

The old Swede proved a fine workman and stayed with us for six months.

Two or three days after we got out of the water, Nina developed a fever, but it lasted only a few days. Baby Frank did not so much as have the colic from the exposure. And it never hurt the rest of us at all, except the scare we got from the high water kept us from buying land in that country. We made plenty of money those days and could easily have bought a big plantation, so I guess after all our minds were badly affected. Frank, years afterward, sold land all over this country, even helped sell a part of the state convict farm, but kept none for ourselves, which didn't seem right to me, as Frank had to live in this, the only country where he could have his health, and oh, I did so want a little home of our own.

I wanted to buy a place and grade up a mound like an Indian mound to build our house on. I was sure that some day this country would be settled up and this rich land would all be in cultivation. I had gone through so much here and on Concordia Island I wanted a home of my own. I think I was the very first white woman to cross Sunflower River coming into this country to live, and I know I am the first white woman that ever came through what is now Parchman, when we were guided by the bits of paper Frank dropped along the dim blazed road through it.

The next morning after the fire was bright and clear; the water had fallen three inches, and I must say right here we didn't have another rain until the latter part of July. We could see all over that six acres of burnt-off land. On and around those knolls the ground was black. The fire made a good job of clearing off all the cane and underbrush, but the trees were putting out their leaves just enough to brighten up our future home, for we built a house there and lived for over a year.

Every man was out bright and early, some to Shelby, some to get the rest of our things and the men's things. And they all had to get enough provisions to last till the water went down enough to get wagons in. Old Swede John was too clumsy to go with a boat, but I found plenty for him to do. I got him to spading up a small garden. The mellow black soil was easy spaded up and we had several shovels among us. The men got to helping him evenings, and I soon had a nice garden. The plants I had saved from my other garden hardly stopped growing. John, not to be outdone, drove posts in the ground every twelve feet, took poles made of small saplings, and nailed them from post to post. Then he cut cane eight feet long, had to carry them three hundred yards, stuck one end of the cane in the ground, then laced them to the poles with strings. That was the prettiest garden fence I ever saw.

The garden was made close to where we built our new house. Then Frank drove a pump. It was the first pump driven on what is now the state farm and was the very best pump water I have ever tasted in the Delta in all the years I have lived here. It was cold, clear, and soft. Then we built our house. Both sides were made like a sleeping porch; the whole top half of the walls swung with hinges from the top so they could be raised like awnings clear around the two sides. The men's bunkhouse was about two hundred yards from us.

By the time we all got our houses built, the water was all gone down, and the Sunflower River was within its banks; where the fire had burned over and where the water had been was a soft green carpet of grass all dotted over with purple violets and other wildflowers. Standing at my house it looked like the Garden of Eden I imagined. How I did love it. All the woods were full of animals again, and birds, and full of workmen, too. We could hear them chopping and sawing and trees falling.

A Crisscross of Paths and Blazes

OUR CAMP ON THE MOUNDS WAS ONE MILE from what was known as the "Cyclone," a stretch of cyclone-swept land from two to four miles wide, starting at the Sunflower River and extending for eighteen miles right to where No. 1 Camp at the state farm is now. The Cyclone was a terrible place. In all that stretch not a tree was left standing. Maybe there would be half a mile where every tree had been uprooted and left lying; then it would look like the wind had lifted gradually and cut the timber off like hay by a mowing machine; then down the wind had dropped to the ground again, lifting trees by the roots. All this had happened years before, so try to imagine what it was like now. Cane, undergrowth, blackberry briars, grape and poison oak and muscadine vines, all growing to enormous size out of that rich Delta ground, interlaced through that fallen timber so that it was one great tangled mat. Not a trail or a path through it.

But the whole country was almost as bad. A man couldn't get through any of the woods without a compass in one hand and a cane axe in the other to blaze every foot of the way. In throwing timber the men had to cut a path to their tree every morning. Then they would estimate the direction they would throw the tree, and each man cut a path to get away in when the tree started to fall, and God help them if they couldn't outrun the falling tree.

Frank came so near getting killed that way. Two men were to saw a tall, clear-bodied tree, no limbs except at the top. He told them to saw and he would keep the wedges driven in. They sawed till the tree began to pop, then took the saw out and began to run; but Frank stayed, kept pounding away at the wedge as it kept trying to come back on them. It finally looked like it was going to fall right, so he gave the wedges one more hard lick, dropped his sledge and started to run. The boys began to yell he was going to get caught. He tried to get out of the path but caught his foot under a vine and fell. That tree crashed down right alongside of him and buried half a foot deep in the ground. It missed his caught foot by about six inches and his head the same. But he wasn't hurt, except his bad knee was out of place. He told the men how to set it, but they were so scared that when it popped in place they pulled harder. Frank yelled, "Stop. It's done. You fellows must think I'm like one of your jointed snakes and unjointed all over."

They all had a big laugh over it, as those chances were all in the day's work.

We had twenty men boarding with us that year. The work now was run on a different plan altogether, as this was a European stave company Frank was working for. They had brought in hundreds of Slavonians and put up their camps about two miles from the mounds. The foreman of their camps was a fine Jew by the name of Minkus. Frank ran the American camp for Minkus. He worked by the month for a good salary and a commission on all staves got out by the Americans. Minkus bought all the staves that Frank and the other boys had saved through the high water by weighting them down so they couldn't float off. Minkus put in a ferryboat at Lemaster's landing, a settlement across the river from us, eighteen miles from the mounds. He got his supplies shipped in to Mound Bayou from New Orleans, and we began getting ours the same way.

When Minkus got the camps ready for his men, three hundred of them came marching by our house afoot, each carrying a suitcase. Then there were three four-mule teams, and the wagons had a frame like a hayframe. These were loaded tier on tier, as high as a big load of hay, with three-gallon kegs. Behind this came six or seven wagons loaded with bedding and groceries. When the men passed our house they were all singing; not loud and boisterous like our men, but low, all keeping time with their one free hand, but not so busy with it but what every man tipped his hat as he passed our house. Of course, we couldn't understand one word, but that was the sweetest music. Leslie said, "Don't those angels sing nice? Did they all fall out of heaven at once?"

But when Frank told me those kegs I saw were full of whiskey, and each man had from two to three kegs apiece, I thought they had all been kicked out of the bad place. I thought our cheerful home life was ruined, with them only two miles away. But Frank told me not to worry, they wouldn't bother us.

"They are polite and quiet," he said. "Tend to their own business, and with all that whiskey they never get drunk. Around their camp they are friendly to everyone, bring out a keg with a nice new straw, or cane, offer you a draw, but if you happen along while they are at work, they pay no more attention to you than they would a rabbit. Of course, they are the finest workmen and timber men in the country. That is what Minkus told me. But he has given them to understand that I am to go around where they are working, and they are to show me how to use their tools that are so different from ours. I can talk their lingo enough to carry on a conversation with them. Besides, they know I am English."

Lucy spoke up. "Frank, you mean when they offer you their whiskey keg with a cane, you will understand what to do with it?"

And I said, "That is right, and by the time you have sampled all three hundred kegs you will know so much about stave-making you won't be able to get home."

Frank said, "You girls are smart," and had business elsewhere. But I knew his failing and couldn't help but be uneasy.

Camp life is always either a feast or a famine. That week Frank killed a bear that weighed 250 pounds dressed. I cooked bear meat every way I could think of, and we sent the Minkus camp some. I didn't cook it every meal, as we got a beef or a hog from Lemaster every week and corned beef by the barrel from New Orleans. We treated our men so well through the feast days that when the famine days came on because of bad roads or high water or missent goods, they understood it wasn't our fault and never grumbled. Those men were the bravest, biggest-hearted men, and from those common workmen came some of our richest citizens in the Delta today. They took advantage of the cheap lands, took care of their money, and fought their way every foot through a wilderness to make this country what it is today, the garden spot of the South.

Frank was introducing the Slavs' style of work to our boys and was among the Slavs a good deal. They worked in gangs, six to a gang, and for his lunch each man carried half a loaf of bread and a pint of whiskey. Our boys told Frank they would be glad to adopt the Slav style of working if they could adopt their style of lunches. As Minkus paid so much for each tree, the more staves they got out of a tree, the better for the company and for the men. It saved not only money but labor, for throwing the large trees was the hardest part of the work. Their staves were hewed smooth as glass, and they used every part of the tree but the bark and the smallest limbs. It was Frank's job to keep account of the stumps, and he said it was hard to keep up with the Minkus crew, for instead of leaving stumps, they left just holes in the ground. For the Slavs literally dug their trees out by the roots. When they got to the woods, they, like our men, cleared around their tree, but then instead of falling their tree with saws, they would surround, and like pigs rooting something out of the ground, dig it out with shovels. And it always fell just where they wanted it to.

Mr. Minkus often took dinner with us, if he happened to be near at noon, and he nearly always had some of his Slav foremen along. It was funny to see them try to imitate Minkus, nodding, bowing, and smiling at everyone, so busy trying to put on airs they could hardly eat. When Minkus left the table he would always give each one of my children a quarter, and the men would do the same thing, then come to me, spread out their hands, jabber and bow and smile. I wished I could understand what they said but knew of course they were trying to thank me. They liked to come and never missed a chance. That Christmas every man among them sent each of my children a pound of candy or fruit, and every package had a quarter in it. You see, I did mending and darning for Minkus: tablecloths, shirts, coats, vests, and trousers, and I wouldn't charge him for it. Buying in such large quantities as he did, he got lots of premiums: white glass dishes, silver knives and forks and spoons, all kinds of fancy dishes, wire baskets for boiling puddings, wooden chopping bowls, all kinds of cooking utensils. So for Christmas he sent me a hogshead full, or almost full, and the men finished filling with the children's things, and sent a box full besides.

I am thinking, as I write, of those wasteful days. The candy we gave away to the Negroes working for us, what the boys didn't eat, for we never allowed the children to eat much candy. I don't even remember what we spent the money for, but I know if I had it now in these hard times I could live high on it two or three years. I have some of my knives and forks yet, and it does me good to look at them these lean Christmas times and think of the past. When I sit down to write, old memories guide my hand. I am living again. I don't have to think of my husband and Nina and Oswald and almost all of our old neighbors as dead, me old and crippled, but as I lived life then, day by day, young and full of life and fun, trying to make our own home pleasant and home for dozens, yes, hundreds, of men. To me they will all live as long as I do, laughing and joking, sympathizing with each other and us, in sickness and trouble, and working, toiling to blaze a way and build healthy homes in this dear old Delta where the happiest part of my life has been spent.

Fall was coming fast. Lucy seemed to have settled down to make her home with us. Her romantic nature had taken the role of persecuted wife in hiding from a bad husband. She still pitied herself too much to work very hard, but she took good care of my children and was good to them. She would wait on table and wash dishes. We needed but one addition to our house to make it snug for winter, and that was a large fireplace. We had that built on the side of our dining room, an old-time fireplace, made of sticks on the inside, board on the outside, like a lath and plastered house only chinked with mud and grass. We could have roaring big fires without danger of burning the house.

Wild animals were plentiful. The long dry summer had dried up all the small streams, bayous, and sloughs, and animals came to the camp for water. We had a wash shed at the pump and kept wash basins and towels, comb and drinking glass and benches to wash on. Of course there was lots of water thrown out every day and a ditch to carry it off. There was water in it all the time, and that was what brought the animals. Raccoons and opossums and wildcats would fight around the pump at night and rattle around among the tin cans thrown out through the day. Moonlit nights we could see them. Some of the boys even declared they had seen bears priming the pump—one would pump while another drank—and one night a quarter of beef Frank had hung on a hook at the end of the house to cool overnight before we cut it up was gone next morning, and the biggest bear tracks led away from it into the woods. But the bears didn't bother me like the panthers and the wolves did. I never could get used to hearing a panther scream, nor wolves howl, though it was an every-night occurrence.

By fall so many workmen had been in the woods making staves and so many wagons hauling them out, cutting new roads, that the whole place was a crisscross of paths and blazes. If a man understood them, he stood a chance in bright daylight of finding his way out, but if night caught him he was hopelessly lost, and between the mosquitoes and sand gnats and thirst and the wolves howling, he would about go crazy. We made it a rule never to let a stranger go by our place after three in the evening. We would make them stay overnight.

One night about dark someone commenced to yell. At first we thought it was a panther, as the screams of a man lost and frightened out of his wits sound so much like the scream of a panther. But that night the screaming kept up and when some of the boys began answering, the screaming began to circle. Then we knew it was a man, for when you answer a panther it comes straight to you, but a lost man circles. The boys kept answering and blowing the horn we kept for the purpose, but the cries kept circling, and they took a lantern and started out. They found the man about half a mile from camp. He was barely able to get to camp; he had been lost two days and a night without a drop of water or a bite to eat. He had yelled until he could hardly talk.

When he had rested up some, he told us he came in from the hills near Charleston, Mississippi, to try to get work. Frank asked him if he still wanted work, and he said, "No, thanks. All I want is to get out of here and get back home. You can never know how thankful I am to you people for saving me. I couldn't have lived through another night. I came to Mound Bayou by railroad, caught a stave wagon and came across the river. The man put me down on what he said was the right road, just two miles from this camp. I've crossed a thousand roads since then and never stopped walking till dark last night. Then the wolves got to howling so I tried to make a fire. Didn't have but one match, so I climbed a tree and sat there till daylight this morning, when I began walking and hollering again."

After the boys got him off to bed, I said I felt so sorry for him. Mr. Perkins, a surveyor for the stave company who boarded with us, spoke up and said, "I don't. Any man with any sense at all brought within two miles of camp in broad daylight, and then gets lost, doesn't deserve sympathy."

Frank said, "Any man could get lost in these woods, certainly a stranger. The same thing could happen to you, Perkins, if it wasn't for your compass."

Perkins looked so disgusted. "Why don't you call me a damn fool and be done with it? Why, I've surveyed land all over the lowlands of the South in worse wilderness than this and never have been lost."

Frank said, "That's no reason why you couldn't be."

Perkins said, "Well, if you ever hear me whooping and yelling, don't answer me, but I would never waste my breath yelling, when I could use my head." At that he got up and went to his tent.

It was about two weeks after that conversation that there came a rain. It didn't rain hard, just a slow drizzling mist, and was dark and cloudy. The boys had all got in from work early on account of the weather, and even when they came in they had heard someone yelling. They thought it was some of the Slavs going in and so paid no attention to it, but when they came in for supper and didn't see Perkins, one of them said to Frank, "You don't suppose that could be him and his nigger lost?"

Frank smiled. "That is Perkins yelling all right, but I don't think he is lost."

The man said, "What do you think he is yelling his head off for then, and the wolves howling already? Not for his health."

Frank told him what Perkins had said two weeks before, and that he figured Perkins was just trying us out. But by that time the cries were getting awful. So a couple of the men began blowing the horn and answering them. The yells stopped circling and in a few minutes down the path, panting and blowing, ran Perkins and his nigger. Perkins walked up to Frank and said, "Thanks for blowing us in to camp."

Frank said, "Don't thank me. I knew you were just kidding. I didn't have anything to do with calling you in. A man with brains doesn't get lost. Besides, it wasn't even dark, and you had your compass on your shoulder."

Perkins said, "Well, I'll be damned. This is the first time I've thought of that compass. I'm sorry I said what I did about that man. I was lost bad today, and if all the boys had thought like you did, taken me at my word, I'd have been wolf bait by morning."

I called him in to a good hot supper. After supper we had a fire in our new fireplace for the first time, and he entertained us with stories of his surveying experiences in all parts of the country, but every time a wolf howled I fancied I could see him shudder.

Minkus now had about four hundred and fifty Slavs in the woods. He had built a large new camp out on Black Bayou, not over three miles from us. Frank was working about a hundred men in his three camps, four with our home camp, so they were looking forward to cleaning up that part of the woods by spring. Every two weeks Frank had to turn in his time for all his work.

One day I will never forget. It was Frank's birthday, the sixteenth of November. He told the boys at breakfast he was going to turn in their time and would get a supply of tobacco and ended with, "You fellows make your orders light as this is my birthday, and I may celebrate it and don't want to be a packhorse today."

All twenty men proposed going with him to help him celebrate, but he said, "No. Thanks just the same, but this is strictly a European celebration. No outsiders invited. I couldn't get in if I wasn't English."

You see, he was going to the Slavonian camp to turn in his time to Minkus. Frank started out laughing, and I stopped him to find out if he would be back by noon, as I was fixing him a nice birthday dinner. He said, "I'll be back before noon unless something happens, and it will have to be serious to stop me. Keep the pudding boiling till I get back anyway."

I always tried to make our Christmas plum pudding on his birthday. We had some for dinner that day, some for Thanksgiving, and saved the rest till Christmas. As the children got old enough I taught them Christmas celebration started on Father's birthday. Those three days nothing but hard times or bad luck stopped Frank from being at home.

So when noon came and he was not back, it was with a heavy heart that I set his dinner for the men. I was afraid he had got a little too much, started home, and his knee had got out of joint. I fancied I could see him crawling along trying to get home. Of course, the men were all sure he was just full and having a big time. No one worked Saturday afternoon, as that was when they all did their laundry work. Three o'clock came, and by then I was so worried I got two of the men to go look for Frank. They laughed at me, but to please me they went.

Sundown came, and none of them were back, and the wolves had begun howling. I was almost wild with worry. I could see the men were uneasy, for five or six of them filled a lantern, took guns, and started out. They told me they would have them all home by ten o'clock. I could see they were making light of trouble, and that only made me surer poor Frank was dead. I hardly know how I got the work done, the children to bed. Lucy got ready for bed after telling me over again there was nothing wrong with Frank but that he was full. She thought more of Frank than of her own brothers, but how she hated his drinking. I told her I was sure it was his knee had slipped out of joint. She grunted, settled down in bed, and said, "It ought to be his neck," and went to sleep.

Ten o'clock came and no news. Nine men gone, and I began to think there must be something to this drunk business. In about an hour I heard what sounded like twenty men coming in the house. I ran to the door sure Frank was in the crowd. It was just the first two men I had sent, making noise enough for ten trying to slip in quietly. When I called them, they said, "Now Mish Hamilton, stop shinking about Frank. He ish havin' one hell of a good time. All full ash hell but ush."

I thanked them, closed my door, and went to bed. I was relieved but mad and ashamed of myself and of Frank.

Next morning was Sunday. About nine o'clock we heard the funniest singing, and here came what looked like an army. A wagon came first, loaded, we found later, with drunk federal officers that had come down to arrest those last fifty Slavs and their boss and send them back to the old country for violating the immigration laws. As they passed our place they stopped, and Frank and his six men dropped out. They shook hands with the entire bunch of fifty men walking behind the wagon and about a hundred more of their friends on their way to Mound Bayou to see them off. They were all jabbering, passing their kegs. Every man had his own keg under his arm. Frank called all our boys out, about fifty in all, as they had come in from other camps. I never did see so much handshaking and laughing and clapping each other on the back. They all shook hands with our boys and gave each a big draw of whiskey. Their boss made a speech, but none of us could understand it. Then the driver of the officers' wagon, a Slav, clapped his hands and yelled something and started driving slow. They fell in line, after giving each man another drink and shaking hands all around again, and started singing, that same odd low singing, and disappeared through the woods. We could hear them singing long after they went out of sight.

When Frank came in he was almost sober. I tried to be mad but couldn't. He apologized and looked so humble, and all the boys crowded around the door, to see he got "fair play," they said. He told us what had happened. "When I got up there yesterday, they were all singing and marching around among their tables. Every man had his keg under his arm; there was a regular feast on the tables and an officer stretched out on each table drunk. When they arrested them the night before, the Slavs asked to have a farewell feast with their friends and drink up their whiskey. As there was no way out that night, and Minkus told the officers he'd be responsible for them, they all entered into the sport. But the officers couldn't stand as much toddy as the Slavs could so they had to stay over last night to sober up. But they weren't steady enough to walk yet this morning and had to be sent in a wagon. The Slavs tried hard to keep them drunk another day but couldn't."

"But what part did you play in that sad story?" I asked.

"Me? Oh, I forgot my part. Minkus was working on the books trying to get everything straight, and I had to help him, as he was grieving so he couldn't sit up long at a time, feeling sorry for those poor devils that were having to go back. Mary, I know your motto is 'Never desert a friend in trouble,' and if ever a man needed a friend to cheer him up and help keep that bottle empty, it was Minkus yesterday. So you see, dear, it was to please you that I stayed."

One of the men let out a sigh, and said, "Poor man. How we all respect you for seeing your duty so plain and doing it."

Of course, I had to laugh.

As winter closed down on us and shut us in, we had lots of rain, but it didn't hurt us as bad as the winter before, for we were on higher ground and were more used to the country. The roads were soon so bad that all hauling stopped except groceries, and we got a regular team-ster, a man named Bob Coleman, from the Lemaster settlement across the river to do that. The winter passed off pleasant enough inside and out. The men got out lots of staves and had them taken up and paid for every two weeks. We had warm houses, plenty to eat, and plenty of

work to do. Most of the camp work fell on me, for Lucy had her hands
full tending the children; all three of them were full of life, Frankie
getting close to a year old, big and fat, curly-headed and pretty but so
badly spoiled he wanted Lucy to carry him all the time. He wouldn't
try to crawl, and when Lucy tried to give him lessons in walking it was
funny to see them. One day she said she could teach him to walk in
just a few minutes, if he would just try. His father said he was too fat
and lazy to walk; I said he was too bullheaded and knew Lucy loved to
carry him. But we all watched Lucy that day trying to teach him. She
stood him down on the floor but still held his hands. Nina was clapping her hands, cheering him. Leslie was stepping around trying to
show him how to take his first step. His father was taking some hams
out of a white pine box, the cleanest box, about four feet square and
two feet deep. As he took out the last one, he wanted to bet Lucy she
couldn't get Frankie to walk for another six months. She was holding
his hands and saying, "Big man will walk for Aunt Lu." But big man
stood about a minute, looking so surprised and amazed, then jerked
loose from her hands, sat down, let out a howl like a wolf, and
commenced to pound the floor with that curly head a few times, then
looked up at her and said "Take baby, Lu."

It was funny, but I was too mad to see the funny side of it. I jerked
him up and plumped him down in that box so hard Nina said, "Mama,
I'm afraid you have broke him." Her father said, "No, but if his little
sitter had been glass he would be pulverized, but even so his suffering is
terrible."

Then I had to laugh, for he got over his second shock, reached up
his hands, grabbed the edge of the box, pulled himself straight up on
his feet and, jumping up and down, yelled, "Take baby, take baby." I
forbade any of them to take him. I said, "You will stay right there till
you walk or crawl, just as you like." He was still standing, holding to
the box. Nina took hold of the box on the outside, laughing and
playing with him. He stopped crying and commenced laughing and
stepping around and around the box, but he wouldn't turn loose.
Then Lucy told Nina to take her hands off, hold them up so he could
see them, and walk. She straightened up, put her hands on her hips,
and said, "Look, Frankie, you can't do this."

He stopped, turned loose of the box, looked at his little fat hands,
twisted them around, reached out, and finally put them on his hips,

and stepped so high, like a blind horse, but he walked from end to end of that box. I could stand it no longer. I picked him up, kissed him and patted him, told him how sorry I was for being so rough with him, as though he understood, then I set him or stood him down and told him to walk to his sister. He sat down and commenced to bump his head and pull his hair and scream as before, "Take man, man." Nina caught his hands and said, "Mama, see what you have done. Made him pull out all those pretty curls. And that is the only thing about him that is pretty. You will have to put him back in the box. It is all to do over again, and I want you and Lucy to let him alone. I am going to take care of him myself."

I set him back in the box, not much gentler than before and said to myself, "You little bullheaded rascal you. It is strange but you have jumped back three generations and take after my Dutch grandfather." But I loved him more for it. It would be just a case of matching wits with him. As he grew older we had to be firm with him, but we were that with all our children. No two of them were alike, and as they grew older each called for a different method of treatment. In those early days I taught them to love their home above any place on earth and taught them to help make it a home.

A camp can be made a happy home as well as any other. I had not seen a woman for over a year, just Lucy and I, and no child but my own, but I determined to raise them right. We kept men around us who knew how to behave. We laughed and joked at all times, for I believed then and do now that blues are the worst disease you can have in the home and far more contagious than measles.

Every afternoon that winter we would have a couple of hours off from work, since sixteen of our men took their dinners with them to the woods. That meant I could make dinner and supper together and would have to heat it over at night, make fresh hot coffee and little things like that. So in the afternoon when the work was over for a couple of hours, I would make cookies: gingersnaps, spice cookies, white cookies. I always kept a large cracker box full on a small table by the dining room door, free for all. When someone asked me why I never put them on the dining table I told them I never saw a boy yet who liked cookies at table, but if he could "snitch" them he liked them.

Another thing we always kept was dried venison. Bob Lemaster brought us a deer almost every week when he brought beef. I always fried the hams and dried the rest for the men's lunches. I would get up at four o'clock mornings and get breakfast ready while Lucy set the tables; then she and Frank waited on the tables while I packed sixteen lunches. I had a long narrow table made like a counter in the dining room against the kitchen wall so the men could set their lunch buckets on it as they came in to supper the night before. We washed them, scalded them, and set them back, and in the morning I would slice my bread and meats and make sandwiches and pies. It is a lot of trouble to put up so many lunches and change them from day to day. Some liked one thing, some another; hardly any two buckets would be alike. Every man's name was on his bucket. When five or six of them would be close enough together at noon, they would take coffee and make it in the woods.

A Souvenir

S
O THE WINTER PASSED, AND EARLY THAT SPRING WE MOVED CAMP.
Moved half a mile back of a new settlement that later became
Parchman but was then called Ohio City. An Ohio lumber company
had come in and put up a sawmill on about an acre of land they cleared
up. They started sawing out gum lumber and put up a big two-story
house and two or three smaller ones. Frank came home every night
while they were building and cutting a road from No. 2 to the new
camp, and he would tell us of the women and children they saw in Ohio
City. Our children stood by him openmouthed, staring like Alice in
Wonderland. Leslie said, "Father, you mean fairies, don't you? We three
are all the children there are, aren't we?"

Nina said, "Oh, Leslie, I can remember seeing some children some
place a long time ago." She broke off, looked bewildered, and said,
"Or did I dream it? I remember Oswald, but God took him."

Lucy and I were as excited as the children at the thought of having
neighbors. I was glad for Lucy's sake, for she had been so good to my
children, loved them as well as if they were her own, and they loved
her as well as they did me—baby Frankie loved her better.

The great day came when Bob Coleman came after us with three
wagons. He had moved the men's things the day before. We started
bright and early as he had to make two loads, and we had to get there
in time to get supper for the men. Try to imagine how bad the roads
were when we didn't have quite three miles to go, and it took us from
early morning until noon to make it! Wagons would bog down, then
they would have to double team, whip, prize, and push. They would
unhitch, take the extra team back, hitch up, try to rush through,

likely as not stall again; by then the wagon in front would be stuck down in another mudhole, and as likely as not, the one behind stuck. So we swapped back and forth. It was funny to see. I was in the front wagon with Coleman. I had Leslie and the baby. Lucy and Nina were in the second wagon.

About the middle of the morning we got stuck in an extra-bad hole; even with the help of one of the other teams, and Bob jumping up and down in the mud knee-deep in his hip boots, calling to the teams, they didn't come. He looked at me, out of breath and so queer, that I said, "What is the trouble?"

He said, "If I could give them one good pop with the whip and cuss them good they'd come out in a hurry."

I said, "Why don't you try?"

"No," he said, "I don't cuss before ladies. It won't take long to get Dick's team." And back he went for the other team.

We got to the settlement at last, tired and hungry and worn out, but happy, and I had to laugh to see how excited we all were. At one house two children came out and stood on the porch. I could hardly hold Leslie. She clapped her hands with joy, saying, "Oh Mama, they are sure enough children, just like us." From there the half-mile to our camp seemed short, we were all so excited.

We were almost out of groceries but got enough for supper and breakfast, and by scraping, for dinner next day, by buying out the sawmill commissary. We had a bill of groceries in Sumner, our nearest shipping point, and the next morning Coleman and one of the mill men went for them. It was late that evening when we heard him coming, and not a thing for supper. We rushed up the fire when we heard the wagons. I was going to have to make biscuits for thirty-five men. Bob drove up outside and I heard him say, "The finest load of stuff in that carload, by Grannies. I forgot what Frank told me to get the first load, but I got what I knew we needed."

My heart sank. Whenever Bob couldn't bring everything, he always loaded up with the things he liked best. I was right. What do you suppose he had brought? One forty-gallon barrel of molasses (and we had plenty), one barrel of apples, one fifty-pound box of fancy cakes, ten boxes of dried fruit, a box of crackers, two hams, and forty pounds of smoking and chewing tobacco. Not one dust of flour. No coffee. No sugar. My sister Lucy very seldom laughed about anything, but when the last thing was taken off the wagon and there was not so much as one sack of flour, and thirty-five men looking to us for three more meals before we could get any more, she commenced to laugh. I couldn't keep the tears back, and I said, "Lucy, you are silly. I can't see anything to laugh at."

She said, "That's what is so funny, to see something happen that you can't laugh off."

She put her hands on her hips to imitate Bob, and in his shrill high voice she said, "By Grannies, them men is all right with plenty of chewing and smoking tobacco and good old ham and gravy. I'm sorry I forgot the flour but they can sop their crackers in their gravy, and if they don't have sugar for their tea they are getting old enough to do without. Just leave it to me, ladies." Then in her own voice, she said, "And that's just what we must do, Mary. That little fighting rooster will make the men like it and save us a lot of work."

Sure enough, we heard the men laughing with Bob outside.

Frank only had two sections to work up on the European stave company's land to help wind up. Minkus was working up all the rest near the Sunflower River. This was February and they expected to finish up by the first of July. But Frank began drinking again. While we were near the Slav camp where whiskey was no treat and there were hundreds of gallons free as water, Frank never got drunk but the one time; but since getting in a settlement, he was getting whiskey all the time. I respected him for not drinking while we were so isolated, away from our kind, and raising a fuss every time he came in the house wasn't my idea of a happy home. Besides, I knew now if I hadn't before, by Frankie's being so much like his father, so sure of himself, so stubborn, that Frank couldn't be driven to do anything. So I didn't say anything to him about it. He knew how I felt about whiskey. Little by little the work fell on me. Frank depended on me not only to go ahead with my work but help him with his. I got along because Lucy took hold and helped me more than ever before, and Nina took most of the care of the children.

Frank had lots of temptation to drink. The country was filling up fast with people, mostly timber men, and almost all of them drank in those days, so besides the saloons in the little towns starting up, there were blind tigers all over the woods. Webb, Mississippi, was put on the map about that time. One of our men named Lake told us, "At Webb they have a killing or a lynching on dull days between paydays and fights or some kind of amusement like that every Saturday night."

I took it as a joke, but in a couple of weeks had reason to believe it a fact. A new man came to work for the company. He was quiet and looked pious as a preacher. He went to Webb with Lake the first Saturday night he was with us. He came back to work Monday morning, but in less than two hours Frank and two more men came carrying him in on a rude stretcher. Frank had tied up his foot, which was split wide open, with his undershirt, to stop the blood. We always kept a complete medicine kit, and Frank had saved more than one life when a doctor was out of the question. So he sent me word to come help him, to bring hot water, epsom salts, and bandages. I took everything, went quick as I could, rolling bandages as I went.

Frank was holding the poor fellow's foot. I fixed hot water and bathed it, handed Frank the things he wanted, and helped him to bandage it. We had to work fast for he was weak already from loss of blood. Frank needed a cord and I hadn't brought any, so he told me to reach in the man's pocket. "He has a cord in there," he said. "He was fumbling with it when I got to him."

So I put my hand in his pocket, got it, unwound the cord, handed it to Frank. I thought I smelled a strong odor. The man had fainted, so woman-like. I finished unwinding the paper, and oh, it makes me creepy yet. A Negro's finger fell in my hand. I yelled, dropped that thing like it was red-hot iron, and started to run. I came near running into Lake as I went out of the door of the men's house. He took it all in at a glance, saw I was completely unnerved. I was trembling all over. It was all I could do to get home, I was so sick and mad. Lake followed me to the house and tried to apologize to me. Told me they had helped string up a Negro near Webb, and that man cut off a finger as a souvenir.

"You see, Mrs. Hamilton," he said, "there is no law in this country yet, and if it had been a white man committed the same crime that Negro did, he would have been served the same way. Women and children have got to be protected. We treat niggers all right down here as long as they stay in their place, but when they commit the crime that one did, they have to be sent out of the world the quickest way."

I said, "That is all right. I approve of that part, but if you have any fingers or toes about you don't bring them in the house."

Needless to say I never went near that crippled man again. I cooked his meals and did everything I could for him except to see him. I asked Frank that night if he didn't think it was the man's bad conscience caused him to cut his foot, and he just said with a teasing laugh, "My dear, I have been wondering all day why it is, since so many thousands of years have passed since Mother Eve's curiosity fell like a blanket on the female species, that you still have your full share. I am no judge of that man or any other."

In one thing Frank and I always had different opinions. He always held himself apart from people, while I always wanted to be friends and neighbors with everyone. I had found I could live without neighbors, but it was a lonesome life. When I would talk about it, Frank would say, "Mary, who is your neighbor and your friend? Neighbors are just anyone that happens to live close enough to borrow coffee and sugar from in a tight, and be sure you pay back with a full measure packed down and running over, or else look to get knifed as soon as your back is turned."

I said, "Frank, why don't you practice what you preach? Just let anyone get in trouble, and you don't stop to think who or what they are. You go the whole length, do far more than your share, and no questions asked, and nine times out of ten when they are out of trouble you wouldn't speak to them if you met them. I can't understand you."

Frank said, "I do my duty as I see it, knowing the one I am helping will repay me with treachery if I give him a chance. I try not to give him a chance." He shrugged and patted my shoulder. "But who knows which of us is right, Mary, you or I."

It wasn't what he would say at such times but the way he looked. I can't describe that proud, lonesome, sad look, as though he was looking back into a past that he couldn't bear to see; but those moods never lasted long, especially if Nina happened to be around. She seemed to understand him as I did not. She would climb on his lap, put her arms around his neck, and call him the sweetest, best father in the world. He would soon be laughing with her as though he didn't have a care in the world. My very heart ached for him, and I determined that even when he was drinking, nothing would make me nag or quarrel with him. I was sure that, with Nina's help, for she had far more influence over him than I ever could have, we could help him work out his salvation without his knowing it.

Frank loved all the children, but this one, Nina, he was so partial to right from the start. He would try not to show it. One day when he was drinking some, just enough to make him talk, I told him it was wrong to make so much difference in the children. He said, "I can't help it, Mary. If you had ever seen my mother or sister you would understand. I don't think many boys ever loved a mother as I loved mine, and my sister. Nina has my mother's face and ways. If I ever try to win back what I have lost, it will be easy through her. She could be identified as one of that old family by her hair alone. For six hundred years, Mary, that gold, bright, curly hair has been in my family. It never changes color from birth to old age. My mother's hair was that color when she died. And those dark gray eyes, almost black, with that peculiar sweet look out of them. I sometimes believe she can see right through the future."

I cried out, "Hush, Frank. I can't stand it. For you know ever since she began talking she talks of no future for herself but heaven."

"Don't say that," Frank said roughly. "I couldn't stand that. I would be sure God was mocking me to send her as a light to right the wrong, then snatch her away. You ask me, Mary, why I don't make friends. I have gone through hell because of another's treachery. I have no friend in this world and want none but you and my children."

But I took this as whiskey talk and changed the subject. I could not help him unless he chose to confide in me, and now I was almost glad he didn't. I didn't want to know. I pitied him more and more every year. I must just try to get as much happiness as I could out of life for my children, Frank and myself, help him overcome his weakness for drink, and teach the children to love him enough to make up to him for whatever it was he had lost or left behind him.

Time was getting along towards June and the last payday. The Yellow Dog branch of the Yazoo and Mississippi Valley Railroad had been surveyed through, and the right-of-way was being cut off. It was cut off to the lower edge of the state farm, and men were making and hauling out ties for it. The woods were full of Negroes and white men. About all the hauling was done by Negroes. We had not had much rain, and the woods were dry, but mosquitoes were bad and wild animals plentiful. The "Cyclone" part of the state farm had not been touched, only a few roads cut through it, but it would take an expert woodsman to follow them. The Slav camp was back on Black Bayou, a flat-banked bayou, crooked as a snake.

On this June payday Minkus came to our camp and settled up with all the men and with Frank. He took dinner with us and told Frank when they got through scraping up to come over to headquarters camp. So he told us all good-bye as he wouldn't be back any more. Four of his men were with him. They all bid us good-bye, and Minkus gave Nina five dollars. When I objected, he said, "You have all been so good to me, mended, darned, and patched and never let me pay you, and I want this little girl to get her a nice doll."

She thanked him and told him she was going to get Frankie a little wagon and Leslie and herself each a doll. He said, "No, that is yours. These men want to give little brother and sister some money."

He told the men to give the other children two dollars each, then he turned to me and said, "These Slavonians love to come to this American camp. The whole four hundred would like to come and tell you all good-bye."

When they were gone I laughed and said to Lucy, "If the whole four hundred had come, we could buy a nice place with about $1200."

Lucy said, "If Frank had $12,000 he wouldn't buy a home and settle down. I sometimes think he is the Wandering Jew. If he ever gets a home, even forty acres, he'll build a house on each corner so you can move four times a year. That is the only way you and Frank could be happy."

Just then Frank came in, and heard the last part of her speech. "You're right, Lucy," he said, "but why didn't you add a saloon in the middle for good measure?"

She said, "Because you didn't give me time; for I do want you to be happy if you ever do settle down."

Frank laughed. "Lucy, you would make a great temperance lecturer."

This was on Saturday evening. Minkus was to settle up with all white hands, Americans and Slavs, Saturday, and on Sunday morning was to go over to a camp of Negroes, teamsters and stavemakers, about five miles from his headquarters camp on Black Bayou. This Negro camp was in a kind of horseshoe bend of the bayou. It was five miles by road, but if he could cut straight through the Cyclone, it wasn't much over two miles. So he set out alone with $472 in a pocketbook, a compass and a cane knife. He told them at headquarters camp he might not be back for a couple of days, as he was winding up everything in that neck of the woods. This was Sunday morning. On Wednesday, the white man running the Negro camp came into headquarters camp to see why Minkus hadn't come to pay off.

They knew at once he was either lost or killed. They searched every foot of the five-mile road, trying to pick up his trail through the Cyclone, but could find no clue. Then they raised the alarm. No one could go in the Cyclone that night, but the night was spent grilling those Negroes at the camp, for with all that money, and with Minkus one of the smartest men in that country and an expert woodsman, it seemed more likely that he had been robbed and murdered than that he was lost.

But Thursday morning searchers in the Cyclone got on his trail. Found he was going way above his camp. He had gone about two miles above the camp, had run into the bayou again, then started circling. Taking in a space about a mile around, he had worn a smooth path traveling. They found bits of his clothes, could see where he must have stayed under one small tree at least three nights. They found his hat, shoes, compass, and cane axe, but not him, and yet they could see no place where he had broken away from that circle.

Early that morning some Negroes, tie haulers, were unloading ties on the railroad right-of-way. They saw a wild man, as they thought, for he was stark naked, come out in the edge of the right-of-way. They began yelling; the man threw up his head and saw them and darted back into the bushes. The tie inspector with them was a white man, and he had just heard about Minkus being lost. He called "Minkus, Minkus," but the man didn't stop. The Negroes had already taken the gear off their mules, and, jumping on the mules, they ran him down, caught him and held him by force. His clothes were all gone. He fought and cried, but finally they calmed him, and he began mouthing "water." They gave him water from a keg on their wagon, but his mouth and tongue were swollen so bad he could hardly drink. And yet that circle he had traveled for four days and nights had taken him by that bayou, to its very edge, at least a thousand times, and he couldn't remember ever getting a drink. His body was scratched and bleeding, but he kept fumbling with something in his hand. The man asked him what it was and he said, "Money. Count it."

The man counted it. "Four hundred and seventy-two dollars."

Minkus reached for it. "All there. Thanks," he said, and started off down the track. Did I tell you Minkus was a Jew? They got him back, and one of the Negroes lent him his overalls and went back to his railroad camp in his shirttail. Minkus was taken to his camp dressed in the Negro's overalls and holding his pocketbook. But he hadn't lost one nickle of the company's money!

Nina Wears Her White Dress

TWO MORE WEEKS WOUND UP ALL THE STAVE-MAKING for that company, and all the men but Frank were scattering out, getting new work. Frank still had about three months' work going over all the timber checking up, so we rented one of the new houses that had been put up at the mill, a big two-story house. We were going to live in a real house at last, and rest, rest. I didn't know I was tired before. Frank could be home only over Saturday and Sunday, but how I looked forward to three months of rest!

We stored everything we didn't need upstairs and only used two large rooms downstairs. Cooked and ate in one and slept in the other. Lucy's bed was in one of the other rooms. That first night we had lots of fun getting supper, trying to cook just enough for one small family of six, but in spite of all we had enough for fifteen, and I caught myself a dozen times starting to set the alarm clock for four o'clock. And I might as well have set it, for I woke up at four and couldn't go back to sleep, so I got up and started breakfast.

I wasn't started good when Lucy came in, saying she couldn't sleep either. "I was sure all along," she said, "if we ever got in a house again we would go crazy."

Well, we had time to look about us and take in the sights of Ohio City. There was the Mills family; Billy Mills was helping Frank, and he had a wife and two children. Then there was Hurst, a northern man, and his wife, who lived in the hotel. Hurst was the mill owner, and his wife ran the hotel for the mill crew, mostly Ohio men. Mrs. Hurst was a perfect lady, but Mr. Hurst was haughty, overbearing. Like so many northern people when first coming to this country in those days, they were too big for the country. Hurst couldn't treat a southern white man decent but was going to reform the South and show the Negroes they were equal to the whites in all things. When a northern person comes to this country and starts that, the Negroes are the first to get down on them and laugh about it. So it was in this case. We told Mrs. Hurst they were making a mistake, but she said she couldn't do anything with her husband.

We hadn't been there long when one Sunday here came Mr. Perkins, the surveyor, like a long-lost brother, a boy bringing his suitcase and surveying instruments. We told him we couldn't board him, but he said he was going to stay anyway, so we had just as well stop making excuses. Frank was at home and asked him why he didn't stay at the hotel.

"You are running Hurst's line," Frank said, "doing his work."

Perkins said, "Frank, you know I am a southerner. Some of my best friends are northern people, but this man is rank, has no sense at all. Do you know what he did when he met me in Webb? Introduced himself, then said, 'I have a rig here to take you out. I'm coming later.' Then he turned to a black nigger and said to him, 'Mr. Jackson, here is your passenger, Perkins.' Can you beat that?"

Frank just hollered, and of course we all laughed. He said he wasn't coming one step with the Negro, but as soon as Hurst got off a step or two, the Negro turned to him and apologized. "Said, 'Boss, dat white man sure is hurtin' hisself an' hurtin' us too. But dah is a white family livin' dah close dat is mighty fine folks.' So I came on, and the first white person I met at the hotel was Miss Lucy. So here I am, and here I stay, and if I can't stay with you, I catch the first train back to Memphis." So he stayed.

That three months passed so quick. Frank was through with his job and was resting up for a few weeks before starting with a new firm, an English and Irish firm from New Orleans. They weren't to start till October, and Frank was home all the time. I was so glad. Lucy was staying at the hotel, helping Mrs. Hurst, and at last she had met the man. A Mississippi man, a widower with three children. I never believed she cared one cent for him, but she wanted to mother those children. The more she thought about it, the surer she was she wanted the job. And he was a farmer. While Lucy had never been on a farm since she could remember, she knew a little farm was the dream of my

life, and thought it the very thing. The man, Charlie Lawlor, was
hauling lumber from the mill and boarded at the hotel a lot. We all
liked him. Frank seemed to think a lot of him.

All this time Hurst was getting more insulting with his race views,
and one morning just before we left there, a squad of horsemen rode
up to the hotel, called him out and told him in a few words that he
had twenty-four hours to get his business straight enough to leave the
country. In less time than that Hurst was gone. A few of his men went
too, and the mill was shut down. Nothing was molested after they
went.

In October Frank's new job was ready for him. Their camps were to be
in a low, wet place, or would be as soon as the fall rains set in, and
Frank didn't think I could stand it, for I was pregnant again. Mean-
while, a Mr. Amens had bought all the cypress timber on the sixteenth section to make railroad ties for the new railroad. A man
named Maddock was to run the job and had already moved his family
there. Maddock and Amens wanted us to run their boardinghouse. We
had a big outfit, and they said they would build a good camp on high
ground. I wanted to get to real work again, and I felt like we needed to
make as much money as we could; so when Lucy promised to stay with
me and help me through the winter, not get married till spring, we
decided to run the boardinghouse.

Oh, how I longed and worked for a home of my own. Another child
coming and still no home. Those days there was no such thing as birth
control. Poor hardworking mothers were supposed to thank God for
every new addition to their family, buckle down and work all the
harder. If Frank would just stop drinking and save like I did, we could
soon have a home. If we were to stay in this country on account of his
health, and I loved every foot of it, I couldn't see why we couldn't save
our money to buy a home where we could raise our children right; and
I could see money in this new boardinghouse. Frank promised to let
me have everything I made. No wonder I went into it happy and
lighthearted.

Frank helped build the houses and get us started. Our living room
was built off a few feet from the cookhouse and dining room. We had
thirty men, most of them our old men, and just the right number to
make some money from. Frank bought a Texas pony and got home

almost every night. This tie job would last several months; there was a good doctor at Dublin, so I had nothing to worry me—for two weeks.

Then we heard Flynn was coming. Was out on good behaviour seven months before his six years were up. Bad as I hated to see Lucy get a divorce, I knew it could be put off no longer. She applied for it at once, and when it was granted and her maiden name restored, she married Lawlor and went straight to his home. How I hated to see her go, and the children took it so hard. Poor little Frankie, now almost two years old, would cry for days after she left, "Lu, sweet old Lu. She gone. Gone."

A Mrs. Lyons and her husband, Ohio people, moved into our house. I gave her their board and three dollars a week to help me. She was a good cook, agreeable to get along with, and so much company when Frank had to be away. Nina was only six, but she needed no help with the children. She played with them, washed and dressed them, and wouldn't let them bother me, not even to undressing them for bed. She would put their nighties on, hear them say their prayers, and sit by Frankie, singing or telling them stories till they went to sleep. She was the first of them to wake up of a morning. She would hurry and dress, get Leslie up, help her dress, then get Frankie up and dress him, then all come into the kitchen for their breakfast. As soon as that was over, out they would go to play all day long. The days didn't seem long enough for her. She was always in a good humor, nothing bothered her; but let other children come to play with them, and she was like a little bantam mother hen, fussing over her two chicks, protecting them. I never worried about them with her.

But Frank kept drinking more than we could afford. One member of the firm Frank was working for stayed in camp with him all the time. A Mr. Reliford, Irish, right from Ireland, and he and Frank were good friends, and I was sure he liked to drink. Now I don't want you to think Frank was a gutter drunkard. He never got sloppy drunk and had no other bad habits at all. He would not gamble, and I had no right ever to be jealous of him. He held himself above anything like that. But it was just the silly things he would do when drinking. Money was no object. He was always rich. I tried to tell him we must look out for ourselves and our children. I said, "Frank, if you were just half as careful and particular when you are drinking as you are when you're sober, we would soon be well-to-do."

"Now don't you fret, my dear Calamity Ann," he said. "We have never gone to the bottom but once, and that was an accident and not very good judgment on my part. But you and the children will never suffer."

I was sure we wouldn't if my strength held out.

One Saturday in November Frank came home, but only for a few hours. He had to go back that night. The children were all in bed and we thought them all asleep. He had kissed them all goodnight, but here came Nina, insisting on saying her prayers to him. When she got through she kept looking at him like she wanted to say something. She threw her arms around his neck and said, "Father, there was something I wanted to ask God to do for you, but I was afraid you wouldn't like it."

He looked so puzzled and said, "Nina, you couldn't say anything that would hurt me."

But she slid down off his lap, and said, "That is all right. I will whisper it to God. Goodnight, Father. I'm so sleepy."

Frank sat there until he thought her asleep. Then he got up to go. He kissed me good-bye, and said, "Mary, I don't believe Nina is well. I know she is always a good child, but the last few months she is more angel than child. Oh, my God, if anything were to happen to her what would we do?"

Mrs. Lyons spoke up and said, "Frank, if anything happens to her it will be because you are so partial to her. She is a fine child but really no better than the other two. You make such an idol of her I'm afraid she will be taken from you."

Frank looked at her so straight, and said, "No, she won't. I couldn't stand that and wouldn't try."

He opened the door and went out. He jumped on his horse and left in a gallop. Mrs. Lyons said, "I'm sorry I said anything to him, but maybe it will sober him." I was afraid it would have the opposite effect, but I could do nothing. I had to go to bed—if not to sleep, to rest for tomorrow.

I got up next morning feeling like a trouble was hanging over us, and I couldn't shake it off. I plunged all the harder into work, but work as I would, it grew stronger and stronger. If I could just have a good cry. But how foolish, I thought. I couldn't cry. For one thing I had nothing to cry about, and for another, I didn't have time. Mr. and

Mrs. Lyons had been called away that morning, and I only had a Negro woman to help me, Aunt Sue. Aunt Sue couldn't go ahead like Mrs. Lyons, and my work was so hard I almost overcame the feeling of trouble ahead. I left the care of the children entirely to Nina.

It had been a wonderful fall. We had very little rain—bright sunshiny days and nights just cool enough to have a little fire in the fireplace. The children stayed outdoors all day in the sunshine and played. One day that week I said to Nina, "Why do you play so hard? You don't look well." She looked sort of pale and peaked.

"Oh yes, Mama, I am all right. My stomach hurts all the time, but I am well, and Mama, I love to play with Frankie and Leslie while I can." She hesitated and looked so far away, just for a moment, then she brightened up and said, "I forgot Ozzie will be there."

I said, "Why do you talk like that, Nina? It is wrong. You are by far the healthiest one of the children, and I don't like to hear you talk about dying."

"Mama, I'm sorry. I say that before I think." So she ran off to play, and it seemed like she had forgotten it; but I didn't forget it. Nina had always been a strange child, and her beauty, along with her constant talk of death and heaven, made her seem at times almost unearthly. But it troubled me and seemed to be a part of the feeling I couldn't get rid of all those beautiful late fall days.

Just a few days after that, Frank got word that a big shipment of groceries he had ordered for both camps was at Dublin. He got wagons ready to start after them Saturday morning, and he stayed at home Friday night so he could get an early start with them next morning.

That night he helped Nina get the children ready for bed. I was in the kitchen. After she got them ready and off to bed, she climbed in her father's lap and said, "Father, I want you to rock me and sing to me, but don't sing those old war songs. Sing something good. Father, I am awful sick, but I don't want to worry Mama. It is my stomach. It hurts all the time. Do you think it could be that marble I swallowed a long time ago? I heard Mama and Aunt Lucy talking, and they said the doctor said it was liable to kill me some day years and years from the time I swallowed it."

It was with a heavy heart he sang to her, and when she went to sleep he came in the kitchen and told me what she had said. It was the first time we had thought of it for many months. It had been three years and over since she swallowed it. We decided she had a little malaria. Frank made out a small dose of calomel, told me to start giving it at four next morning, and when he got loaded up in Dublin he would bring the doctor out with him Sunday morning. He had to go and come with the teams as he was the only one that knew the way.

I got up at half past three next morning and made Frank some coffee and toast. While he ate, I started breakfast but went in the house with him to give Nina her first dose of medicine. I woke her up and told her we were going to give her some medicine, that she was going to stay in the house all day and not to try to take care of the children. I ended, "Then tomorrow when Father gets back, you will be well."

She got out of bed, threw her arms around Frank, and said, "Father, please don't go. If you do I will never see you again."

Frank sat down, took her in his lap, and said, "Nina, baby, don't talk like that. If I thought you were bad sick, nothing on earth would take me, but the teams are all ready to start and can't go without me. This pretty weather can't last much longer, and if it starts raining we can't get a team over the roads. Now you be good and take your medicine, so tomorrow when you hear me coming you can come to meet me."

She laughed and shook her head, then looked at him so straight and said, "Father, when you come home tomorrow, and I can't come to meet you, because I'll be gone to heaven, will you promise to stop drinking so you can come to heaven, too? I heard you tell Mama once if you ever got to go home it would be because of me. Well, I'm going up there, Father, and as soon as I get there I'm going to find your mother, the one I am so much like, and I'm going to find God, and tell them both how good you are, and how bad you want to go home, and that you're going to stop drinking."

She stopped, threw her arms around his neck, and hugged him tight. Frank couldn't speak. She sat back quiet on his lap for a minute, and then said in a little voice, so sober, "I did want to stay with Leslie and Frankie. Father, do help them with their prayers. Mama is always so busy."

I slipped out and over to the kitchen. I was sobbing and crying until I could hardly do anything. Used as I was to her grown-up ways, it seemed like I couldn't stand it to have her talk like that. Frank came in the kitchen just then and tried to speak, but like me, he broke down. When he got control of himself enough to speak, he said, "Mary, do you believe she is in any danger of dying? Never in my life have I heard a little child talk as she does. Just six years old. It's not right. If I thought she knew what she was talking about, no power on earth could take me away from home, but she can't, it's impossible, and those teams are all started, will go as far as they know, then wait for me. What must I do?"

"Well," I said, "you will have to go. I can't believe she is in any danger, Frank, for she played yesterday. She hasn't a bit of fever and hasn't had. But I know she is a long ways from well. I am a little afraid of that marble. She doesn't complain of but one thing, her stomach. I will keep her close today, give her medicine, and she will be all right. But when you come back, bring the doctor. As for her talk, we are to blame. She is sensitive, and she has always talked about dying ever since Ozzie died. She heard you tell me if you ever went home it would be because she made it so you could, and she thought by 'home,' you meant 'heaven.' Then the day Lucy left she said, 'I could go so much better satisfied if Frank would quit drinking.'

"I flared up as usual, and said, 'That's the only fault he has.'

"Lucy said, 'Yes, but that is bad enough to keep him from ever helping you get the home you want so bad.' Then she laughed and said, 'His drinking is the only thing that will keep him out of heaven. He will go there flying if he doesn't do some silly thing while drunk to keep him out.'"

It was so plain when we got to studying about it, how that sensitive, loving child had overheard us talking at different times and got things confused. She loved her father better than anything on earth, and anything to do with him stuck in her little head. Frank went away in better spirits, I know, though the teams had to wait on him, and I was late with breakfast just a few minutes.

When the Negro woman, Aunt Sue, came to help me, I sent her to get Mrs. Mills to come stay all day with me, give Nina her medicine, and help with the children. She came. Nina's medicine made her sick but not sick enough to keep her in bed, and that night she got both children ready for bed as always, then got back in bed herself. When I got in from the kitchen she begged me to go to bed. Said she didn't need anyone to sit up with her. I took her in bed with me so I could take better care of her. I was up with her several times through the night, but was so tired and worn out I couldn't stay awake very long at a time, and she seemed better. When the alarm went off at four o'clock I didn't hear it, but Nina woke me, and I got dressed. She was sitting up in bed watching me, her eyes so bright, and she was smiling. I stooped down, kissed her, and said, "Nina, you are so much better. I wish your father could see you now. Now tell me you feel all right."

She said, "Go get breakfast started, Mama; then come back. I have something to tell you."

I was so lighthearted; I soon had a fire, got breakfast almost ready, and went back in my room to see what she wanted to tell me. The minute I saw her, I knew without asking. She was lying back on the pillow, her little face pinched and drawn. The pallor of death had spread all over her, but she smiled, "Oh, Mama, if I could just live till Father gets here."

I tried to move, run for help, but I was paralyzed for a moment. She said, "Mama, ring the bell. When the men come, get someone to go for Aunt Sue. Let her finish breakfast, and you stay with me."

I went like in a dream and started ringing the bell. But I dropped the bell and ran as hard as I could go. When I got far enough away so I thought I wouldn't scare her, I screamed, "Help, help, quick. Nina is dying."

Men came running to the door. I told them to go quick for Aunt Sue, Mrs. Mills, Mrs. Maddock. I hurried back, and Leslie was standing by Nina's bed. Their arms were about each other, and Nina was whispering to Leslie. I never did know what they were talking about. When she saw me, Nina said, "Quick, Mama, bring Frankie."

I woke him up, set him on the bed by her. She brushed the curls out of his eyes and said, "Oh, you sweet boy." Then she fell back, said, "Hold me, Mama, I am tired." She sank back into my arms, then brightened up. "I hear him," she cried.

It was coming daylight. Someone went to the door and said, "It is Frank." We could all hear his horse galloping. He came rushing in like a madman, ran to her, and took her out of my arms, choked with sobs so he couldn't speak. She reached her little cold weak arms up to his neck, and said, loud enough for us to hear, "Father, don't forget to come . . ." and was gone.

The house was full. Someone took her out of Frank's arms and laid her on the bed. Frank fell face forward on the floor. I thought he was dead, but he had only fainted. When he came to himself, he got up, shook off all help, turned a deaf ear to everybody, walked out and sat down outside the door. He had never spoken. I went to him, dropped down by him, took his cold hands in mine, and looked up in his face that was as pale as hers. His poor agonized eyes were staring, but I knew he saw nothing I could see.

"Frank," I said, "she died so quiet and easy, believing she was carrying a message to God for you."

I was remembering little Oswald's death, and how easy Nina's was compared to his. We had stood that; somehow we could bear anything.

Not until they began asking us where she was to be buried did we realize how awful it really was. It was all right to live in a camp in the wilderness, but to die here was different. We did not know of a graveyard in the country that we could reach, nor a preacher. How could we bury her like that? But Frank said, "Mary, as it has to be in the woods, let her rest just across on that ridge where her playhouse is. The last time I was home she took me out there and showed me her playhouse. We don't need a preacher."

I had far nicer clothes to bury her in than we could buy. The white silk dress her Uncle Jim had given her on Concordia Island with the hem out was just right, as it was all the fashion when I made it for little girls' dresses to come to their insteps. So on Monday she was laid to rest in her beloved woods, under a holly tree that was full of berries, where the birds could feed all winter and sing, and where the children could play on warm days.

As soon as she was buried, Frank came to the house with us, stayed just a few minutes, then kissed the children and me, and said, "Mary, it is cowardly to leave you, but I can't stay here tonight."

Almost before I could answer he was on his horse and gone. As he passed her grave he uncovered and bowed his head for a minute, then put spurs to his horse and left in a gallop. It began clouding up and the next morning there were about four inches of snow. All I could see of Nina's little grave was a white mound, the green holly trees full of red berries at the head, birds twittering and singing. I had breakfast for the men on time, and they were so gentle and good. Every table of them insisted on waiting on themselves.

That day at noon Flynn came walking in. Frank had written him he could come to us, and help me, as Lucy was gone now. Flynn was the same man, only worn and older, and someway we looked for no more treachery from him. During his prison term we had been his only friends, sending him a little money every month, writing to him. He had never seen Nina, Leslie, nor Frankie, but one of the first things he did between times helping me was to get out timber and build a little house over Nina's grave. Frankie took up with him, trotting after him everywhere he went. Flynn's coming was a great help to me. He was one man who could do everything and do it well. He fixed his bed in a corner of the kitchen, so he could be right there to help me. He kept big fires and lots of wood cut, did all the hardest cooking, and waited on tables. If we had been good to him, he paid us back that winter. No one around there had any idea he had ever been Lucy's husband, or that he had been in prison. Lucy's name was never mentioned between us.

Thanks to Flynn I could take up more time with my children. But I was worried bad about Frank. He never came home now more than once a week, and then never stayed but a few minutes. And every time he came he was drinking. I couldn't bear to think that Nina's death, instead of helping him, had hurt him, and I determined as soon as my baby was born to go to him—it made no difference if his camp was in a frog pond.

When he came home just a few days before Christmas he had a bad cold, and I was so afraid of pneumonia, I begged him to stay at home. He said he couldn't. Said his cook had gone out for Christmas, and he didn't know what to do. I told him to take Flynn back with him, and I would get Aunt Sue to help me. So Flynn went. Christmas night closed down on the two children and me alone, but I felt a kind of happiness sitting by the fire telling them stories that cold snowy night.

In a Circle Like a Man Lost

W E HAD A FEW NICE DAYS AFTER CHRISTMAS. Work hummed—
the men were clearing out the timber fast, and we could hear
them working on the new railroad. Flynn came back from Frank's
camp the first of January and again took almost all the work off me, but
I had plenty of excitement for a few days. One of the men caught a
stray dog, a big hound. He tied it up with a long chain, and everyone
that came within the length of that chain got bit unless they got out of
reach pretty quick. Mrs. Maddock, a neighbor woman, was pregnant
and was excitable and nervous. One day she went to the pump to get
water. She was laughing and talking to her two little boys that were
with her. She had forgotten all about the dog till it sprung out and on
her. It knocked her down, tore her clothes nearly off her and bit her
pretty bad. They got her home and in bed. She wasn't hurt so much as
frightened to death, and to make it worse her husband was away on
business. Frank happened along and he went to Dublin for a doctor,
but we soon saw she couldn't wait for a doctor. Aunt Sue took his
place. Less than two hours after the accident, she gave birth to twin
girls, born a month too soon.

Our supper was over, and I had got Leslie off to bed and was trying
to get Frankie to sleep so I could go down there and stay till the doctor
came, but try as I would, he wouldn't go to sleep. Aunt Sue came by to
tell me she had to go home. That woman mustn't be left alone down
there, so I wrapped up Frankie and myself and started. Aunt Sue said
Mrs. Maddock was getting along all right, but that the babies were
"making a mighty heap of funny noise."

When I went in I saw the room was cold. I threw the stove drafts open and went to the bed. The babies, lying by their mother's side, had been washed and dressed and covered good, but they were cold, and like Aunt Sue had said, were making the queerest noise. The mother begged me to take them to the fire and get them warm. I told her they were dying, but she wouldn't believe me. Frankie was scream- ing at the top of his lungs, he was so scared of the babies and the noise they were making. I filled the stove with big wood, sat down, held my hands over Frankie's ears so he wouldn't hear the babies, and rocked him a few minutes. I got him to sleep, slipped him in bed with her little boys in the next room, and went and got a blanket.

I warmed the blanket good and took up those dying babies. I didn't much more than get sat down with them by the stove than here came Frankie screaming and crying. "Oh, Mama, take me, take me. Throw those old rabbits down." A few days before a man had caught a rabbit alive and told Frankie to hold out his hands, he had a pretty pet for him. Frankie ran to get it, and when the man jerked it out from under his coat, it hollered not so very different from these babies, and it had scared Frankie nearly to death. He thought these babies were rabbits.

In spite of all I could do, he climbed up on my lap, fighting and screaming. I couldn't keep him off. I tried to get up, but I couldn't. Just then the lamp went out. Like many others, Mrs. Maddock had neglected to keep her lamps filled with oil, and it had just burned out. At about the same time one of the babies stopped making any noise. There I was—one dead baby, one dying, and a terrified two-year-old boy almost having spasms, all on my lap, and the room in darkness. Frankie was afraid of the dark, afraid of the babies. At last—it seemed hours but was probably no more than a few minutes—the other baby got quiet. I knew it was dead. I got Frankie quiet enough so I could talk to him. I got him down on the floor and told him to hold tight to me, and I would give those babies back to their mother. I had to walk slow and careful as it was black dark. I laid them down on the foot of the bed, straightened them as best I could. I asked Mrs. Maddock where to find a match. I picked Frankie up and held to the wall to guide me to a table. There I found matches and struck one, found the oil, and carried it back to the stove. Then for the first time I thought to open the stove door to give a little light, enough to fill the lamp by. From the time I was a little child, I had been taught to keep our lamps filled, and before we had lamps, extra candles handy in case of sickness. I lit the lamp, shut off the stove draft, and told Mrs. Maddock I was going to run home to leave Frankie and would be right back. I took him home and put him in bed with Flynn, looked in my room to see if Leslie was all right, then went by and got Aunt Sue and took her back with me to Mrs. Maddock's.

The doctor got there about midnight. Mrs. Maddock got well, but she had a hard time. Her husband got home the next day and buried his babies. I felt so sorry for them. They wanted a little girl so bad. They both had thought so much of Nina, and Mrs. Maddock had often said, "If my baby is a girl and like Nina, I will be the proudest woman in the world." Now it was all over.

One good thing was I got to talk to the doctor, Dr. Harrison, the one Frank had spoken to for me. Dr. Harrison was one of the finest doctors I ever knew and one of the finest men. We knew him for years afterward. After Tutwiler was built up, he moved there. He told me there was a Negro nurse at Dublin, a good old woman, and he advised us to get her and bring her out. She wouldn't charge much till I got down, and if anything happened before he got there, he said she was almost as much good as he was anyhow. So we sent for her the next day—Aunt Silvy, her name was. It was a good thing we did, for it came a big snow and the roads were almost past traveling except afoot or horseback. On the twenty-second it came a regular blizzard, snow and sleet. Cleared off about the twenty-fifth but turned so cold, with snow a foot deep. I told Flynn to keep the chickens up. They had a good warm house; we gave them hot feed. But as the men were coming to dinner, one of them noticed the chicken house closed, thought we had forgot to open it, and to oblige us opened it. Several flew out, and eight of them froze so near to death before we could catch them that they died.

We had such big fires that cold spell I was afraid we would burn the house down, and even then, sitting by the fire, you had to keep turning around and around to keep from freezing. We could hear loud popping like from a gun outside in the woods. Frank said it was the trees freezing and bursting; great limbs would break off and lots of trees fell. At the Maddocks' house, Maddock and his wife slept on one side of their room and their boys on the other side, about a five-foot space between the beds. Christmas morning a limb dropped from a tree that stood at the end of the house, came down endways through the roof, and stuck as straight up in the floor between those two beds as if it had been set out there. It didn't hurt anyone, and Mrs. Maddock told me afterward she was glad it fell, as she had been trying for an hour to get her old man up, and in three minutes after it fell he was up and had a good fire burning.

Frank was staying home nights this terrible cold weather. We had a time getting breakfast and cooking all during that cold spell. Had to melt snow for water. Couldn't cut meat to fry, had to chop it off with the cleaver and boil or roast it.

The twenty-sixth of January, 1899, dawned clear and cold, eight below zero. Frank said that morning, "Wouldn't it be the devil to have to go for the doctor today?"

And about three o'clock that afternoon I told him he could go, I would need a doctor before midnight. How I did pity him having to get out in that cold and snow! I got both children to sleep by seven o'clock. I was suffering pretty bad but was so thankful Aunt Silvy was with me. I was so much better off than when Frankie was born, but I couldn't help but think how like that other stormy night it was. That was a hurricane, and this was the coldest blizzard I could ever remember.

My baby was born at eight o'clock, a sweet little girl. I was so glad it was a girl. Someway I thought she would take Nina's place. Aunt Silvy had her bathed and dressed when Frank and the doctor came. Of course they both had had some whiskey. I don't believe they could have lived through that cold without it. When they got warm, Flynn had them a good hot supper, and after looking over Aunt Silvy's work, the doctor stayed all night.

Next morning bright and early they were up, had breakfast, and were ready to start. Frank wanted to see the children before leaving, and the doctor wanted to hear what they had to say about the new baby. So Frank got them by the fire and Aunt Silvy showed the baby to them. I was afraid it would scare Frankie like the Maddocks' babies did, but his father told him it was a little baby sister the doctor brought for him and Leslie. He peeped at her, and she opened her eyes and blinked. He said, "'Tis a baby, Father, not a rabbit."

Leslie looked at him so hard. "Frankie, you are crazy, and the doctor had nothing to do with bringing her. I knew all the time God would send her back. That is the reason I didn't cry so much. I ask God to send her back every time I go to our playhouse."

The doctor asked her what she meant and she said, "We had a sister, such a sweet sister. God took her away up in heaven, and made an angel of her, and that made her little and sweet. Father, is she still named Nina? She looks like she did only her hair is brown."

I thought to myself, "You funny child. So that is the reason you never cried."

Frank picked her up and kissed her and said, "Leslie, you are right. But her name is Edris, the angel that went to heaven to live, but her love for the ones she left on earth was so strong she had to come back to earth and to her loved ones."

The doctor said, "Frank, where do you get all that? Not from the Bible. I didn't know you had it in you."

Frank laughed and said, "Dr. Harrison, you've never seen anything but the business and fool side of me, but I have a sentimental side too, and Leslie started it working. No, I didn't get that from the Bible, but from Marie Corelli's 'Field of Ardroth.' What Leslie said is true, and that is why I gave her the name; besides, Edris is a good, old name, five thousand years old and more. But we had better be riding. Mary, I have a carload of groceries in Dublin, and I expect it will all be frozen, potatoes, onions, and cabbages, so I won't be home for three or four days as I must get it hauled."

I asked how he expected to haul it when he couldn't put a wagon on the road. He said he left them making a sled, and by wrapping gunny sacks around the mules' legs they could make it, even if the snow was not frozen, till they could walk on top. So he and Dr. Harrison left.

I was doing fine and felt I was lucky after all, although living in a camp. Wasn't almost all the country camping? I had had only one cloud in my sky: Frank's giving up and going to pieces like he had since Nina's death. I had felt sure he was trying to drink himself to death, but now I believed Leslie's little childish thoughts had made him stop and think. How I did pray that little Edris would grow more like Nina and in time would come to take her place. And she did. All her life she has shed her sunny nature on all around her, always looking on the bright side, turning a deaf ear to her own troubles but always helping others.

By the first of February the weather had moderated some, but the exposure to the bitter cold had given Frank pneumonia the next day after the baby was born. I knew nothing about it till he was up. I kept fretting about him not coming home, till Flynn told me, after he was out of danger.

"What was the use of worrying you before?" he said. "You weren't able to sit up, let alone go to him. By the way, Mary, I think you ought to go to Frank's camp. He is with his own countrymen and is drinking entirely too much. They are putting up a new camp out on the new railroad, a little station called Bray. Frank's company is putting up a bucker there to trim the staves down and get them ready to ship to Europe. They expect Frank to run it. You will live out there in a real house. Captain Thomas of Memphis has bought a big tract of land and is opening up a plantation there, and the bucker is on his place. They are going to have a station there and a store, and they are building a nice boardinghouse."

I asked Flynn where they were getting all the lumber, and where he was getting all his information. He said, "The lumber is coming from the Ohio mill, and Frank gave me the information last time he was here. Frank don't want you to move till you make the move to Bray, but I think you ought to go to his temporary camp now, on account of his drinking. Then, too, he needs me to cook for him, and you should come, too."

I thought over what Flynn said, and I saw he was right. The last of February we sent Aunt Silvy home. Paid her twenty dollars in money, and she collected up two barrels full of meat scraps—ham and shoulder bones and meat skins—enough, she said, to make a crop on. She called down every kind of blessing she could think of on me, and some I am sure she never had thought of before. We have lots of Negroes, but few Aunt Silvys. She was so good and so happy.

The first time Frank came home after that I begged him to let me move to his camp. He gave in, and we moved. I couldn't help but think of what Lucy had said about Frank moving, but instead of having a house on each corner of a forty-acre plot, we were moving in a circle like a man lost and were getting nowhere. Or were we?

This camp was in a low place, deep in gumbo mud, but the buildings were by far the best we had ever had in camp, with puncheon walks a foot high from shanty to shanty. Charlie fixed me a large chicken house; as spring opened up my hens started laying, and how they did lay! I had the Giant Brahma chickens, snow-white with a little black fluff of a tail, black head and neck, and no comb at all— the healthiest chickens and the finest layers I ever had. We were never without game chickens as long as Frank lived, and he had Frankie and Leslie loving a cock fight as much as he did. Frankie had one fine game rooster, an Indian game.

I had my usual thirty-five men to cook for. I had a Negro girl as nurse for the baby, but I never let them out of my sight. I made Leslie understand she was to take care of herself and Frankie. While Leslie wasn't as gentle and kind as Nina, she was strict with Frankie and with herself. She had her own ideas of right and wrong and religion, and with my help managed fine.

I liked Frank's bosses. The Irishman stayed at camp all the time, as did one of the Englishmen, Mr. Ray. We boarded them, and as they paid good board we could afford the best. I had cooked so long I thought I really knew how to cook English-style. But I didn't have time to take the pains I wanted to, as they were working some Negroes, and the Negro boy helping me had to cook for them. So Frank went to Memphis and got a German cook by the name of Stine.

He was good, but, like all professional cooks, was cross. He told Frank to give him a Negro boy to help him and to keep me out of the kitchen. "I know my business and don't want no woman telling me what to do," he told Frank. So Frank gave me strict orders not to step my foot in the kitchen, nor let the children. Not even as a shortcut to the dining room.

I was disappointed. I said "Frank, why did you get that kind of a man?"

"Well," Frank said, "I had to take what I could get; besides, he is one of the finest cooks in Memphis. He must be, by the price I have to pay him, so don't you go interfering with him. Let him do all the cooking, and you rest and play with the children. And listen, Leslie, don't you and Frankie go in there bothering him. He is a redheaded goblin and may eat you up."

It wasn't but two days later that Frank came in the house with Frankie on his shoulder, Leslie trotting by his side, and said, "Mary, I bring you the conquering heroes. They have routed the goblin in the kitchen and found a friend in our new cook."

It seems Leslie had run in the kitchen and said, "Good morning, Mr. Goblin, are you going to eat Frankie and me up?"

Stine said, "I eat bad children when they bother me."

"Oh," she said, "we are good, and besides Frankie and I have a rooster that eats goblins just like eating corn. So if you look like you are getting hungry we will bring old Game in and he will eat you."

He looked at her through his nearsighted eyes, and said, "Little girl, you're a game yourself, so let's shake and be friends."

Frankie was standing in the door, and he sidled up to the cook, held out his hand, and said, "Hello, Mr. Gobble."

"Young fellow, my name is Stine."

Leslie said, "How nice. We have a cat named Jack Stine." So Jack Stine he was to them, and they were good friends as long as he was there.

I had a harder time making up with him. He made a yeast that would have bread ready to bake in two and a half hours after making it up, and every time I could make an excuse to be in the kitchen I was there trying to watch him. At last one day he said, "Mrs. Hamilton, I told your husband before I came here I wouldn't stand any interference from women. I can't stand women poking around my work trying to find fault. If my work don't suit you, I will get out and you can take the kitchen."

I said, "Hold on a minute till I tell you what I am poking around your kitchen for, then if you still object, you can go. You say you are not going to stay but two months, and after you leave I will have all this work to do again. I am sure I have had at least twenty men cooks and from every one I have learned something that was such a help to me, till I began to think I knew it all, but since you came I feel as if I know nothing at all about cooking. I would freely give you a month's wages just to learn how to make that quick yeast alone. I want to help you just so I can learn."

I could see him begin to brighten up, and I went on. "I won't interfere with your work. I want you to make out a bill for everything you need to make cakes and decorate them. It makes no difference how much it costs, I will see you get it. We keep everything necessary for common cooking, but I have had to do the work alone so much I have never had time for much fancy cooking. We make plenty of money but can't save much; all I get out of it is a living and the pleasure of knowing how to cook and handle this work the easiest way. So if you will just let me be your pupil, we will get along together fine."

He looked at me and said, "Do you mean to tell me you have done all this cooking for this crew of thirty men and more?"

"With a breathing spell of a month or six weeks about once every four months," I told him. "Cooks are hard to keep in the woods."

"Well," he said, "I am going to do for you what I never did for a woman before. I will take you, as you say, for my pupil, but if you show signs of wanting to teach, I expel you."

That night when I gave Frank a list of stuff as long as my arm and told him to have it sent by express, his face looked as long as the list. But he got it all. Such light bread, rolls, French, plain, sweet, and fruit, every kind I had ever made before, but he made them so quick and with so much less trouble. I was as good on meats and fish as Stine was but knew nothing about cakes, fruit salads, or dozens of other things, compared to what he did.

One day he made a fruit stack cake almost a foot high. Was going to make a kewpie on top of it. He got his white, green, and brown icing spread on the sides and the top, still warm and not quite firm. He called me to watch him make the kewpie. I was bathing Frankie and didn't stop to take him out of the tub. I told Leslie to take him out and dry him and put on his clothes. When I got in the kitchen, Stine had his cake on the table. He was standing back and admiring his work, squinting through his thick eyeglasses, paste tubes in his hands. He was so tall and redheaded he did look comical. Just as he said, "Now we will begin with the feet," Frankie ran up and said, "Jack Stine, please show me the feets."

We looked down at him. He had broken away from Leslie naked and wet. Stine looked him over, laid his tubes down, and picked him up. I thought, "Young fellow, you are in for a spanking," but instead Stine said, "Why bother making kewpies when here is a better one?"

And without another word, he deliberately set Frankie down on top of that cake, then stepped back and said, "Behold! The cake is finished!"

Frankie tried to get up but was stuck fast. He threw up his arms and yelled, "Take me, Mama. Me don't want no cake." I picked him up. I was laughing so I could hardly lift him down. So was Stine. But not

Leslie. She got in with a towel on her arm in time to see it all. She was mad at Frankie for running away from her, but she was madder at Stine. She shook her fist at him and said, "Old Jack Stine, you have made me mad. I wish you had to lick that stuff off that nasty boy. I came in here to spank him when I caught him, but now I can't. Mama, you take him back, put him in that tub, hold him up and I'll take the broom and scrub him."

I could see no way to carry him, as he had got it all over his hands even, but I coaxed him to walk and climb in the tub. I rolled up my sleeves, washed him good, set him out of the bath, and asked him if he wanted to go with me and get more cake or stay and let Leslie dress him. "Me stay here. Don't want no nasty cake. Me had enough." He shook his curly head to show us he meant it.

When I got back to the kitchen, Stine was repairing the damage done to the cake, but he didn't have enough icing left to make a kewpie and so made a bunch of violets instead. I asked him if he scraped all that icing off and threw it away. He raised his eyebrows and said, "No, why should I? Wasn't the boy clean, just come out of his bath? If we never eat anything dirtier than that, we'll be all right."

I told Frank not to eat any of it, told him what Stine did and said. Frank laughed and said, "Stine was right. If the boy was clean, the cake wasn't hurt, but it won't do to advertise the story."

But I believe the men would have forgiven him even if they'd known it, on account of his beer. He made a hop beer that was almost like the lager beer. He kept a thirty-gallon barrel on tap all the time, strictly homemade. It was kept under a tree on a little platform with mugs hung by it, free for all, with a little faucet near the bottom of it so it was handy. Stine was the finest cook I ever saw.

I had plenty to do those days besides helping in the kitchen. We were getting ready to move to the bucker at Bray as soon as our house there was done. Frank was staying out there now, and I was left to wind up our business at camp, pack up and move. I had to take an inventory of everything left in the commissary and all the other things we sold them, for the camp of Negroes was to stay in the woods. Besides I had to cook for our men till the last day, for Stine was gone, his two months up.

The morning the teams came for us, moving started early and lasted all that day and the next. I had to stay till everything was moved.

Flynn went with the first load and took care of the cooking till I got there and then helped me to get straight. About two weeks after we got settled in Bray, he came to me one day and said, "Mary, I am going to leave. I have heard Lucy lives near Sumner. I believe it would kill me to meet her. I have lost her. If I could have been man enough to have stayed straight, life would be so different. She was such a child when we married, and no one but God in heaven ever knew how much I loved her and will as long as I live. I was contented as I can ever be without her, here with you and Frank, but since I have heard she is so close, I can't stand it. I hate to leave you and Frank and that sweet baby, but I might as well go, for I can never repay you all for what you have done for me."

I told Frank about it that night and said that he must give Flynn some money. Flynn wouldn't take a cent for what work he did, but we had made him get some clothes. So now Frank bought him a ticket to Memphis and gave him fifty dollars. He cried like a child when he bid us good-bye, calling us his only friends on earth. So ended Charlie Flynn, wrecked and ruined for a foolish love. We never heard of him again.

The Coming of Civilization

OUR NEW HOME IN BRAY SEEMED TO US A SMALL PALACE. When we moved, the railroad was all graded up ready for the ties as far as Tutwiler. The bucker stood on one side of the railroad, our boardinghouse just opposite on the other. Woods were on all sides of us but the right-of-way. When Leslie first saw it stretching away, she looked up and then down. She pointed towards Drew, where the dump stretched as far as she could see, and said, "That end goes right up in heaven." Then she turned and pointed towards Tutwiler, where the dump made a curve and she couldn't see far, and shuddered. She clutched Frankie's hand and said, "That end goes to the bad place, and you are so bad, Frankie, you will get right in it before you know it."

In a few days the work train got closer, throwing off rails and ties. Negroes were driving spikes, with two or three white men overseeing them. Leslie stayed on the front porch all day long watching, but guarding Frankie, keeping him from going closer. The train got almost to the curve one day, then—bell ringing and whistle blowing—came flying back. Negroes were singing and yelling and running up and down the flatcars. Here came Leslie in the house, sobbing and crying. It was so seldom she cried that I thought she was hurt or had let Frankie get hurt, but when I asked her what the trouble was she said, "Oh, I feel so sorry for those poor Negroes. They are going right back for more of those old ties and will build that road right into torment. Then those white men will shove them off in the fire to burn up."

I thought it was about time to explain it to her. I told her to get Frankie and come in. I told them all about the railroad, work trains, passenger trains, freight trains, and what they were for, but above all, how dangerous they were, and to stay off the track and keep Frankie off. She said, "I wish we were back in camp. I hate this railroad. It is no good."

I said, "Yes, Leslie. It brings everything we wear and eat, and it will bring civilization to our country."

I was working while I was talking and must not have spoken as plain as I should, and she had worked herself up to a fury anyway. When I said "civilization," she stamped her foot and said, "Mama, you don't need to tell us any more. If they are to hitch old damnation to that train and bring it in the country then I want Father to move us out."

I heard someone laugh and looked around. There stood Frank, his eyes twinkling. He stooped down and spread out his arms. "Come here, both you little misguided limbs of Satan. Your mama hasn't time to teach you the difference between civilization and damnation."

I said, "I want to hear you explain the difference."

He said, "That railroad is bringing plenty of both to this country, and there is no use to go back to camp to hide. We have got to face it and fight damnation and adjust ourselves to civilization, a disease spreading all over our land. I say, Mary," he broke off, "you are going to have two more boarders for the best room. They will be here for dinner. They are northern, but not like friend Hurst. They represent the Cedar Rapids Land Company that owns all this cutover land, all the Cyclone land, and all the land Minkus and I worked over. There is a world of timber in this country yet, and I expect I know this part of the Delta better than any man in it today. One of these men, Mr. Busby, wants me to work for them. So when I am through with this damned job—" he thought of the children and said, "Little lady, I beg your pardon, and you too, young fellow."

Leslie said, "That's all right, Father, I say that lots. When Frankie don't mind and gets in meanness I pull his ears and say 'Damn, damn' about two times, and he just flies. You see, Uncle Charlie always said that when he hurt himself, and I asked him if it was bad, and he said, 'Not so bad, for it cures a hurt quicker than anything.' So I tried it on Frankie and it works fine."

It was the first time we ever heard her swear, but it was a habit we never broke her of. She was the most religious and strict of all our children, but swearing was something useful and necessary to her. It wasn't just letting off steam, it was a weapon to be used when everything else failed. That first time, her father tried to look solemn, and said, "Leslie, don't pull Frankie's ears any more for they are too large now, and I wouldn't say 'damn' either. It is swearing, and ladies don't swear and pull little boys' ears."

They both looked so funny I knew he was bound to laugh. I wanted to laugh, too. I told them to run out on the porch and play, for poor Father was about to cry. He dropped his head and covered his face with his hands to keep them from seeing him laugh. As soon as they were gone, I laughed, too, but asked him what he thought of his daughter. He said, "She swears like an old veteran, but it is our fault. I didn't think Flynn would swear before them. I am sure she knows lots more 'swears' as she calls them."

"If she does, she had better keep them to herself, or I will—" I hesitated, and Frank said, "Well, what will you do?"

"Spank the fatal fire out of her," I said sternly.

"Whoop," Frank laughed. "In other words, you will spank hell out of her and tell her so, which would be far worse than what she said. There is but one thing for us to do. She is as good in her way as Nina was. She has her own ideas of right and wrong. We must set her a good example, conduct ourselves right, and ignore her swearing. Let her see we pity her, but don't go spanking her."

Frank was sure children could be raised without spanking them, without using the rod at all. I told him as I had before, "If I had nothing to do but take care of them, I could do that, but with three children to take care of and thirty men to cook for and very little help, I only wish I had a spanking machine. But that reminds me, Frank, you haven't explained to me why it took you and Mr. Reliford so long to say good-bye when he left. You don't look so cheerful since."

"I'll tell you very little, as you think you know so much. You think I was drunk, and I was not, just drinking a very little. I have been keeping their books, you know, and suspecting a lot, and when Reliford told me he was pulling out of the company and going back to Ireland, it put a bee in my cap. There's something dead up the creek and I am laying low watching for the next move. Meantime I'm going to help Busby on the side."

"Frank, has the company paid you yet for those commissary and camp outfits?"

"Not yet; but don't worry, they will," he said.

From then on there was a cloud in the sky; none of the men knew it, and work ran on as smooth as ever. They were making lots of staves, and shipping had already started in a light way. The railroad was completed to Tutwiler and a boxcar depot. A few freights were running and a daily passenger train went to Tutwiler, stopping there an hour, then coming back.

About the last of August, Frank was sick with a touch of malaria. He wouldn't give up to go to bed but couldn't work. He took some calomel, but it didn't help much, so he made up his mind to go to see Dr. Harrison at Tutwiler. The train would leave our station at Bray, or Minot as it was now called, about twelve o'clock. He was having a hard chill when the train came, but he went anyway, with his coat buttoned up to his chin. He was shaking like a leaf.

When he got off the platform an hour and a half later, he was carrying his coat on his arm and walking fast like he always did when he felt well. When he came up to the house there were a few men still on the porch. They began asking what was wrong with the train, for every window light was broken in the only white coach. He said, "Just give me time to see if I am all together. Yes, we had a wreck. The worst accident I ever was in but one. That time a mill blew up and every man in the boiler room was killed but me." He broke off talking, looked so funny and said, "Well, every man in that coach was killed but me. But I guess my malaria is gone. I say, Busby, if you men get malaria, don't forget to try my remedy." He tried to laugh but was so shaky we could see he was nervous.

He said when he got on the train here there were three men in the coach; two were sitting in one seat and the third about four seats ahead. He sat down in the seat just behind this one man. He said he could tell those two that were together were drinking, but the third man seemed to be a stranger to them, as all were strangers to Frank. The two drunk men were cursing and swearing about what they were going to do. He guessed from their talk they had had trouble in Tutwiler the day before and were going back to settle it. He tried to raise his window to get some fresh air, so the man ahead of him came back and raised it for him and asked him if he wasn't sick. He sat down by Frank and got to talking. He asked Frank if he knew those other two men. When Frank said he didn't, he said, "They got on at

Ruleville. I think they are hunting trouble." Frank told him they were going to the right place to find it, for he knew every man in Tutwiler, and they would find all the trouble they were looking for.

Just then the train blew for Tutwiler, and as it began to slow up, one of those men came running to Frank's opened window, peeped out over his shoulder and began shooting at someone on the platform. The other man was shooting through his window, and shots were returned from outside. The man beside Frank was hit, just a flesh wound. Frank said, "Drop to the floor." The man dropped and began crawling to the back door. So did Frank, pistols cracking all around. When they got to the door and both got to their feet, the man started to jump out onto the platform. Frank said, "You'll be killed. Get out on this side." He said, "I'm not afraid," and he hardly hit the ground before he was shot down dead. Frank dropped on the other side, rolled down the dump and was saved. One of the bad men was killed outright, and the other died before the train left to come back. Several citizens of Tutwiler were wounded but none of them killed. So stray bullets killed one innocent man and saved the other by scaring the malaria out of him.

When he finished telling us, Busby asked him if he wouldn't have to be a witness. He said "No, they won't need a witness," and if it ever went to law we never heard about it. All parties were satisfied, all got what they were looking for except the two innocent bystanders, and what they got was just part of living in that wild country. I believe though there was more justice in the law those days than there is now. It was a freer country; if you didn't want to get in a jam, you could generally stay out of it by minding your own business.

We were having a time right then to keep our own business straight and keep from going to the wall. Not that we had far to go or much to lose, but what little we had we had got by hard work and by being strictly honest. I admired Frank for that; for he was honest, didn't gamble, and wouldn't tell a lie to anyone, unless it was me. He drank and made some bad trades while drunk, but when he saw things looking shaky, as they were now, he kept a pretty level head.

The company we were working for was going to the wall fast or pretended they were. They wanted Frank to take over the business as a sham sale, they to reap the profits still, but Frank to take the risks, though at a good profit. He had been looking for this proposition ever since Reliford left, and when it came he told them "no" flat out. He told them to pay him everything they owed him, and he would quit. He had made up his mind at last to buy a little piece of land over on the Sunflower River and work for Mr. Busby selling land. I was so happy to think I was going to have a home at last. But he told me not to get so shouting happy till we got our money out of the company. We were paying our own money out for supplies and had sold them a good bit on credit. We had got not a penny out of them since moving to Minot, although we had made a little money on cash board. The two northern men paid cash, I had some transients, and I sold dozens of lunches every day to train men and others. Sold all the bread and rolls I could make. But the men working for the company couldn't pay us till they got their money. When it came, their board would be taken out, as Frank was bookkeeper, but it didn't come.

It seemed to be a game of freeze-out, but it was diamond cut diamond, or English against English. They were all alike, all the English I ever saw or heard tell of, coolheaded and stubborn. They finally told Frank they thought they had a man to take his place.

"We don't want any hard feelings, for you have been white with us, Frank," they told him, "but business is business, and when our Mr. Mann from Shelby comes, will you just turn everything over to him?"

"Hell, no," Frank said. "I won't turn over one thing till you pay me every cent you owe me and buy out this house as you promised. And your Mr. Mann nor his men don't so much as hang up a hat in my house till you settle with me."

"But Frank," they said, "we have sold out to Mann, lock, stock, and barrel. He will settle with you. He is honest."

Frank said, "Sure he is honest. He has taken an honest place. But he doesn't owe me anything and never will. I am dealing with you, not Mann."

"Well, you make out your bill and we will pay you the first of the month, if you will turn over the books to Mann so the business won't stop. I give you my word of honor, we will pay you, Frank," said the man who was talking for the company.

"I love your word of honor, sir, but there is no use talking any further. When you or your man from New Orleans comes and settles with me in cash for everything you owe me, then and not till then will I turn over house, mill, and books. That is provided you do this within one week. After that, you don't get the books at all. They are my books. I paid my own money for them, and my and your dealings don't concern this Shelby man at all."

"Frank, you're not making anything by this stubbornness."

"I know where I stand, sir, so good-bye."

"Listen, Frank," he said, "that Shelby man is sending a man here tomorrow to see you. Please treat him decent."

"Thanks for the suggestion. What is his name?"

"A Mr. Fly."

"All right. Maybe Mr. Thomas will board him. I won't, unless he keeps his hat on."

"You're crazy, Frank. This place has got to go on."

"It will. I am still bookkeeper, foreman, and boarding boss, the whole works. Haven't been fired, nor quit, and don't intend to quit till you settle with me; and if settlement doesn't come within a week, you will have to send a bookkeeper from New Orleans to copy my books, and that will take a week longer. I am only standing up for my rights, so why prolong this painful interview? The first thing you know we will both be weeping."

Frank walked out, and the man left, too.

The work went on as usual. Frank knew he had the law on his side and the men as well; but he knew if he ever gave possession in any way, he was gone as far as our getting our money was concerned, so he locked all the books up in our big zinc trunk, and I carried the key.

The next day a man got off the train and came over to the house, carrying his suitcase. Frank sat down on the front steps. The man halted and told Frank he wanted board for a few days.

"Nothing doing, stranger, we are full up. Can't keep you at all."

The man said, "Well, if I can get dinner and leave my suitcase here till I look around . . ."

Frank said, "I have no room for any of Mr. Mann's men, Mr. Fly."

I don't know where the man stayed that night, but he was all over the works, at the mill, and out in the woods. He didn't come to the house again until next day just before train time. Frank and Mr. Busby were having a hot argument over something on the front porch, and here came Mr. Fly.

He broke right in and said, "Mr. Hamilton, I was sent here to check up on everything and see if we could come to terms, but I can't get any sense out of you."

Frank looked at him a moment, and said, "Young man, I wish you wouldn't interrupt when men are talking." And he turned and went on talking to Mr. Busby. But the train was coming and had to be flagged, so Mr. Fly, as he turned to go, said, "What must I tell Mr. Mann from you, then?"

Frank whirled around and said, "Tell him to go straight to hell, and don't you interrupt us again."

Mr. Mann wrote us. They wrote us from headquarters in New Orleans. Frank paid no attention to either of them. In a week they wrote from headquarters that Mr. Mann would be down a certain day bringing our money and his bookkeeper, and that he would buy out the house and pay us all they owed us. Frank made arrangements to move us over on the Sunflower River in one of Mrs. Lemaster's houses till we could build our own house just across the river on our own eighty acres we had bought from Mr. Busby. I was happy, oh, so happy. But I knew our trouble wasn't over, for if Frank got to drinking over this settlement with the company we were lost. I talked to him as I never did before. Told him he had to promise me he wouldn't take a drink until we were settled up and away from here. They knew his weakness, and if they could catch him drinking knew they could settle any way they wanted to, but as long as he was sober, I knew we were all right. I told him, "Frank, if you go to drinking, I will take things in my own hands, I warn you. If you think I will stand by helpless and see all my hard work go for nothing, you'll have to guess again."

He said, "All right, Yank, I guess I will stay strictly sober, but I would love to see what you would do if I did get full!"

Well, he got to see. It was like this. By the day they came in, we had tagged every article in the house we could let them have, with the price on it. I let them have forty-five feather pillows with two cases each. I kept back just six and the children's bed and two complete beds besides, but only four quilts, two pair of blankets, and twenty sheets. I kept just enough dishes to set table for six, no kitchen or stove vessels, for I wanted a complete new outfit. I was so tired of boardinghouse things. I saved all my two-pound cans and unsoldered them instead of cutting them open, so I had a good many of them. Saved a thirty-gallon barrel of vinegar, plenty of sugar, and all kinds of spices, flavorings, and large jars, as Mrs. Lemaster had a fine orchard and garden and had sent me word I could have all the fruits and vegetables I wanted.

The day the men were to come to settle with Frank at twelve o'clock, a man came walking in about seven o'clock in the morning. He was well-dressed and introduced himself as a man wanting to buy some timber. He said Frank had been recommended to him as the man who could tell him more about the timber in the Delta than anyone else. He wanted Frank to go with him to the woods. Frank told him he couldn't, as he would be pretty busy all day, but that if he was around tomorrow he would help him. The man said, "Let's walk around awhile, I want something to drink."

They were sitting just outside on the porch; the windows were all up and my work table was near the window where they were. I heard Frank say, "I don't care if I do." As they started, I called Frank. He came in, all smiles. I said, "Haven't you got sense enough to know what that man is up to?"

He winked at me and said, "Little Calamity Ann, I never break a promise." And he went out. I was mad all through. I knew there was trouble brewing, and I got ready for it. I knew there was a blind tiger behind just about every tree for miles around. Well, about nine o'clock, sure enough here they came back, both of them staggering. Frank's derby was on the back of his head, and when they got to the front steps he couldn't get up without the other fellow helping him. Leslie came in and said, "Mama, Father is sick or awful drunk."

I had been watching them and praying for strength to help me be cool and keep me from killing somebody. My little home, my happiness, were all swept away. My faith in Frank was gone. I went in to the office where they were. They were sitting down by Frank's desk, each with a quart bottle almost full. I walked up to Frank and said, "You told me a black lie. You broke your promise to me." Then I turned to the man and said, "I don't know what business you are here on, but I suspect it's no good, so please leave my house. I am going to lock this house up."

Frank said, "I shay, Mary. You are mishtaken. This ish good friend of mine. He show me one grand way to settle wish them."

I paid no attention to him but asked that man again if he was ready to go. He said, "No, indeed. I came here to see Hamilton, not you, and there isn't a woman living can dictate to me. Frank, let's have another drink." He picked up his bottle. I snatched it from him, snatched Frank's and slammed them together, breaking them all to pieces. Then I grabbed up the shotgun and by that time he was up and starting toward me. I threw it in his face and said "Now get out."

He turned and made one leap for the door. I followed him, still holding the gun on him. "I'm going to count ten, and if you aren't across that railroad I will kill you."

I meant it, but just as I said "nine," Frank reached over, took the gun from me so gently, and said, "The poor devil was paid to do what he did."

I looked at him, astonished. He looked perfectly sober, but so amused. He said, "You are a gritty little devil. I haven't broken my promise, but got to test you out in case I had. The minute he came in this morning I had an idea he was sent, so played up to him to find out. I didn't swallow one drop, but he got drunk trying to make me drunk. So now can you trust me to finish this settlement, and you attend to your dinner? Let's have a nice dinner. I don't want a hitch anywhere. They are looking to find me drunk, but they will get the surprise of their lives."

An official of the company, along with a bookkeeper, got off the train a little after twelve o'clock. They began paying off by Frank's books. He held out all board money. They paid us every cent they owed us and bought everything, so all they had to do was to put in a cook and go to cooking. They gave Frank a check on some New Orleans bank, and he wired down to see if it was all right. It was. Our check called for near $900, and we had enough groceries to do us a couple of months. I tried to get Frank to turn over the books, so he could move with us next morning, but he wouldn't. He stayed behind and held the office till they copied the books. They offered him ten dollars for books he hadn't paid but three for, but he told them he had had them so long they were like old friends, and he didn't mind waiting around the extra week a bit.

So the next morning just the children and I started with our little household goods to drive to our new home and quit camp life forever.

We had two wagons, with Bob Coleman and a Negro driving. In a way I hated to leave the camp life, although my new home filled all my thoughts, and I felt like singing with Leslie on the road, "I'm going to my good new home," with Frankie chanting after her, "Home, good home . . ."

"Home, Good Home"

EVERYTHING WE SAW ON OUR WAY WAS SO STRANGE AND NEW. When we got on the ferryboat—the first Frankie had ever seen and the first Leslie could remember—they were scared but didn't cry. Bob Coleman put the bars up at each end of the flatboat after we drove on, and this, with the side bannisters, made a pen for us. As soon as Bob started pulling on the rope that stretched from one bank of the river to the other, and the pulley that held the rope to the boat railing began to squeak as it turned, they forgot their fear. When we got across and they saw their first field of cotton and corn, their eyes opened in wonder. When we came to the Lemaster orchard loaded with late peaches, apples, and pears, I could hardly hold them on the wagon. They amused everyone who saw them with their odd ways and questions.

We lived in the yard with old Mrs. Lemaster and her old maid sister, two fine old ladies known to everybody as "Grandma" and "Aunt Bet." I liked all the Lemasters. I went there with the intention of liking them whether I really did or not, but I really did. They were old settlers and owned a nice plantation. There were two girls and four boys, all married but two, when we first knew them, and all living right around in that neighborhood. The old man was dead. The boys were every one brave, healthy, and strong and were all good neighbors, southerners of the true old southern stock.

My house was a two-room log house, but it was fine, and I baked in Grandma's stove in her house till Frank could get one. It was fun. They gave me cornbread every day for dinner, and I gave them light bread when I baked. Our log house had a fireplace, so I boiled meats and vegetables and made coffee at home. As soon as I got straight, I got into the fruit. I used every can I had saved by unsoldering them, sent for and got sealing wax and lined those tin cans with writing paper, and didn't lose a can. Of course Grandma got half. It was fun for me and for them, for they were workers, and I tried to help them in every way I could. There was so much that I must learn from them. Wasn't I going to be a farm wife now? I was so glad.

They had seventeen cows, and I learned to milk that first week. Aunt Bet and Blanche, an eighteen-year-old girl, Grandma's baby, did the milking once a day. They let the calves have all the top milk; then they would take about two quarts from each cow, just the strippings. Even that was more than they could use, for they couldn't even give away milk and butter, as their children and neighbors had cows of their own. They churned every day, keeping back what they could use of the buttermilk, and gave me all I could use. Then they dumped the rest in the hog trough out in the lane, but as the hogs roamed at large, unless a few happened to stray around the house, they didn't get it. When they wanted to kill a hog, they just went to the woods and shot what they wanted to dress in one day, for the woods were full of hogs, and if they didn't belong to one Lemaster, they did to another, so what difference did it make?

How I did enjoy the few weeks we were there. Bob Lemaster killed a deer the first week and brought the hindquarters home to Grandma. His wife and Blanche were there, and Jim Lemaster, his wife, and boy. I helped them cook it as I was making hot rolls for supper, enough for all. We had fried venison steak, roast apples, and good coffee with rich sweet cream. Next day I asked Bob what he did with the rest of the venison.

"Left it in the woods," he said. "We never save any but the hindquarters. Our women won't cook anything else."

I told him the next time he killed one to bring it all. So you see, again I found neighbors. You can find them everywhere, and they are far more important than money. You can live without money, or could in those days, but not without friends. I always looked for friends and not for trouble. Trouble was something I found without looking for it.

One Saturday along late in the afternoon someone began to yell across the river in front of our house. The ferryboat was on our side.

Grandma said, "That's Hamilton. Let's go down and see him swim across."

I took Edie, Blanche took Frankie, and Leslie raced ahead. We all got there in time to see him get as high in the saddle as he could as his pony jumped off the bank into swimming-deep water. He had his things strapped on the back of the saddle. The pony swam like a duck. They came out on our side and Frank was as dry as if he had been on dry land. This crossing at the Lemasters' was the only shallow crossing for miles up and down that deep and treacherous Sunflower River at that time; it had a solid bottom and none of the shiny black quicksand that made most of that river so dangerous.

We were all so glad to see Frank. The Lemasters all knew him, and I could see they liked him. Grandma told him she had some good cold buttermilk hanging in the well for him, and nothing would do but we must eat supper with them. Bob and his wife were there, and Bob had everything ready to go headlighting for deer. We had an early supper, and after it was over they took guns and a big headlight and went up the river a few miles in a boat, then drifted back down slow. If there was a deer on the bank, they would shine the headlight at its eyes. It seems when a deer sees the light at night he stops and looks. Then the man behind the light shoots; a good marksman never misses, and both Bob and Frank were good. It is strange, but a real hunter can always tell the difference between a deer's eyes and cattle's eyes. They got home about eleven o'clock with two big bucks. They opened and hung them in the smokehouse till morning. And I want to tell you, there wasn't a pound of that meat wasted.

The next day I cut off all I could get from the four shoulders and one hind leg, ground it up with fat meat, and made sausage. I boiled up all the rest except the hams and saddle, as the back is called, and which I would call the choice piece to fry. I took all the boiled meat and made hash, meat pies, and patties. They helped me make it and helped eat it. Bob's wife got to be a fine meat cook, and there was no more wasted venison.

Sunday afternoon Frank took the children and me across the river to see our new home, "seventy acres more or less," just across the river from the lower edge of Mrs. Lemaster's land where Bob Coleman lived, and not over half a mile from her home. That "more or less" played hob with us later. When I stepped out of the boat onto our own land, I felt like falling down on my knees to thank God. My prayers had been answered at last, a reward for my hard work and patience with life as it came. I was sure Nina's farewell talk with Frank had finally taken root, and that our years of happiness were beginning. Frank took Edie out of my arms and tossed her to his shoulder. "Now ride your horse, little lady, into your home."

Frankie said, "Let me ride."

Frank said, "Not much, young man. From now on you are a man, my partner."

Leslie said, "What about me, Father? I would make a better partner. I'm bigger."

Frank said, "Oh, you will be nurse and Mama's little cook."

We were at the top of the river bank, all out of breath, for the bank was at least a hundred feet from the river to the top, but it was a gradual slope. About halfway to the top was a good spring, where we got all our water after we moved. Frank said, "Do you want to rest a bit? You point in the direction you want to go. I want you to pick out a house site."

I was too excited to rest. I saw a small cleared space and said, "Let's go over there." We went. There was a path leading to it. It was a little cleared spot of about half an acre.

"An old corral," Frank said. "This is cutover land. Some men camped here last year."

I said, "Right here is my garden," and then I saw about a hundred yards away the biggest holly grove I had ever seen, with the biggest holly trees.

"Oh Frank," I said, "a little house built in the middle of that holly grove would be like paradise." And I commenced to cry. Nina's holly trees she loved so well.

Leslie said, "I know the angels planted them for us. Maybe Nina helped before she came back."

Frank blew his nose and asked me what I was crying for.

"Just the same as you are blowing your head off to keep from crying pure joy."

We walked over to the grove. Frank took his hat off and said, "I never thought till that odd child spoke, but I feel like this is holy ground. Nina's house site."

He, baby Edie, and I sat down on a log to talk while the two children romped and played. We planned out the house, just two rooms and a porch to start with. He had already had Bob Lemaster deaden the trees on thirty acres by cutting a ring around them through the bark to the sap, which was the first step in clearing up land. Frank had made two payments on the land and had a good job with Mr. Busby, selling land.

Frank told me there were about eight sections of land sold up and down the river on our side; clearing up and building would be starting right away and it would settle up fast. He was going out next day to Merigold to get lumber. He had it all figured out, was going to do nearly all the building of our house himself. I begged him to get Bob Coleman to break up a turnip patch on that corral. He got turnip seed, radish seed, lettuce, and carrot seed. Mrs. Lemaster gave me a gallon of shallot onions, so I soon had a late garden.

Every day when I got my work done, I would leave Edie with Grandma, take the other two, and go across the river in a dugout to help Frank, and every day I took a rose bush or a peach tree and set it out. Everything I took grew. Every moment I wasn't handing Frank nails, hammer, saw, plank, or water, I was working and had both the children working. Sometimes Frankie would say, "I can't carry this stick. Too big."

"Well, then leave it and get one you can carry. For this is your home as much as it is mine, and you are your father's partner." Then he would work and tug and grunt. I got my idea right there to raise my children to believe they were a necessary part of the home—not to drive them to work, but to make each one believe that without him and his work, home would soon go to pieces. And all my children loved their home more than any place on earth.

Frank hewed all sills and blocks out near the house. Our worst trouble was in making the house storm proof. We had heard so much about the cyclones, and it seemed they all came down the river and struck out across country just about where our landing and house were, although Grandma told us not to worry, as a holly tree couldn't be blown down in a storm. But Frank was afraid, and so he put in studding it seemed to me every foot. He worried me to death with those studdings. He would nail one end hard and fast, then start a spike in the other. About every ten minutes, just when I was busy doing something else, he would call out, "Mary, walk out a bit and tell me when this is straight. Take your time, look good."

So I would get out to what I would think was the right distance, look, and to make it look more important would wave my hand in one direction or the other and say, "Just a fraction of an inch that way." Just whichever side the children were playing on, that was the way the studding leaned. He nailed several on that way one day, then came down the ladder and walked out to view his work. All at once he threw his hammer away and jumped like a bee had stung him. He was so mad he couldn't speak, but I knew as soon as he could he would start swearing, so I said, "Frank, dear, please swear in French or Italian or Indian, so Leslie won't understand you. She is so bad about that."

That kind of sobered him a bit, but he looked at me so hard, his eyes just shooting sparks, and said, "Mary, you did that through sheer damned meanness."

"Now Frank, you knew I was no carpenter. Besides, what difference does it make? Those studdings are all inside the house, and let's not start our new home with a quarrel."

That settled it. He grinned and said, "I ought to do you like you do Frankie. Take you across my knee and spank you. But instead I'll fire you. I am going for Bob Coleman."

Just what he should have done in the first place. No one could do to suit him, for he didn't know how it should be done himself, as that was his first carpenter work; but at last we got it done, right or wrong, mostly wrong. He had boards rived out to cover it, but to make a neater job made a shaving horse, as he called it, and took a drawing knife and shaved the boards down thin and smooth and nice, as we found out when the first storm came.

Our house was ready now, but we couldn't move till Frank went and got a stove and cooking vessels. We needed almost every kind of furniture but beds. I had $175 saved back. It was my own; I had earned it in the boardinghouse. How I planned! I was going to get lumber to make another room later. That would still leave me over $100 to get what furniture I wanted. A plain No. 8 stove, for I was so tired of big ranges. I wanted everything small, to fit the house and our needs. He had some money too, I had no idea how much, but I felt safe, for he hadn't been drinking since he began to wind up his job at Bray.

The day after the house was finished, Mr. Busby came by to get

Frank to go with him to Arkansas on a land deal that would take a week or ten days. They had to go through Memphis, and Frank was going to buy the things we needed there and ship them back to Merigold. He paid Jim Lemaster before he left to go for them and help me move. They had got a ferryboat down for a while until Frank could get time to make one. He wrote me from Memphis that he had shipped our things and what day he would be home. I thought his handwriting looked shaky but thought nothing of it.

So the great day came when Jim went out to get my things from Merigold. I could hardly wait till he got back, but when he did I thought I would die of humiliation. There was one great big sec-ondhand boardinghouse range, so large it took four men to get it off the wagon, and then they couldn't get it in the kitchen door and had to set it down outside. The stove pipe looked like a smoke stack. There were a few stove vessels, no two pieces the same size, and none fit the stove. There was one tub and a washboard, one wash boiler, a rocker, and three straight chairs. There were enough plain groceries to do us three or four months. Jim said there was some lumber at the station for making a ferryboat. But I was just standing looking at that stove. I wanted to sink through the ground. I could see they were all sorry for me, but they were all loyal to Frank.

Grandma said, "Now, Mrs. Hamilton, you should be proud of all these groceries and that big fine stove. Frank knows you bake such fine light bread, and he won't eat any other kind, and he is thinking about his and the children's bellies. He might have had a drink or two when he bought it, but he knew what he was doing."

Well, when he came home what was the use of asking him if he was drunk when he spent my money for those things? I might cause him to tell a lie. We had a home anyway. There was no use to cry over spilt milk. The Lemaster boys joshed him enough when he had to tear out half a side of the kitchen to get the stove in and tear out and rebuild the flue. Bob Coleman said he didn't mind a house-raising, but Hamil-ton's smokestack was a little too much. When they got the door facing and about two feet of wall back in place, it looked better, and in time I got to like the old stove. I never asked Frank a word about it, but I knew he didn't have over five dollars left, and he put that in paint, nails, and caulking for the boat. Every minute he had he was making something: a barn, a chicken house, a smokehouse.

After he got his ferry made, that brought in a little money, as he charged people to cross on it, and he traded his pony to Blanche Lemaster for two good milk cows with young calves. I had a good milking pen, calf house and pen. I milked regular twice a day and got around five gallons of milk and a pound of good solid butter every day. We had rails split and a fence put around the garden to keep the cows out of it. Already we had turnip and mustard greens, radishes, carrots, and onions. We didn't care much about greens, as Frank wouldn't eat them cooked with fat meat, and just boiled in salted water and seasoned with butter they didn't have so much taste.

One day Aunt Bet was at our house for dinner, and I was putting on some turnips and greens to be cooked together, southern style, but in clear water without meat. She asked me if we had ever cooked the turnips and greens together that way before, and when I said "No," she screwed up her mouth, winked at me, and said, "Let me cook them, and I'll guarantee Frank'll never know the difference."

She took a piece of fat meat, boiled good, then put in the turnips and greens, but took the meat out before it got tender and started to cook to pieces, and said, "Now put a little butter in so you can say it is seasoned with butter."

Frank ate plenty. We all did. When Aunt Bet asked him how he liked turnips and greens cooked together, he said, "Fine. So much better than either cooked alone."

After that little by little I fooled him in vegetable cooking to the last, but never in fish. And I never got him to eat a bite of cornbread nor biscuits till the last year of his life.

He was taking the greatest interest in our home, working every minute he was there. He traded work with Bob Lemaster in sawing down all the trees near the house except the holly trees. He sawed down all that were near enough the house to be dangerous in a storm except one great big gum. It had been topped when young, either by a storm or another tree falling on it, so it wasn't very tall but was tall enough to have smashed three or four holly trees clear across the house. The gum was over five feet through near the ground and had the biggest, bushiest top I ever saw. I tried to get Frank to saw it down too, but he said, "There's no need, Mary. A storm that would blow that tree down would send us all to kingdom come long before it would hit the ground."

But I was afraid. Every time I saw a cloud coming I was sure this was the time. It was getting so late I thought we would have no cyclones before spring, but Frank had to be away from home so much selling land for Mr. Busby, that I was afraid, with just the children and me there alone. Afraid of storms, of Negroes, as the country was beginning to settle up, but more afraid of wolves getting my calves, as we could hear wolves howling every night. Frank made heavy shutters over the windows so I could shut them on the inside. He always told me to get everything done before night and get the house shut up, and if I heard anything or anybody prowling around outside, never to open the door. He never knew when he would have to go or how long he would have to stay. I had a good gun and could shoot it.

Late that first fall he got word to go to Arkansas on another land deal. It was warm for that time of year, and the wind was blowing from the south. Towards night on the day he left, clouds began scudding across the sky. I got all my work done but milking. The cows were late coming up, and when they did come they were restless, and kept sniffing the air and snorting. I knew we were in for a rain, as a big cloud was coming up out of the southwest. There was lightning, and at the first hard clap of thunder the cow began to kick. So I turned the calves in to get their milk and carried what milk I had to the house, strained it, and ran back to turn the cows out and shut the calves up from the storm and from wolves. I could see by now it was a storm and a bad one. The cloud had turned green. I knew it was hail. I got one calf in the shed but the other one was running, jumping, playing.

Frankie was yelling to me from the porch, "Put my Dixie calf in the house before he gets hurt."

I couldn't do one thing with it. Then Leslie hollered, "Mama, turn that damned calf loose and get in the house."

I literally picked that calf up, shoved it in the shed, and ran, or tried to run, to the house, for the storm had broken in all its fury. I got in the kitchen door, and it was all Leslie and I both could do to shove it to and lock it. By that time the hail was splitting those nice thin shingles of Frank's and coming through on us. He hadn't got the kitchen sealed overhead yet. Then I saw the oven door of that big old range was open. I thought sure we were all going to be killed, but I shoved Edie from my arms into the oven and made Leslie and Frankie crouch down under the oven door. I finished covering them with my body and got my head and as much of my shoulders in the oven with the baby as I could. The sound of those hailstones splitting those shingles was just like corn popping, only much louder. It didn't last but a few minutes, but it was long enough to tear that kitchen roof all to pieces and to ruin the shingles all over the rest of the house.

After it was over and things got quiet, I asked Leslie if she wasn't afraid to swear. She said, "No, I had to, to make you come in the house. I didn't have time to pray. I had to take the quickest way. If you had sworn at that calf you wouldn't have had half the trouble with it."

When I looked out next morning expecting to see the holly grove cut to pieces, the leaves all torn and ragged, I saw them instead looking brighter and greener than ever. Then for the first time I thought of the big gum. I went around the house to see which way it had fallen, but there it stood, gaunt and ugly, not a leaf on it. The leaves had been falling anyway, but the hail whipped them all off clean. I felt friendly towards the old gum tree, like we had all suffered together.

Frank came back from that trip sober as a judge but with very little money, as he wouldn't draw any till near Christmas. He intended to save some money for Christmas after paying what he owed for work around the place, but when he paid up, he only had enough left to get some necessary things and to recover the house. He didn't use a drawing knife on the shingles this time. I did so want him to get ahead enough to have a pump driven. I had to carry every drop of water from the spring under the hill, and it was hard work.

Mr. Busby told Frank if he would go to Minot and get his pony, he could keep it and use it. He wasn't much of a saddle horse but was good for working. Frank made a slide to haul water, wood, or anything else. Grandma said he could keep the pony in her pasture, so he went after the pony. Told me to go over to the old lady's that evening and watch him swim the pony across the river there where it was shallow.

About sundown we heard him hello. We all went down to see the fun but had no idea how much fun we were going to see. Frank got down and raised the stirrups so he could sit high in the saddle, got on, gathered the reins tight, and put the spurs to him. The pony jumped off the bank into six feet of water, went to the bottom like a rock, and stayed there. Instead of swimming he walked across on the bottom. We could just see the top of Frank's head and the tip of the pony's tail.

Frank managed to get his mouth above water, and when the horse got to where he could get his nose out he blew like a whale. How we all laughed! I laughed till my side hurt. We couldn't go up to Grandma's but went straight home, as the weather was so cold I was afraid Frank would have a chill. One of the boys took the pony to the lot, and we went straight home in the boat. Got a good fire going and dry clothes for Frank, ate a good hot supper, and it didn't hurt Frank at all.

It wasn't long till Christmas, and no money yet. Frank was feeling so bad about it. We didn't really need anything, if I could just get a few things for the children and manage a good dinner. All four Lemaster families had invited us for dinner, but we both believed every family should make Christmas a home day, and as it was our first Christmas in our new home, even though it was just an everyday dinner, it would be a happy one. I had made pies, cakes, and all kinds of Christmas "doings" as Aunt Bet said, for every one of the Lemasters, but none for ourselves. Our hens hadn't laid an egg in days.

I had made Leslie a doll, Frankie a pig and a dog, and Edie a white rabbit out of cotton flannel. I had plenty of sugar and so made them some candy. Frank had just one twenty-five-cent piece in money. A day or two before Christmas he caught the pony and rode to Merigold; he was so sure his money would be there, but it was not. He got the children an apple apiece with that quarter and put the rest in peppermint candy. I never saw him look so down as he was when he came back. I had it in my silly head he was grieving because he couldn't get whiskey. Christmas Eve morning he came out to the cowpen where I was milking and said, "Mary, what are we to do about the children? I can't face them in the morning. All they can talk about is Santa Claus and what he will bring."

I said, "Frank, is that what is bothering you? You are silly. I have made them some little things and am going to make more today. They will have a fine time. They will hang stockings that will be filled and running over not only with things they love but with happiness, if only you don't put a chill over them by moping and being blue for nothing. They would rather hear you sing and tell stories than have anything you can buy them."

He said, "If that is the way you look at it, I surely can do my part, for it was my damned foolishness put us in this fix."

I said, "Frank, you never heard me say so, did you? Now you run on, and if you can't bring a cheerful face into the house the next few days, don't bring any."

"All right," he said, "and I am not sure but you will get a present tomorrow that you will value, Mary. I am not sure yet."

I went to the house with a lighter heart and was ashamed to think I had thought he was missing his whiskey. I mopped and cleaned the house, as I always kept everything clean. I got the children out where Frank was piling brush, cutting down and cleaning off a couple of acres around the house. He wasn't going to plant but about four acres the next summer, as he would have plenty of steady work and not much time to farm. When I got rid of the children, I made some sugar cookies without eggs. I had colored sugar to dip them in. I made little animals, with currants for eyes and made hearts and stars. I could think of a dozen things to do that I hadn't thought of before, for I felt like, as Leslie would say when she was pleased over anything, "God is just about to do something for me."

And sure enough that afternoon Grandma sent me a five-pound bucket full of sausage and some spareribs. Bob brought us a hind-quarter of venison, and Aunt Bet sent me a half-bushel of the finest big ripe pears, yellow as gold. I had helped her gather them late that fall, a big box full. She said then they would be ripe by Christmas. I had forgot all about them, but I thought now, "Cast thy bread upon the waters, and after many days it will return to thee." And right then I needed it so bad.

That night we romped and played with the children. Little Edie sang herself to sleep in her chair, or she thought she was singing. We got the other two to sleep, then we filled their stockings with home-made candy, everything I could make, topped off with their apples. I had my table all set for breakfast, so I put some cookies in each of their plates. I set Frankie's pig on one side of his plate, his dog on the other; put Leslie's doll by her plate and had both its hands in the plate; set Edie's rabbit in her plate. It was a comical sight, and when their father woke them next morning they clapped their hands and squealed for joy. Edie, not quite a year old, hugged her rabbit up to her and rocked and tried to sing. Her father said, "Edris has the real Christmas spirit. Just watch her squeeze that poor bunny and sing."

I said, "Yes, it is hard to tell which is the happiest, she or the little birds out there in the hollies. Just listen, Frankie, you and Leslie, they are singing their Christmas carol, 'Peace on earth, goodwill to men.'"

Frank went to the door, looked out, and said, "Mary, come here. Isn't that a beautiful sight? There are hundreds of robins in those trees eating berries and singing to the sun just peeping over the tree-tops."

"And to our little home. Frank, this is my first Christmas without one cent, but the very happiest one of my life."

He looked at me and said, "I see you will have to get that present." He looked at his watch and said, "I have an invitation to go to Grandma's at eight o'clock this morning. I won't be long. When I come back I am going to light all those brush piles and have some homemade fireworks."

I had started dinner when he got back. He went out and started the most of his fires. Soon Leslie and Frankie were out there with him. He was telling them stories, while they all worked throwing brush on the fires. So I picked Edie up, went out where they were, set her down close enough to a fire to keep her warm, and commenced to pick up brush and listen to Frank's stories too. He was telling Frankie of how in India he had been a messenger for Lord Roberts, how on the line of march he would have to gallop ahead to map out the way and send back a map every five miles. Frankie said he would love that, but Frank told him, "You just think so. When I first went to India I used to think all I lived for was to get to gallop by the side of the royal carriage escorting some of the royal family through India, and then I got the chance. I was detailed as one of those to escort the Prince of Wales on a tour through India. He rode in a closed carriage drawn by four horses, a mounted soldier at each wheel. I rode at one of the front wheels, sword gripped tight in my right hand, bridle held in my left, keeping my horse's head not four inches ahead, nor four inches behind that wheel, at a trot from eight in the morning all day long, with one hour's rest at noon. The third night when I started to dismount, I fell and lay in a high fever for more than a week."

Of course the children had to stop and try it, with a piece of brush wood for a sword, marching up and down, their arms stiff and straight, and Frank stopped working and sang a rollicking wartime gallop, just to see who would tire first. They both soon tired and came back to the easier work of throwing brush on the fire. They were having a big time working, thinking it play.

Frank came over to me where I was and said, "Mary, I have made up my mind to quit drinking. When I came home from Memphis after running through your money as well as what I had left, and you never said one word, just went to work harder than ever, I made up my mind. It was such a pleasure to me watching you planning how you would buy enough stuff to make another room and furnish all the house. I left here with high hopes of helping you. God above knows what I did with the money. I don't know. I paid forty dollars for that damned old stove. If you had raised hell with me when I came home I could have stood it. I would have some excuse to keep on drinking. You don't know what a cad I've felt ever since Nina talked to me. When I realized how miserable I had made her, you, and all of you, I hurried back that morning to promise her I would quit. But when I got back and found her gone, I determined to finish up, end it all, but I can't forget her and how she talked that last night. Right now you won't believe me, but I will make you a promise. I went over to Grandma's to drink an eggnog at eight this morning, and until eight o'clock next Christmas morning not a drop of whiskey, wine, beer, or anything of the kind will I touch, to prove to you I mean what I say. After that I may take a drink now and then, but I will never make a fool of myself again. But I can see lots of hard work and suffering ahead of us if we make a go of this, Mary."

I said, "Frank, if you stick to your word and really quit drinking, work is nothing. I don't care if I have to crawl, am not able to walk to work. Hard work never kills, and your drinking is the only cloud in my life." But little did I guess then what a job I had taken on my hands for the next four years.

That night Frankie had been in bed about fifteen minutes, and Frank and I were sitting by the fire, when here came Frankie in his long nightshirt, marching stiff and straight. He was the whole show, horse and rider both, one-two, one-two, he came, stepping high like a horse and stepping so fast that when he walked straight against the wall he struck it with such force that it threw him down on the floor and woke him. As he woke he mumbled, "Damn Prince of Wales," the first oath I ever heard him swear. Without another word or a look at us, he got up and started back to bed. His father called after him,

"Young fellow, you shouldn't blame the Prince of Wales. You should guide your horse better."

That was the first time Frankie walked in his sleep, but it was the beginning of a watchfulness that we could never let up after that, for as he grew older he grew worse and worse about sleepwalking.

How that reminds me of that first year. The first of February it was cold and looked like snow. I was out milking when I heard what sounded like little chickens cheeping. I went in the new stable, and there was a hen with sixteen little chickens. I had missed her but thought wild cats had got her. I caught the chicks and put the hen up. What was I to do with the chicks? It was snowing by that time, and they would freeze outside. Then I thought of my big stove. It had two warming closets, the lower one on the floor. It made no difference how hot the stove got, it was never more than seventy degrees in that lower warming oven. So I put the chicks in there with a board across the door to give them plenty of air. I kept a little fire all night to keep them warm. When I would go to bed of a night I would fill the stove with big wood, shut off all drafts, then get up at midnight and fill it again. I raised every one of those sixteen chicks. So the old stove was being a help to me after all.

Storm

THE REST OF THAT WINTER PASSED OFF with lots of lonely days and nights and weeks, with Frank away, out helping sell land, but he was staying strictly sober. He was telling me, though only me, more about his business.

The roads were so wet and muddy it was almost impossible to get wagons over them, but a small steamboat had started running on the river once a month. Mr. Lombard had about 4,000 acres and was clearing it up with Negro labor; he had a nice house on the river, and his wife and child stayed there about half the time. They were about three miles above us, and the steamboat went that far and turned back. A Mr. Potter had bought a section of land joining us down the river, and a family named Swann joined Potter on the back, with his house built right on the edge of Black Bayou. Joining us up the river was a man by the name of Millen who had bought that section, and a family named Davis got a section above him. The Lombard place joined Davis. Two families bought a section each across the river, joining the Lemasters. Our settlement sprang up overnight like a mushroom. All these families moved in the first spring after the fall when we had moved.

As the country was filling up so fast and work was so plentiful, we decided it was best not to farm at all, just have a good garden truck patch and about two acres of corn to feed hogs on. I knew what was really holding Frank back was that he didn't know anything about farming, and he wanted to wait and watch the others, since he could make more by working out than by farming with no experience.

Meantime the state bought all the Ohio land company's land from

Mr. Busby; it took in all the Cyclone land and started to open up the state convict farm at Parchman. Lucy's husband, Charlie Lawlor, bought 160 acres joining the state farm at Parchman. The Cyclone was still a wilderness. When the convicts began clearing it up, it was like mowing wheat a strip at a time, and the guards only had to guard the rear. No convict, no matter how desperate, would venture out ahead in that tangled mat.

When I saw everyone else clearing land I was sorry we hadn't cleared up more, but we had the finest garden in the country. Frank got all the farm magazines he could and began studying up on farming for next year. When he wasn't on the road, he was making staves out of his own timber and timber he bought here and there. He had two men helping him. It was getting to be late spring and we had had a couple of severe storms. I had been after him so hard to saw down that big gum in front of the house that one Saturday he said, "I'm going to saw your bad tree down, Mary, while I have these boys to help me. It will take half a day to saw it down, but there will be enough stove wood in it to last you two years, and you'll never know a minute's peace, nor give me one, till it is down."

They began chopping out the notch on the underside the way they wanted it to fall. They had not been thirty minutes when he came in the house. He was white and shaking. I said, "Frank, what is wrong? Are you hurt?"

He said, "You know, I never went to that tree before we started notching it, it looked so solid, but it is nothing but a shell. It is going to be a hard thing to swing it off the house. You send Leslie with the other children up to the garden, and tell her to keep them there if she has to tie them. And you come out of the house."

They took the calves out of the lot and took them up to the garden. I got all my pet chickens up there too, but I had one hen with ten chicks, and as fast as I would drive her away from the tree, back she would go and call her chicks. She could see the sawdust falling and thought it was something to eat. At last Frank yelled to me to leave that damned old hen and save myself. I ran to the children. The tree was cracking and popping. There were two of them driving wedges to keep it off the house, and the other was chopping fast as he could. I gathered the children all up in my arms, hugged them tight, and shut my eyes. Down crashed the tree. It shook the ground where we were.

The men began laughing and talking, and I opened my eyes, for I knew they were safe and the house as well. It didn't even touch a holly. It fell just where they intended it should, but Frank said it was the hardest hour's work he ever did in his life. We saw one little chicken running around alone, yipping as loud as it could. One of the boys asked Leslie where the hen and the rest of them were. She looked around and said, "I guess they're all in the bad place. I hope they are."

Her father said, "If they were under that tree when it fell, they got a fair start in that direction." And he was right, for we never saw but the one of them again. That tree was hollow twenty feet up.

The next day was Sunday, hot and sultry, but clear, and when Mr. Lombard with four or five other men came by going to Black Bayou on a fishing party, Frank went with them. They had come downriver to our landing in boats. They had a couple of Negroes with wagons meet them at our landing and loaded their boats on their wagons with plenty of beer and lunch to go along. After Frank went with them, I hurried to get all my work done, bathed and dressed the children, and sat down to read a book called *In His Steps* that I was so interested in. Just as I sat down, it thundered, but when I went to the door and looked out there wasn't a cloud in the sky. I went back to my book and was so deep in it that when I heard a rumbling a little later I never thought but what it was a train, not stopping to think I wasn't within eighteen miles of a railroad, till Leslie brought me to my senses saying, "Mama, you better help me put the windows down and close up the house."

Then I recognized that awful roaring, growing closer fast. I ran and looked out the door. Yes, here it came down the river. It looked like smoke from the smokestack of a train, only ten times bigger. Great limbs flying through the air in that black cloud narrow at the bottom and growing wider at the top like a great funnel. It wasn't one minute after Leslie spoke that it was on us. We bolted the door. I took Edie in my arms and Leslie and I both held Frankie. I wanted to run out front to that old hollow gum tree, but Leslie screamed to be heard above the roaring, "No. The old big stump behind the house."

How we ever got there I don't know. Edie was screaming, so was Frankie. We huddled up on the far side of that stump, away from the house, our backs to the storm. Trees were falling all around us; the tall hollies' tops were sweeping the ground almost, but not one broke. I thought of what Mrs. Lemaster said, "A holly never falls in a storm." Their bushy tops seemed to be protecting us, for while we were covered, half-buried in trash, small limbs, and twigs, nothing heavy enough to hurt us reached us. In five minutes it was over, but during the worst, Frankie kept screaming and holding so tight to Leslie and me that Leslie jerked loose from him, stood up, and folded her arms like her father always did when he was worried about something. I reached up and tried to pull her back down, but she stepped out of my reach and yelled, "Let me be. If God wants me, let Him take me standing up. I don't want to be blown through Frankie's big mouth."

Well, it left us, just like a train passing, but what a sight. I could have walked on fallen timber from where the cyclone left the river as far as I could see. There were seven big trees fallen around our house; any one of them would have reached it if they had fallen towards it. We had a complete garden fence of fallen trees, but just one that did much damage. That was a top that blew out of one big tree and landed upside down in the middle of our garden. And not a drop of rain fell. It was just like a whirlwind. After it was over, and I was satisfied we were all together, with nobody hurt, I went around the house to make sure the house was all there. For the first time I was glad Frank had put all those extra studdings in it. That and the hollies saved it from being blown away.

After we got in the house and settled down, I asked Leslie what made her act like she did. I asked her what she thought about. She said, "If I tell you you will be mad, but I thought how silly you were acting, just after reading that book *In His Steps*. What would Jesus have done? Do you think he would of huddled down behind that stump where he knew he was safe and helped those big-mouthed kids cry? I thought you would of looked better praying."

I said, "I didn't notice you praying."

She stamped her foot and said, "How the devil could I while you were all making so much noise? But I thought a prayer for Father. I wish I knew he wasn't dead." And she burst out crying. I hugged her up, told her I was sure he was safe, as the storm didn't turn, and it would miss him.

"I am not mad at you, Leslie, for speaking your mind. I only wish the rest of us were more like you, cool and sensible in trouble."

But she wouldn't be comforted till she saw her father with the others coming about an hour later. They were walking. Left their boats, wagons, everything. They stopped at our house, all of them. The storm had struck them full force. They were eating lunch when they heard the storm coming. They jumped up and some of them started to run back in the woods. They had been drinking and their minds were fuddled. Mr. Lombard said to me, "That old reformed sinner of yours was all that saved us. He yelled, 'Get in the boats and go for the other side,' and he yelled at the Negroes to rush the mules across."

They all did what Frank said. One boat with Frank, Mr. Lombard, and another man in it was lifted literally up out of the water and slammed down on the bank. They lay flat on the bank till the storm passed. Trees were blown almost across the river. Leslie listened to all they had to say till they told about the boat with her father in it being blown out of the river. She could keep still no longer. She walked up to her father, patted his hand, and said, "Father, you weren't afraid, were you? You knew God was close, for I asked Him way down here," and she put her hand on her heart, "to take care of you. I couldn't ask Him out loud for poor Mama and those kids were making so much noise I just had to think, and you thought it too inside of you, so He was there."

Mr. Lombard looked at Frank and said, "You lucky scamp, to be the father of such a child." He reached out his hand to Leslie and said, "Shake hands with me, little girl. I want to be your friend, too. I think maybe it was your God that saved us all."

She gave him her hand and said, "I like you. Yes, I will be your friend."

From that day he was our friend, and that quaint child with her common sense and old-fashioned ways was the beginning of it, for in the years to come he thought so much of all our children.

That storm about ruined our corn. It missed Mr. Potter's place, crossed Black Bayou, and cut across the state farm, following the old path of the Cyclone. That storm was the beginning of our troubles. We hadn't got over the damage it did till a flaw was found in the title to our land. Not only ours, but all the land up and down the river on our side for ten miles. It was some old Indian claim, I think. Everybody went together and got a lawyer. Our part cost fifty dollars for the lawyer and four dollars an acre to get it straight. Coming in together with our third payment on the land it was bad, and I could see our home slipping away. We pulled through somehow, by borrowing fifty dollars, but I knew my hope of a pump was gone. I was catching water enough for wash water and to water the stock, but all the rest had to be carried from the spring halfway down the river bank.

The rest of that summer passed off slowly. I canned lots of stuff from the garden, and we dug plenty of sweet and Irish potatoes to last us all winter. Frank stayed in his timber camp most of the time except when he was out with Mr. Busby. I was alone with the children almost all the time with the howling wolves and screaming panthers for company, for it was raining all the time now that fall was coming on and was so muddy we couldn't get out to see our neighbors. I had got acquainted with them all, and those hill folks were fine neighbors, but I valued our old friends the Lemasters most.

That fall Frank hired a sixteen-year-old boy, Will Paine, by the month to stay and help us. We were going to clear up some more land ready to burn off in the spring, to pay off that debt. Not much, fifty dollars, you say, but a fifty-dollar debt means a hundred before you get it paid. I was determined not to pay out any more on land clearing except what we paid the boy Will, so I worked with him. I was determined to save our home if it killed me. And it came so near doing that, before it was over.

Frank was still making staves and was at home only nights. I could trust Leslie to see after the children and to go ahead with the work, so I would get up mornings at four o'clock, get breakfast and Frank's lunch, see him off, then stack my dishes, go milk, come back and wake Leslie and Frankie, fix their breakfast, mix my light bread, put it to rise, and show Leslie how high it must rise till it had to be molded out. She would tap the bell one time for bread and two times at eleven o'clock for me to come get dinner; if any of them got hurt, she would tap it lots. Frankie's job was to watch the ferryboat and, if anyone wanted to cross, tap the bell four times.

Then I would pour the dishwater for Leslie; she had a box to stand on to reach the pan. She could dress and feed Edie as well as I could. Frankie had all the stovewood to carry in. You say those children, mere babies, couldn't do that. But I taught my children to work according to their age and strength. I always thought if a baby could be taught to feed every three hours, it was as easy to teach it other things as well, and they could all dress themselves before they were three. I taught them right from wrong, to respect others' feelings, never to meddle with anything that didn't belong to them; and I spent lots of time seeing they did what I told them. They both thought we couldn't keep house if it wasn't for them. I always praised everything good they did, shamed Leslie over a fault, spanked Frankie. Their dispositions called for different methods. I had to be strict, for I didn't have time to fool with them. So you see I could trust them. I had to.

After I poured the dishwater for her, I would go out where Will was clearing land. He was a good, hard-working boy, but I could keep up with him. We had a big Cuban machete, two or three cane axes, and a chopping axe. We would cut all cane, vines, and saplings six inches and under and shove it all back. Some weeks we would cut down two acres, some three, but how we worked to do it. I worked so hard to save my home and my children. Will worked so hard to keep a woman from getting ahead of him. Sometimes when the bell would ring for eleven o'clock I would almost wish I could die, but when I got home and saw how the children were trying so hard to help me, Edie running to meet me with her little arms stretched out, crying, "Good Mama, good Mama," and Frankie meeting me with a water bucket for me and a little one for him to go to the spring for water, well, it would rest me.

Leslie got so she could bake the bread. I always baked eight loaves in a pan. I would set it on the oven door to rise, leave a little fire, and show her how full to let the pan get before shoving it in the stove. She could heat up the stove, and when the bread needed turning, she would pull it out on the door; then she and Frankie would both get a cloth and turn it, shove it back into the stove. When it was done, she would pull it out on the door and let the fire die down.

When I would go in at night just before sundown, I had to milk and carry up the night water. Will always got the heater wood and sometimes had time to help me with the water. When I got supper over and we were all gathered around the fire, we would each tell our experiences of the day—mine and Will's generally of the snakes we had killed or the rabbits Frankie's bulldogs had caught. These bulldogs were a pair Frank had bought, as I had to be alone so much. At this time they were a little over a year old, trained as watchdogs at home and on the ferryboat. They always went with the boat, Bess swimming alongside it, Bell riding on the boat. We had trained them that way.

One day I was at home getting dinner and Frankie came running to tell me there was a man with a lot of cows wanting to cross the river. I said, "I'm so tired I have a notion not to go."

But Frankie said, "Please go, Mama. I will run the pump all the time. I need a nickel."

We had a pump pitcher attached with a short joint of pipe to go down in the hull of the boat to keep the water pumped out and a little stool by it for Frankie to sit on and pump; every time we put a team across we gave him a nickel. So I took him and his dogs and put the man across. He had three head of cattle. When I told him the charge was thirty cents, he said, "That is not enough, lady."

I said, "That is our regular charge for a team, and it is about right."

But before I finished speaking Frankie walked up to the man, took his hat off, and said, "Sir, if you want to give us a dollar it is all right. My mother is so tired I couldn't hardly get her to come at all."

I told him to hush, and come on, but he waved his hand towards the ferry and said, "Besides, sir, it is worth half a dollar just to run that pump. Whew, I am so hot." He brushed the curls back out of his eyes like he was wet with sweat. It was a cold day, and the man just hollered and laughed and gave Frankie half a dollar. I told Frankie he couldn't have it, but the man insisted and went off laughing.

Frankie, the little rascal, was all business and always felt his importance.

About this time Frank was called off on business to be gone four or five days. Just as soon as he was gone, one of the men who worked with him making staves came to the house in a great hurry and asked if Frank had gone. When I told him he'd been gone since daylight, he said, "I tried to get here before he left. He wanted me to go to Shelby for him this morning. Did he say anything to you about it? He was to leave a couple of dollars here for me if I didn't get here before he left."

Frank had left me three dollars but hadn't said anything about giving his stave man any of it. I knew both of the men making staves with him had already been advanced about all he would owe them, as he had made half the staves himself. But I gave the man two dollars and he left in a hurry. Next morning, Saturday, bright and early, our old enemy Mr. Mann of Shelby came back with our stave man and began looking over Frank's staves, which had all been hauled and stacked across the river. Then he came to the house, and said to me, "Tell Hamilton I will take the staves at the price agreed on. I will send teams out Monday to haul them."

I smelled treachery as I knew him of old. Those staves when Frank sold them were to pay off our debt, give us enough to live on till spring, and pay Will until late spring, so Frank could stay at home and prepare our land for a good crop. So I looked at Mr. Mann and said, "Those staves won't be touched until Frank gets home."

He said, "Surely, you don't think there is anything crooked in this."

"Just so crooked I will shoot the first man that loads a stave," I said.

He looked so sneering, and turned away and said, "That would be bad, lady, but we will see."

I got straight in the boat and went across to see Jim Lemaster. He thought like I did but told me not to worry, they would keep their eyes open and see the staves weren't moved till Frank got back. I knew I could trust them and so went home; but I was so glad when Frank came home Sunday unexpectedly. When I told him about Mr. Mann, he was so mad he nearly exploded. For one of his own stave men to sell him out like that and try to play such a dirty trick on him! He went over to see Jim, and Jim had got wind that Mann was sending in teams by two o'clock Monday morning to steal the staves.

Frank had me set the alarm for midnight. I got up and made him some good strong coffee. He took his gun, put a few extra shells in his pocket, lit his pipe, and started. Jim Lemaster was to join him on the other side of the river where the staves were.

They hadn't been sitting there any time, Frank said, when they heard the wagons coming and a white man on horseback leading the way, calling back to the drivers to keep quiet. They got close and heard the white man say, "Some up here in front, some around back here, and load quiet."

Just as he rode around to show them the way to the back, the Negro with the wagon in front picked up a stave from the stack where Frank was sitting, and Frank threw up his gun and shot in the air. The Negro dropped the stave and ran screaming that he was shot. Frank hollered at him to come back and get his team, and then he called out, "And the rest of you see how quick you can turn these teams and get out of here."

But he said he was wasting his breath, for the teams were already turned and almost out of sight. The next day Frank loaded the staves on a barge and sent them downriver and sold them. And that settled his second deal with Mr. Mann of Shelby.

Shantyboat

THE LEMASTERS NEVER MIXED MUCH with any of the hill people in the settlement that had sprung up around them, but we were friendly with them all, except one family. This family was named Taylor, and they lived in a shantyboat. They came from the Lombard place up the river and tied up their boat at the Lemasters' landing. The Taylor woman was middle-aged, a spiritualist and a rounder. Boarding with her husband and her was a man named Jackson of the same type as the woman. They studied spiritualism books and practiced it. The man claimed to be a medium and the woman wanted to be. Her husband, Mr. Taylor, didn't believe in it and didn't approve of it, nor of his wife and this man Jackson reading and studying together so much. They had two nice, mannerly little girls, and a boy sixteen years old. They were her children, not his. He was their stepfather, but he was better to the children than she was. She was too busy running around over the country trying to be friends with everybody.

I met her one day at Grandma's. I had the children along, and the way she tried to make up to Leslie gave me the shivers. She told me Leslie would make a wonderful medium. "I wish I could just teach her. I could work wonders with a child like that. Now I can't do anything with my two little girls. Mr. Taylor don't believe in it."

I spoke up and said, "Neither do I, nor Mr. Hamilton. Don't name it to him ever. He would be furious." And I got up and left.

Of course I told Frank about it, and he said, "Be sure you don't ever take the children there, nor ever invite her here."

"Of course I won't, nor her children, though they are nice-looking children."

He said, "Old man Taylor is a very good old man, but we can't risk having anything to do with that class of people. I want you to understand, have nothing to do with them at all. You hear, Leslie? You're to have absolutely nothing to do with that woman."

He seemed unnecessarily worried about it. I sent Leslie on some errand out in the yard and said to him, "Why are you so bitterly opposed to Leslie seeing that woman?"

"Because Leslie, young as she is, is hunting something to believe, hunting, listening. She is an odd child, and I would not have her with that woman to practice her black art on Leslie for one hour for a thousand dollars."

So I almost quit going to Grandma's for fear I would meet her.

One day not long afterwards, I looked out and saw her coming to the house. Frank met her at the door. She had a nice fish, and she handed it to Frank and said, "For the little girl." Frank thanked her politely but refused the fish. She glared at him and said, "You mean this as an insult."

Frank said, "No, Mrs. Taylor, not that. But we all have the right to choose our friends and our children's friends, so good afternoon."

And he came in and closed the door. She left, muttering something about that "old foreigner."

I said to Frank, "I am ashamed of that, Frank. I am afraid you have made a dangerous enemy."

But he said, "Such people are far more dangerous as friends."

He had made an enemy. That woman caused us more trouble than anyone on earth ever did. But you will see.

We were getting along so well with our clearing that Frank took a job helping put up a couple of houses for Mr. Lombard. It took him almost to Christmas to complete them, so I got quite a rest. I put in my time sewing for myself and my neighbors, getting ready for the winter. I did all the Lemasters' sewing and lots for the hill people. Bob Lemaster was almost always hunting, and he kept us in fresh meat— bear, venison, and beef. And we caught lots of fish alongside the ferryboat. Grandma gave me four stands of bees, and Frank fixed me a nice place for them under a white mulberry tree in the edge of our little orchard. One cold day in December, Will and I took some sheets and went up the river in a sassafras dugout. I sewed the sheets around those bee gums (hives), and we brought them home. Next morning we took about ten pounds of honey out of each gum, enough to last all winter.

I liked Will. He would do anything I asked him to. He told his mother I was just like a brother to him, and we did work together like boys. The day Will left to go home to spend Christmas, he said to me, "Mrs. Hamilton, I will back you down sawing up that big gum log for firewood this morning."

I said, "No, you won't. Get the saw ready while I finish up the housework."

He was talking about a big gum log that had fallen in a storm and had been trimmed up ready to saw off into blocks. I went out and together we sawed off sixteen blocks. He turned them all up on end to split when he came back. We did it to get Frank to brag on us, but instead he said he had a notion to spank me for doing it and to kick Will for letting me.

Christmas this second year wasn't so good. Frank had got stuff to make plum pudding and had toys, fruit, candy, and nuts for the children to make up for last Christmas, but we were all older, wiser, and workworn. It just wasn't as nice as last Christmas. Something we had then was missing this year. Still, we were cheerful and happy and thought we had overcome all trouble. We had paid our debts, made our fourth payment on our land. We were sure of our place or thought we were.

For Christmas dinner we had a real old-fashioned English dinner. Frank had bought a sow with thirteen pigs, fat and nice. He killed one of the pigs and we roasted it whole in that big stove. I stuffed it; Frank fixed braces for its legs so it would look like it was running and put a splint in its mouth. I filled the pan it was roasted in with carrots, potatoes, stuffed head of cabbage, and apples. When it was roasted a golden brown, Frank put a red apple in its mouth. I can't say whether that was English-style or Yankee superstition on account of its being the thirteenth pig, but if it was to stop bad luck, it didn't work.

Will came back New Year's Day and work started with a vim. We were clearing land every day through January, and along about the last of February we had cleared all we wanted and were waiting for a good day when we could catch the wind right to set it afire. Frank was helping Mr. Lombard with his mill and with a house for his mill foreman and bookkeeper, a Mr. Whitforth, a very fine man. Mrs.

Whitforth, his wife, was related to the Lombards, and she was so sweet and good and smart. She had the most beautiful clear skin and such pretty gray-green eyes. I liked her better than anyone I had met for a long time, and she was about my own age. They had one little girl, Alice.

The Saturday after we finished clearing, Frank sent Will over to Grandma's for something, and he came back with a bit of gossip. It seemed old man Taylor had got drunk, and someone told him Jackson and his wife were too thick. He got drunker and went up to Mr. Lombard's store hunting Jackson. He got to swearing and cutting up at a great rate in the store, and when Whitforth couldn't stop him, get him out, or get him quiet, he finally had to knock the old man down.

"Old man," he said, "I feel like killing you. You go home and don't come here drunk again or I'll hurt you."

Taylor went home, found Jackson there and ran him off, and gave his wife a beating.

Will heard all this gossip at the Lemasters'. As he was passing the Taylors' shantyboat on his way home, the little girls hailed him and told him to pull up by their boat. They had a blackboard and an easel, a big doll, and a doll bed. They told him they were going to leave and couldn't take the things and asked him to bring them to Leslie. Leslie was so proud of the things, and we were so glad to know the Taylors were leaving, although if they had stayed five years it wouldn't have bothered us, as we had never met any of them since the day that woman brought the fish.

Frank had to go over to the Lombard place the next afternoon, so I got ready and went over to Grandma's, mostly just to give Leslie a chance to thank the children. Frank was going in a canoe. I told him he must take Leslie as far as the shantyboat, for it was nothing but right for her to thank the little girls, and as they were leaving anyway, it wouldn't matter. So he took her. I told her to stay ten minutes, then come on to Grandma's, and I would be there waiting for her.

She got to Grandma's almost as soon as I did. She commenced to cry when she saw me, and said, "Let's go home, Mama. I want to go home. Mrs. Taylor is going to kill Mr. Taylor, and I don't want to see her. He is leaning against a tree on the bank, asleep. When she saw him, Nettie and the other little girl had to hold her to keep from shooting him. Oh, it was so awful, Mama. They could hardly get the gun away from her, and she said she would kill him before morning, so help her God."

Grandma said she had heard that Mrs. Taylor had sent for her boy, and they were looking for trouble, so I didn't stay long but started back home. When we got out in the road I met Mr. Whitforth going over to the mill. We walked on down to the landing together. He told me he came down from Lombard's with Frank in the boat but got out above the shantyboat as he had had trouble with old man Taylor the day before and didn't want to pass the boat. I told him he would have to pass him anyway, as he was sleeping off his spree between the shanty-boat and the landing. Just then we came opposite him. Whitforth looked at him and said, "Poor old man. He is all right when sober, but let him get full and he has no sense at all."

I said, "The people that told him all that stuff about his wife and Jackson are worse than she is, and if this leads to serious trouble, they are to blame for it."

Whitforth said, "There won't be any trouble. When he sobers up they will forgive each other and everything will be fine till next time."

We were at the landing by that time, and Frank was there with the boat to pick us up. Whitforth said, "Frank, I wish you would come with me tonight, as I will be alone at the mill."

But Frank told him he would be over soon in the morning and Whitforth went on. We crossed the river. When we all got out, Frank pulled the boat high up on the bank as he always did, wrapped the chain around a sapling, and tied it. We went home and ate supper. Will was there before us, doing up the night work.

About bedtime Edie began crying with earache and nothing we did helped any. She almost went into spasms. Frank and I were both up with her till after midnight, when she wore herself out crying and went to sleep. Will couldn't sleep and so sat up with us. Our dogs barked almost all night; about eleven o'clock, they tore out like they were going to take someone down. Frank went to the door and called them back. He could just see the bulk of two men, and he said he thought it was Burl, a Negro living just above us, for the dogs knew him. We all went to bed soon after that, got up at the usual time, and after breakfast Frank started to the mill. Will went down to the boat to put him across.

Before they got to the river, a man coming downriver who had crossed at Lemaster's landing waved to them to stop. He stayed and worked at Bob Lemaster's. He asked Frank if he knew old man Taylor was dead. "Shot about eleven o'clock last night. Two loads of buckshot right through his heart. Tore him almost in two."

Frank said, "Was he shot as he slept on the bank?"

"No. Her boy came home late yesterday evening, talked a long time with his mother, then went up the bank where the old man was, roused him, led him down, got his clothes off, and put him in bed. Then he came up to Grandma's and said he had straightened things out and that he was going back to where he was working. Frank, you ought to go over there. I'm going for the coroner."

Frank said, "No, I'm not going. I never have messed with them and don't intend to now."

The man went on, and Frank started on to the river, still intending to go to the mill. But when they got to the river, the boat was not there. Frank went downriver, Will went up. Will got about halfway to the shantyboat and saw our boat floating down the river, not far from our bank. He shoved a short log lying in the edge of the water out with a pole to the boat, stepped off the log into the boat, paddled as fast as he could to our landing, and called Frank. "I want you to see the boat, Frank. I haven't touched a thing. I stood up and paddled."

Frank stared down in the boat. On the seat in the end of the boat were two empty buckshot shells, not fired more than five or six hours before, and a ten-cent square of Star Navy tobacco with one corner bit off and the teethmarks showing. They knew something was wrong. Was it a plant to try to lay the killing on one of them? What could it mean? We talked it over and agreed it was best not to mention it to anyone. Frank warned us again not to say one word of it to anyone, while he went over to see Mr. Lombard about it.

Well, how could we work? The whole place was stirred up. They got the coroner and the officers in. It was plain that either Mrs. Taylor, her boy, or Jackson had killed the old man in cold blood. Jackson couldn't be found. Part of the crowd was for putting Mrs. Taylor in the river. The little girls were quizzed but wouldn't say one word, and neither would their mother.

Frank told Mr. Lombard about our boat, and about the two men passing our house about eleven o'clock. He asked Frank who all knew about the boat, and when he told him just his wife and a boy staying with him, Mr. Lombard said, "That old woman did the shooting, either she or Jackson, and I believe they stole your boat. Her boy may have had a hand in it, and he stays on your side of the river. Those are the shells he was killed with, but he was shot from the foot of his bed, and those shells were placed in your boat, and that tobacco, to put the blame on one of two men, Frank: either you or Whitforth. It's a good thing your child was sick last night, as you wouldn't have any trouble clearing yourself, but Whit stayed alone at the mill last night, and him and the old man having had that trouble at the store—well, you better just not say anything about the boat, and don't let the boy. Old lady Taylor is already hinting she can name the man that killed him, and that it wasn't Jackson, nor her boy. So keep this dark. It looks to me like the old rounder aims to hang it on Whit."

Frank told Will and me this and told us not to mention it. It was on my mind almost day and night, and I could see Frank was worried, but he wouldn't let us talk about it. But when Will and I were at work we talked about it, and about our boat, and wondered what it could mean, but we never breathed a word about it outside. I never mentioned it to Leila Whitforth, but I knew she was worrying herself sick over Whit's having been alone at the mill that night.

They put the Taylor woman and her boy in jail, and the little girls were cared for by someone over on Sandy Bayou. Jackson they never caught. The case was set for the next term of court in May, and we settled down to work.

One morning in March when the wind was high and blowing away from the Potter place towards our house and barn, Frank and Will set the clearing afire. There was a small bayou running through our place the full length of the clearing, and before we set the fire we burned off the bayou bank, so there was no danger of the fire getting to our house. Then Frank and Will went to the far side of the clearing, twisted dry grass together, set it afire and dragged it along the edge of the dead cane and dry brush. From our back door it looked like a solid wall of fire almost 400 yards long and ten feet high, and it made as much noise as a cyclone. You could hear the cane popping a mile, and the smoke was so thick you couldn't see the sky. I was surprised to see how well the fire did its work, for it burned saplings six inches through to ashes, and whole dead trees burned up till you could hardly see a piece of them.

After the burning the farm work began in earnest. Frank had bought a mule from Mr. Lombard and rented another one, for he himself was going to plough this year. He had never ploughed in his life, didn't know one plough from another and wouldn't let anyone tell him anything, but it looked easy. The morning we started the ploughs going, Will was waiting for Frank to go ahead, so Frank commenced fumbling with the gear, and said, "Will, you get those bull tongues rigged up. I'll be back in a minute."

Will said, "I thought you were going to use the turning plough to flat break for your early corn."

Frank said, "The bull tongues, do you think I don't know what I am talking about?"

Just then Jim Lemaster walked up. I slipped out and stopped him, begging him to see if he could show Frank which ploughs to use without hurting his pride. I went with him. He spoke up and said, "Hamilton, I came over to see if you could lend me your bull tongues, as you won't need them breaking your corn ground. And you are right about these cutters on every kind of plough you use the first year. Let me help you rig up those little turning ploughs—help you, not Will, for he is making a mess of it."

Will had the ploughs about right, but Jim undid all the boy had done, then showed Frank piece by piece just how to rig up for break-ing. I slipped back to the cowpen to wait till Jim came by. When he came he was grinning to himself and didn't know I was about. I said, "Jim, don't tell that on Frank. This is serious. Our home depends on his starting right. You're the only man in the country that he'll listen to, but if he ever gets it in his head you are laughing at him, you can't help any more. If you will happen along every day or so and kind of steer him along, I will do all your wife's sewing."

He promised to do all he could. After he left I made some excuse to go back out where Will and Frank were ploughing. Will ploughed by where I was, stopped and took a drink, and commenced to laugh. "Mrs. Hamilton, you said if I laughed at him you would fire me, but a puppy would laugh. You see them poles he put up at each end of the field with a white rag on each? He told me they were to keep our row straight and for me to match him and go straight. Well, I have ploughed for five years, and I came out right at the pole, but he came out fifty feet below."

He was ploughing towards Frank now, and I was walking along close enough to watch his work. Will said, "Mrs. Hamilton, can you sew leather on your machine?"

I said, "Why yes, Will, if it is thin. Why?"

He said, "You'll have to make a leather seat for Mr. Hamilton's pants. He'll have the seat dragged out on these little snags by noon, he pushes his plough so hard. He keeps his feet five feet apart, but that is the only thing that keeps him from turning a somersault over the plough when it hits a snag or stump."

I said, "Will, you shut up," and walked faster and came up to Frank. He stopped and asked me how it looked. I said, "Fine."

He said, "I'm afraid not. You see, this is my first ploughing and the first mule I ever tried to handle. That makes it hard. Now if I had a horse to do my ploughing, I could do better, but this damned old mule is as hardheaded and contrary as a Mississippi nigger."

I thought to myself, "No more so than you are," but I said, "Frank, please listen to me. We want to make a go of this farming, and you have got to take it easy. You work too hard. Walk slow and straight, don't push your plough. You are going below the subsoil, killing yourself and the mule."

I had got him to stop and rest himself and the mule, but he flared up now and glared at me. "What do you know about farming? I suppose you want me to plough like I was on the line of march, escorting this damned old mule like I would the Prince of Wales. Mary, you better run on to the house. The children might appreciate your advice. I don't."

I went but couldn't help flinging back at him, "I'm all right when you want me to cut cans, clear land, do a thousand other kinds of slave work," and went to the house, disheartened, sore at all the world, Frank in particular.

When I got to the house Frankie and Leslie were fighting. It was so unusual, and coming as it did when I wanted to work my temper off, it made me hasty. Leslie had her hands twisted up in his curls pulling as hard as she could. He was biting her shoulder like a bulldog. When I jerked him loose he almost took the piece out, and she had enough hair in her two hands to make one big curl. I didn't say one word, just bent his head down. How I did spank his little sitter. When I felt a little bit relieved, I popped him in a chair so hard, then I turned to

Leslie. I had never really spanked her before, but I must be just, so I grabbed her and gave her the same treatment. Frankie was getting out of his chair, but I popped him back and said, "You both sit right there till you say you are sorry, kiss, and make up."

Leslie jumped out of her chair, folded her arms, glared at me so hard, and closed her mouth so tight it looked like a thin slit. When she spoke, her voice was cold as ice. She spoke low. I never saw her look so. She said, "I am ashamed of you, Mama. You are acting like a damn fool, trying to make us tell a lie. Frankie don't care, the little coward, but I will die first."

Frankie came up to her with his arms spread out. "I love you, Leslie. I want to kiss you."

She jumped back and said, "Get out. I don't want your lies. She can make you tell a lie because you are a coward. Get back or I'll kick my foot right in your mouth."

I said, "Leslie, come tell me all about it. Maybe I was too hasty, but surely I haven't tried to make you tell a lie."

She said, "No, I won't come to you. Unless I can say what I have down here"—she put her hand on her heart—"I believe I am going to burst."

"Listen, Leslie. Say what you think. Maybe I was wrong."

"Wrong, you were worse than wrong. You were a mean damn fool, grabbed us and spanked us without trying to find out what it was about; but the spanking didn't hurt like your trying to make us both tell a damn lie. Every time we would say we were sorry we would be telling a lie. I am not sorry. You think I would be dirty enough to kiss him and say I was sorry, and you tell us, both you and Father, that God hates a damn liar; then you, not Father, beat us half to death to make us tell one."

I was so ashamed and hurt. I hadn't stopped to think; I just got mad at Frank and Will Paine and took my spite out on the children. I stood cowed and ashamed to face her so much like her father. No, he might never learn to plough, but he would never try and force a child to tell a lie. I broke down and began to cry. She came up to me and put her arms around me, crying. "Oh, Mama, I am so sorry. I had to talk like I did. I do love you, and if you never try to make me tell any more lies, I will never say any more swears."

I said, "Yes, oh yes, I promise. Now tell me what you were fighting about."

"Well, Frankie went to the top of the river bank and saw Grandma's geese in the river. He came to the house and said he was going to teach our chickens to swim while they were little so when they got big they could beat Grandma's. He and Edie began throwing them in the rain barrel. As fast as I could take them out I had to wrap them up, and when I got back, they had all the rest in the water. I slapped Edie and ran her off. I shoved Frankie down and had got the most of them out when he commenced to bite me. You must think I was a fool to take that. If you hadn't come when you did, I would of had all his hair pulled out."

I jumped up and said, "Do you mean you didn't get them all out of the water?" I was running to the rain barrel. There they were, ten of them, drowned. I said, "God, what can I do?"

Leslie said, "Nothing now. If you had asked what the fight was about instead of spanking us you could have saved them. If that had of been my little girl and boy fighting, I would of asked them what they were fighting about, then I would of got those chickens out of the water and wrapped them up. Then I would of grabbed that bad boy and spanked hell—no, I didn't mean that, but that was what he needed."

I thought so too, but I said, "Leslie, let's be friends. I need you. I am having a hard time and so are you. From now on you make these children mind you if you have to spank them every day. I am blue. I feel trouble ahead. What it is I can't tell, but you are going to have to take full charge of the children. I am going to have to stay in the field all the time."

I called Frankie around and made him get a board. I reached down in that water, took the chicks out and made him carry them to the river and throw them in, as I went to the spring for water. I gave him a good talking-to and gave him to understand he had to mind Leslie no matter what she told him to do; if he didn't I would spank him till he couldn't sit down for a week.

"But Mama, you have done that already. I don't think I could sit down now. But I will mind her." And he nodded his curly head.

When Frank came in for dinner he was played out, but he wasn't beaten. But by night he said that was slow work, ploughing. He would finish planting Mississippi-style, he believed. Said he wouldn't make anything just scratching the ground the way they do, but the land would be in good shape. Every time a little difficulty came up about the work, I would send for Jim to drop by, and by easing Frank along like that we got along, slowly, but very well. We got all our cotton and corn planted and garden made, but oh, how I had to work.

I had given up washing in the daytime. I would put on wash water after I came in from the field, while I was getting supper of a Thursday evening. Leslie helped wash the supper dishes, then I got the children to bed and started my week's washing. I would hang out my clothes about one o'clock Friday morning. There was a panther would come across the river every night after dark, about 200 yards from our house, and just about one o'clock every morning go back across the river to the far side, screaming. I never could get used to that terrible, hair-raising scream, and it seemed every time I would hang out my clothes that panther would start. I would almost jump out of my hide, so I got so I would make Frank get up and come out to sit on the step and hold the light, while I hung out the clothes. Then I would go to bed, set the alarm for four o'clock, get up, get breakfast, milk, get my churn ready, and be in the field almost as soon as the men were. It seemed Frank couldn't work in the field except when I was with them. He just couldn't realize how hard it was on me.

By May, in court week, we had our corn worked out and a fine stand of cotton, with part of it worked out. Had just started the six-inch shovel around it. Will was ploughing and Frank and I were hoeing, when a man rode up, a sheriff, and began reading a paper to Frank. It was a summons for us both as witnesses in the Taylor case. Everybody around there was being summoned, he said.

I told the sheriff I didn't know anything about it, but our oldest little girl would make a good witness if she was old enough. She wouldn't be six until fall, but she knew the nature of an oath and could tell a straighter story than half the grown people he would get as witnesses. He asked Frank to call her out where we were, so he did. Frank told her to tell the sheriff what happened on the shantyboat the day he let her off there. She told him straight. When she was through the sheriff asked her if she knew what became of people that swore falsely, told lies. She said, "Yes, sir. They go to the bad place. You see, God won't forgive a lie."

We sent her back to the house, and the sheriff said, "If that child wasn't so young, she could send that old woman to the pen for life."

We had to go to court just a week from that day. I had to take Edie with me. We got an old man in the settlement to stay with Will and do the housework and tend the cows. The first day we got there they got Frank on the grand jury, but the rest of us just sat around waiting to be called, wasting time when I should have been in the field. Aunt Bet, Sally Lemaster, and I were the only women there. Then the last of the week the trial was put off. Frank told the judge he wasn't a citizen of the United States and got off the grand jury, and we all went home.

I was worn out but glad to get home to the children and to work. Will didn't do much while we were gone, and we were terribly behind. It is funny how hard it is to get caught up with your work once you get behind, but at last we did. We got the cotton hoed over the first time, but it looked like the weeds just sprang up behind us as we hoed in that rich land: cockleburs, lambsquarter, poke weeds. We could almost see them grow, and the middles between the cotton rows had never been touched. The weeds in them were knee-high, and thick as the hair on a dog's back. But everyone's cotton was the same.

It was hot weather about the middle of June, and we had started hoeing over our cotton a second time. I wasn't well and wondered that morning if there was any chance to pull through the day. I was hoeing in the field with Frank about ten o'clock when a man rode up on his horse and asked us how we were getting along. Frank knew him, called him "Sheriff Ridell," and talked to him a moment, never dreaming of trouble. Finally the man said, "Hamilton, I have a hard duty to perform. I have to put you under arrest."

Frank said, "Ridell, you are joking. Arrest me? What for?"

He said, "It's no joke. That Taylor woman has made a confession, she calls it. Says you went in your boat, shot the old man, jumped back in your boat and left, while she begged you not to kill him while he was asleep. Says you told her you couldn't stand it to see her suffer any longer, so they have you for first-degree murder."

Frank was white as a sheet. I was paralyzed. I was clinging to Frank, crying. I couldn't stand up. Frank put his arms around me to hold me. The death of all my children was nothing compared to this. I had not the least doubt as to his innocence; I knew he was as innocent as my children. I remembered when he had refused the old woman's fish, and how she left muttering "old foreigner." I could see it all, and I knew now I had felt it coming since the day they found the shells and tobacco in our boat. It was Frank she had intended to lay it on all along. I must keep my head clear to help him. I straightened up and said, "Frank, don't you judge all Americans by that old devil. You will find there is justice in this country. We can prove you never left the house till hours after he was killed. We were up till after midnight with our sick baby, and Frank never left the room, and the boy staying with us was sitting up with us."

Ridell said, "She can't hurt you, Hamilton. Everyone knows she is lying to save her own neck, but you will have to go and stand your trial."

Frank said, "I have been in America twenty years and have never got tangled up in their laws. I have tended to my own business and have never meddled with other people's affairs. Now this, coming as it has, means loss of our crop and our place, unless I get a speedy trial."

All the time we were talking we were going to the house. Will had to come to take Frank muleback as far as Sandy Bayou where the sheriff would furnish a horse. How could we face the children to tell them? We thought of telling them he was going on business, but no, they would find out, and how Leslie hated a lie. I knew I was trembling so I could hardly walk but thought I was hiding it. Those sharp eyes of Leslie's saw it.

The deputy sheriff stayed on his horse at the gate. Frank went inside to dress. He told me to send Mr. Lombard word, and he would tell Mr. Potter as they passed. He said, "Go ahead, dig up everything you can, but above all push the work here."

He was dressed. His chin quivered as he turned to me and said, "Mary, I've lived long enough to know the law is the last place to look for justice or truth. If anything happens and I don't get back, if you can't hold the place, for God's sake, don't let the home be broken up. Keep the children together. We have friends I think that will help you get started keeping boarders, and raise my children to understand I am as innocent as you and I know I am."

How could I live if he didn't go soon? But Leslie had come in and heard him talking. Her eyes were blazing. She said, "Father, where are you going?"

He told her. She folded her arms like she always did when she was mad. "Father, you mean that old hellcat—," she said, then looked at me and said, "Mama, I must swear or I will die. Father, that is what you get for not letting those men tie an iron to her and throw her in the river where the devil would of got her and took her on to hell and burned her up. I am going with you and stay with you. If they put us in jail with her I will claw her damned eyes out."

Frank said, "You can't go, Leslie. If you want to help Father, you will stay with Mama and take care of the children and help her." He turned to go.

She threw her arms around his neck and commenced to cry. "Oh, Father, I will be good and help Mama and never swear about anything except that woman."

He kissed me and kissed the children. They all said good-bye in their different ways. Little Edie cried because the other two did. Frankie handed him his slingshot and said, "Take this, Father, and when you get to the jail, shoot old Mrs. Taylor with it, then come home."

When they were gone I left Leslie to take care of the other two, and I went across the river to see the Lemaster men and get someone to go let Mr. Lombard know. I hurried back home and found Mr. Lombard on his horse talking to the children. He had come to see Frank about some work and had ridden up and asked Leslie where her father was. She was sitting on the back top step, she and Edie, Leslie with one arm around Edie, both of them crying; Frankie was on the bottom step playing with his slingshot to keep from crying. I came through the house in time to hear Leslie say, "He is in jail with that old hellcat that killed Mr. Taylor. Now she says Father did it."

I stepped out the back door. Mr. Lombard tipped his hat and said, "Is that so, what the child says?" I told him all I knew. He said, "I was uneasy about Whit but I never dreamed she'd try and lay it on Hamilton. He is the last man in the country to have picked on, but she can't do anything."

I told him how Frank turned her off that day she came to the house with the fish for Leslie, and how she had gone off muttering. He said, "I will go right down. Don't you worry one moment. I'll take care of this. I would keep Will at work if I were you. Frank can't get back under a week."

He turned and left. Leslie ran to the gate after him and said, "Mr. Lombard, you said once you wanted to be my friend. Well, please bring my father home when you come."

He said, "Little girl, I will bring him home if it costs $10,000, and I won't come back till I do."

I took up my work. I must work for Frank, too. Will and I were back in the field that day by one o'clock, working as we never worked before. That was Thursday. We worked till Saturday night. Saturday night I washed. I was sure Frank would come out all right. Everyone in the neighborhood had been in to see me and assure me of their help and sympathy, and all were sure he would come out all right. Witnesses had been summoned to be there Monday morning, as he was going to have his trial that day.

When Monday came there were many went up and volunteered as witnesses. Of course Will had to go. His oath alone would have cleared Frank. But he never was even called on. The character witnesses alone were sworn and so were Burl and the other Negro that passed our house the night of the killing when Frank went out on the porch with the lamp to call the dogs back. They said they saw him plain, that he scolded the dogs back and they both knew his voice. They said he turned back in the house and shut the door, and they didn't go a hundred feet before they heard two shots. They could tell they had been fired inside a house or boat, but they got opposite the shantyboat, a half-mile, before the screaming started. They had kept all this dark till the old lady laid it on Frank. Then they went and told Mr. Potter.

So Tuesday Frank got home. Mr. Lombard came by with him and called Leslie. "See, little girl, I brought him back."

She said, "Oh, thank you, but did it cost you $10,000?"

Mr. Lombard laughed, "Oh, no, he isn't worth that much."

Leslie said, "He is worth that to us, and I do love you for bringing him back. Don't we, Frankie?"

Frankie looked up and said, "He is all right, but I like his horse."

Science Says "No"

E VERYONE HAD TOLD FRANK HE WOULDN'T NEED A LAWYER in the
Taylor case, but he was so afraid of American laws, he had
gotten one. That cost him fifty dollars, and with the other expenses
that mounted up, we had to put a mortgage on our place. We had to
work ourselves almost to death, literally, to clear our crop. But we laid
it by, the first of August. Will went home to stay till next spring, and
Frank got some carpentry work to do for Mr. Lombard. I thought I
would get some rest, as I was pregnant again and was breaking fast in
health as well as spirit. I could hardly see any light ahead now with the
mortgage hanging over our heads.

But I didn't get any rest. Frank's trial was hardly over when, along
the latter part of August, malaria hematuria began going over the
country. Several died with it, and many in our neighborhood were
having chills and congestion, which was so apt to run into hematuria.
Hematuria is the last stage of malaria. It comes on with a hard chill
and vomiting and the skin turns yellow and the urine to blood. Unless
a doctor gets to the patient in two or three hours, the bowels and
kidneys lock, and it is nearly always fatal. When one in a family has it,
others in that family generally have it, and sometimes whole families
are wiped out with it. That was how it was then. I was sick myself but
just couldn't give up. Sometimes when I could hardly hold my head
up, I was up day and night with a neighbor in sickness.

One Monday morning I started washing. I could wash daytimes now
that crops were laid by and I didn't have to be in the field. A Negro
came riding one mule and leading another one with a sidesaddle on it
and handed me a note. It was from Leila Whitforth and said, "I have

just been taken with hematuria. I am not uneasy about myself, but I must see you. Come at once if you possibly can."

I had come to think a lot of Leila Whitforth, and I was uneasy if she wasn't. She was pregnant, and I was deadly afraid of that hematuria, although she had had it before and got well. I knew she had worried herself almost to death over the shantyboat trial, same as I had, and worse, for she knew Whit had no one to prove he was innocent, as Frank had, if the old woman decided to try laying it on him.

Well, I left my washing in the tub and hurried as hard as I could. I got myself and my children ready, and we walked down to the river and went across on the boat. I gave Leslie a note to Grandma to take care of them till I could get back. Leslie walked up the river bank to Grandma's, and the Negro took Frankie up behind him, Edie in front. I had never ridden a mule before and was afraid, but I rode on. When the Negro caught up with me, we rode fast, I was so worried about Leila. As we rode up, Mr. Whitforth came out on the porch leading Alice, his little girl, by the hand. They were both crying. The Negro nurse and two or three other Negro women came out of the house wringing their hands. The nurse ran up to me crying, "Why were you so long? She tried so hard to live till you got here. She wanted to tell you something."

I jumped off the mule and ran into the house. She was just breathing her last, but she was looking at me, trying so hard to speak that her eyes were just agonized with the effort. Her poor lips moved a little, but the fool Negro woman had followed me in and was still moaning and crying. I dropped on my knees beside Leila's bed, put my head down close to her lips, and felt her cold mouth as the last breath left her, just a little less than two hours after she had taken down sick. I got up and staggered out on the back porch. I was never so sick in my life.

But I was the only white woman there, so I had to pull myself together, straighten her, and close her eyes—eyes I was bound to see the rest of my life, for next January when my boy was born, his eyes were like none of my other children's, but like hers: bright, talking eyes, as they had to be, for his voice was as still as hers. Wasn't it that shock of seeing her terrible effort to speak and tell me something that caused my baby's dumbness? Science says no, that would not mark my child, but common sense tells me it did. I worried some over what it was she had wanted so much to tell me—was it something bad? But my life was too full of real worries to leave much room for imaginary ones, although a woman always has room for one more worry.

They told me she had asked that I make her burying clothes, her underclothes. She was to be buried in her wedding dress. I sat up all that night to make them and had to dress her with the help of a Negro woman. The next afternoon Mr. Whitforth took her to her home to bury her, and I had to stay and tend to little Alice.

Frank heard about her dying and went home that night. He went over the river and got the children, and he and Leslie got supper and breakfast, and he milked. Next day at noon he came for me. I got home and managed to get through my work, then tumbled into bed, so sick. But I had to finish that washing next day, and I did. The day after that I went to sit up with a sick child having spasms. I helped save the child, but when I got home I was nearly dead for rest and sleep. I wanted to go straight to bed, but they had supper ready and Frank said I must eat. I sat down, ate a few bites, drank a little coffee, and my head dropped in my plate. I don't see how I ever got up next morning and worked all day, but I did.

Soon the crops were ready to gather. The cotton all over the country was rank and tall, but not taller than the weeds in the unbroken middles, for we just cultivated the narrow rows where the cotton grew. It grew a bale to the acre even in that new ground. We shipped it in the seed on a little steamboat. The boat came up when cotton picking opened up, and dropped off bagging of the sort that cotton is baled in now, only it was long enough to hold a bale in the seed. They called them "worms" or "snakes." The cotton was stuffed in them, and when we had enough for a shipment it was hauled to the river and loaded on barges, then the boat took it downriver to gin at Vicksburg.

Court week was coming again when the Taylor woman's trial was to come up. Two days before her trial was to be called, I was starting to wash. It was too wet to pick cotton and I wanted to get my washing all done, housecleaning off hand, and bake bread. An old friend of Frank's, an Englishman, was coming to stay with Frankie and Leslie and keep house while we were at court. Frank had to go as he was the main witness against her, with what he had seen and what Leslie had heard on the shantyboat the day the old man was murdered.

It had been unusually warm for that time of year, and the wind was blowing from the south. About daylight it started raining; there would be quite a shower that would last just a few minutes, then it would look like it was going to fair off for maybe half an hour; then it would pour down like a cloudburst again. About ten o'clock in the morning my wood began to run low. I wasn't through washing, and I began to fret about it. Frank said, "I know where there's a dry ash snag near the house, just about six inches through, that I can cut down and cut off enough to keep your fire going, as soon as this shower stops. Does that suit you, Calamity Ann?"

So the next time it slacked up he took his axe and went out. Both dogs followed him. We couldn't see him as there were a few bushes and trees between him and the house, but it was right on the road to Burl's house, the Negro living on the Millen place. Well, we had another shower and another. We had heard Frank chopping and heard the snag fall, but Frank didn't show up. Directly after the snag fell we had heard the dogs bark like they were about to take someone down, and at times we could still hear them yap like they were after a rabbit.

I said to Leslie, "I wonder if Frank quit getting wood and has gone rabbit hunting. I am out of wood." I went to the door intending to see.

When I opened the door, there he stood, dripping wet, blood trickling down his face, with a look of horror, hate on his face. He was crazy as a loon. I had never seen such a horrible sight before and never have since. He didn't know me. He looked at us all like he suspected us of treachery. I spoke to him saying, "What on earth is wrong, Frank? You are hurt."

He glared at me and said, "I was told, sir, that you were a detective and would help me find that shadow that struck me down from behind. But you look like a damned fool instead of a detective."

I was never so scared in my life, and Frankie and Edie began to whimper. I turned to Leslie and spoke low. "For God's sake, get the children out of the house. Hide the gun, knives, razor." She did and hid the children as well.

I had to humor Frank. I told him I was a good detective, but I couldn't do anything unless I could look at his head to see if I could find some evidence. He came in, sat down on a chair, and bowed his head. Long ago he had been hurt in England in a steeplechase, the time he got his knee hurt, both legs broken, and his skull fractured.

They had put a silver plate in his skull. Near or almost on that silver plate there was a round hole in his head about as large as my little finger, but the blood was oozing out of it so I couldn't see how bad it was. It didn't look very deep. I told him if I could wash it I could find out something.

He said, "Go ahead, but hurry. It was a shadow of a nigger on a horse."

I hurried and got some water and a little soft cloth, but when the first drop of water touched it, he jumped up and screamed. I never heard such a scream. I thought he was going to kill me. Instead he cursed me and said, "I have a great notion to severely kick you, sir." And he did kick, but I got out of his way. I knew I couldn't do that for long, so I pointed out the door and said, "There goes your shadow. Run!" He flew out after the shadow.

I got the children in the house and locked the doors. I never put in a worse four hours in my life. It kept fairing up for a little while, then pouring down rain again, and there wasn't a soul passed the house all day. The children were all scared and crying. I was sure a limb had fallen and struck Frank. Oh, how I prayed someone would come by! I was afraid to leave the children and afraid to stay with them and leave Frank wandering around outside. Besides, the river had risen so I couldn't get to the boats to cross it.

It was four o'clock that afternoon when it stopped raining and began to turn cold. Frank came to the door and knocked, saying, "Open the door, Mary. I am almost frozen. I have been out all night and am cold and wet."

His voice sounded natural, and I opened the door. I could see he was still groggy, hadn't come to himself. I humored him and, believe me, I didn't offer to dress his head. I got him to sit by the fire. I had plenty of heater wood. How I did wish he would change his wet clothes, but I didn't dare run the risk of exciting him by asking him to. After a few minutes he looked at me so pitiful and said, "My head is killing me. It seems to be on fire. Bob and I got lost last night, and it poured rain all night long. I walked and walked to try to get home. If I could get dry clothes . . . "

I said, "Frank, I will get you some clothes, if you will let me help you put them on."

"I will," he said.

I got them and helped him, and in doing so I saw his poor head. The blood had all dried up; his hair was all matted in dried blood. He was meek as a lamb, but I was afraid to say a word. Just as he got dressed, old Francis, Burl's wife, came in the kitchen and called me. I went to the door.

She was scared bad and had been running. "Ol' Miss, is Mr. Hamp dead? I just found out."

Frank came tearing out of the other room cursing. He looked wild again and was using language that couldn't be printed. "If I get my hands on him I will tear him limb from limb with my bare hands. Burl did it." But she was gone.

I could see Frank was better. He asked me if it was yesterday he got hurt. We told him it was this morning about ten o'clock. I asked him if he would let me dress his head, and he said, "Yes, you should have done that long ago."

I bathed it good. When I got it clean, I could see what looked like a .22 rifle bullet hole. He said that just as the snag started to fall, he went back to a big gum log more than five feet through, lying near, and was standing against it with his back towards the road, watching the snag. He said he heard a horse walking down the road, and when it stopped right behind him, he started to turn.

"I just half turned my head when I got that blow on it. I grabbed at the log to keep from falling, then everything went black, but I am sure I saw a Negro, and that it was Burl."

His head dropped forward, he mumbled something about being sleepy, and he was asleep before I could get him in the bed.

As soon as I was sure he was asleep, I took the children out of the house. The sun was setting clear, so the rain was over. We went out to where Frank got hurt, as I still believed a limb had struck him. But there wasn't a limb near the log anywhere. There were his tracks in the mud where he had stood backed up against it like he said, and tracks where he had fallen and tried to get up, and it looked like he had crawled away and up to the barn. And there were tracks of a horse coming down the road to the log, then going away.

Frank slept till five the next morning and got up feeling better. His headache was gone, and although his head was awful sore for several days, his mind was all right. He said the blow was on the edge of that little silver plate, and it was a miracle he ever came to his right mind.

We had no positive proof, but we were convinced that it had been done to get rid of Frank as a witness against the Taylor woman. That somehow she had hired Burl or some other nigger to do it. He was well enough to go to the trial the next day, but it was put off once more and the woman got out on bond. She made another so-called "confession" at the last minute, clearing her boy, and saying Jackson alone did the shooting with her help and approval. Jackson by now had had plenty of time to get clear out of the country. Everybody knew it was money he sent that fixed the bond for her bail. The law wasn't as strict on women those days as it is now. She took her children and pretended to be going to Clarksdale to live, but she skipped out of the state, and we never heard of her again.

But the harm she had done had put us in debt we never got out from under, and I believe it was the worry she caused that sent Leila Whitforth to her grave, and Leila's going like she did brought me suffering I live with daily even yet, by marking my baby born the next January.

The Last of "Home, Good Home"

CHRISTMAS WAS COMING AROUND AGAIN. We had talk of a school to start the first of the year in one room of Mr. Potter's store, if we could get up as many as five children. By sending Frankie, not yet quite five years old, we could. We had to sell our cows to get good clothes for Frankie and Leslie to go to school. It lightened my work, but it was a blow to me, and it hurt us to have to do without milk and butter. Leslie could read and spell some and started in the second reader. Frankie took an old blueback McGuffey speller I had, and they both carried slates. Frankie broke his the first day and then had to carry the pieces.

I will never forget the first day they started school. They were both neat and clean, and I was proud of them. Leslie was so good; she was attractive, thoughtful of others, smart, and full of dry wit. Frankie was an unusually pretty boy, with yellow curly hair and big blue eyes. He was sober, self-conceited, and full of business. When he was little I was sure he was going to be a great preacher some day, but when somebody asked him what he was going to be, he swelled out his chest and said, "Well, sir, I am going to be a brakey on the Yellow Dog Railroad."

He was dressed that first school day in a light gray suit I had made him, with pants and a white waist. I made his pants to button to his waist, with no opening in them except on the side. I told him if he had to be excused to tell Leslie and let her wait on him. He got along fine until afternoon; he was outdoors, back in the house, all over the place, but about the middle of the afternoon he walked up to Mr.

Martin, the teacher, and said, "Mr. Martin, I want to borrow your knife."

Mr. Martin opened it, gave it to him, and told him to be careful, as it was sharp. Frankie opened it and went outside. In a few minutes he was back in and handed Mr. Martin the knife, saying, "Here. Take your old knife. Look what you made me do. I don't like your old school. I'm going home."

By that time the room was in an uproar, children pointing and laughing, and Mr. Martin trying hard to keep from laughing. The boy had tried to unbutton his pants and couldn't. He was too proud to ask Leslie and so borrowed the knife. He couldn't make a slit in them without cutting himself, so he had gathered up all the slack in front, twisted it and twisted it until he could saw across it with the knife, and then he sawed. There was a hole in the front of those pants as big as a saucer, and to make it worse he had got his underclothes, too.

Mr. Martin told Leslie to take him home "so his mother can fix his pants." Leslie gathered up his things, her eyes just blazing, gave Frankie a shove, and said, "Yes, she'll fix his pants. When she gets through with him he'll have the seat tore out of them, too."

They came home, but Frankie didn't come strutting in like he started off that morning. He was a very sorry-looking little boy. "I am sorry, Mama, but it was the teacher's fault. He had no business giving me the knife."

Leslie, practical as always, said, "No, Mama, it's your fault. If you had made his pants right, there would have been no trouble, and he can't go with me anymore till you do."

I put in the rest of that evening making new fronts to his pants, for I didn't tear up the back of them, as Leslie said I would. So he never had any more trouble of that kind.

That week Jim Lemaster's house burned down. They lost almost everything they had. All the neighbors came together to help him rebuild, every man giving him two or three days work. As Frank was the best carpenter around there and Jim was one of his best friends, he helped all he could. His only trouble was leaving me. My health was bad, and my time not two weeks off. Frankie and Leslie were going to school, and Edie was not quite three, at my heels every way I turned. There wasn't much traveling, so I didn't have to worry about the ferryboat, and every morning when he left Frank would say, "Mary, don't you go near that ferryboat today under any condition."

But one day when Frank had been gone about an hour, a Negro came along with a four-mule team and wagon wanting across. He lived at Mound Bayou, was a good old Negro and one of our best customers. His team had always been gentle and no trouble. But I told him I couldn't put him across that day. He said, "Miss, I has a sick baby at home and haves to hurry. You knows, Ol' Miss, if I haves to go to the other ferry ten miles down the river and ten back, I can't git home tonight. I'll give you fifty cents and do all the work. You just go over to bring the boat back."

Well, I went. I felt sorry for him, and too we did need money so bad. I took Edie to the river, found her a place on the bank to sit, and told her to stay there till I got back. The Negro drove on the ferryboat, left his team standing there, and went back to unfasten the boat and hook the back gate. I had gone on in front of the team and fastened the front gate. Our bulldogs were with me like they always were, Bess to swim across, Bell to ride on the boat as we had trained them to do from the time they were puppies. Bell always inspected everyone that got on the boat. If she didn't like their looks she would lie down in front of them, look straight in their faces and growl, and if they moved, would show her teeth.

This time I had told Bell to stay with Edie, but she didn't understand that the boat could go without her. When the Negro untied the rope that held the boat to the bank, she saw it start to move away from the bank. It had never gone without her, and it couldn't this time. She ran and jumped clean over the gate onto the boat. That scared the mules. They started backing and kicking, and the Negro couldn't hold them. The boat began to turn. One corner ground up on the bank, and Edie tried a flying leap like Bell's. She jumped on that corner, swung to the banister, and started to come to me on the outside holding to the banister. I began crying and pulling on the rope, trying to straighten the boat. I knew the mules were going to break the banisters loose the way they were lunging and kicking. They would either kick her and kill her with their hooves or knock her into the water, and the river was over ten feet deep there right at the bank.

Bell was standing by me, guarding me. I cried, "Edie, call Bell to you."

Edie called, and I gave the dog a shove, and said "Go." Bell ran to her then; snapping, barking, biting, she turned the mules to the other side. That Negro was crying, praying, and trying to quiet his mules, but he couldn't do one thing with them. I had got the boat straight and was pulling on the rope as hard as I could. I was so afraid swinging sideways like it was it would break the rope. I reached one hand over the banisters to help Edie. I managed to get her over, telling her to stand by Bell and hold to her. I said, "Hold tight to Bell, baby, and if we all get in the river, Bell will get you out if you just hold tight to her."

At last we got one corner of the boat within a foot of the landing block on the other side of the river. I picked Edie up and literally threw her out on the bank out of the way. I made Bell go with her. As Bell jumped over that gate it scared the mules back some, as they were crowding to the front to get on land. I took advantage of that moment, dropped the gate, and jumped on the bank with the chain in my hand. I used the last bit of strength I had lifting that boat onto the landing block, threw the chain over the fastening post, threw myself down out of the way of the mules, crawled to where Edie sat, and lay there laughing, crying, too weak to move. The Negro went to the top of the bank before he could stop his team. Then he came back. He was crying and wanted to go for "Mr. Hamp." I told him if he did, Frank would about kill him. I told him it wasn't his fault and that I would get on the boat, and if he would put Edie on and push us off I could get back all right. I was just frightened.

But I knew long before I got home that I was going to have the hardest fight of my life if I lived through it. How I got home I can't remember to this day. I didn't know when the children came home from school, nor when Frank came. He didn't come home till after dark, and I couldn't tell him what had happened, as I was suffering so much I didn't know anything. So he just thought it my time, and as our nearest doctor was at Tutwiler, Frank went for Sally, Bob Lemaster's wife, and got Bob to go for a midwife living near, Aunt Molly.

I suffered all the agonies of torment for two days and nights; then my baby was born. I came to myself afterwards just long enough to tell

Frank all about my getting hurt on the ferryboat. He wanted to show me our fine boy, but I wouldn't look at him. I didn't want to see him, for if I did I might want to live and I knew I couldn't. But Sally brought the baby to me and put him in my arms. He was so sweet and looked so perfect, but I thought of all I had gone through the last year and knew it would darken his life. I was tired and hurt and wanted to die. I began shaking with a rigour, and that was the last I knew of anything for three weeks.

When I came to myself again, I could hardly see or hear, just blurred forms and voices a long ways off as if through a thick fog. I was burning up, begging for water. They said afterwards I had begged for water day and night the whole three weeks, but the doctor said one swallow of cold water would kill me, and Frank had guarded me constantly so no one should bring me anything but boiled, hot water. That first day that I was conscious a little, I thought I would die for water. Just when I thought I could stand it no longer, Leslie came sliding along the bed, her back to me, and slipped something cold and wet into my hand. It was a snowball. I crammed the whole ball in my mouth. She told me afterwards she had been slipping me snow like that all week, without their knowing, as there was a big snow on the ground. I am perfectly sure that child saved my life.

It was another week before I remembered the baby. Then I saw Leslie trying to feed him with a spoon. I asked how old he was, and Frank said, "Your son Bruce is nearly a month old and hasn't had hardly a drop to eat. He won't eat and can't or won't suck a bottle."

I told Leslie to bring him to me. She brought him over and sat down on the side of the bed. Frank brought the warm milk and gave me the spoon, though he said, "You're too weak, Mary. Don't try." I was shaking and trembling, but I poured half a spoonful of that warm milk into his mouth. It almost strangled him to death. Frank shook him, blew in his face. I think that finished bringing me to my senses that I have never again entirely lost.

By the time Bruce was a little over a month old, I was able to sit up, and between Leslie and me we had got Bruce so he could take the bottle. I knew there was something wrong with his throat, and when they saw I knew, they told me he had never cried nor made any sound since he had been born. But he grew fast, and when he was five months old, he, Frankie, and Edie all took whooping cough. All that

saved Bruce was a young Dr. Smith who had just come to our settlement. I think Bruce was his first patient. He stayed with him day and
night. We had a hard time getting milk that agreed with Bruce, and
when we finally did, we bought the cow—an old, ugly, long-horned
cow, mean and hard to milk, who gave very little milk. Frank couldn't
milk her at all, so I had to do it. After Bruce got so bad sick, the
doctor had us keep the cow up, dry-feed her, and milk straight into
Bruce's bottle, half a bottleful every three hours. By the hardest work,
we pulled Bruce through, when stronger and older children were dying
of whooping cough all around us.

Leslie was with it all the time and never had it. She said it was
because God knew I couldn't spare her, and I think she was right. We
had had to take her out of school when the baby came. She had just
turned her seventh year, but lots of girls of fifteen are not half as good
or dependable as she was, and she took almost full charge of Bruce. I
was not strong since the day of the ferryboat, but my fighting spirit had
come back, and I was more determined than ever to save our place.
Frank and I were both working hard for that end. We had cleared off
the debt and the mortgage, but Mr. Lombard had talked Frank into
building another house and getting a sharecropper on our land to help
work it. I begged Frank not to do it. Begged him if he just must build,
to build two more rooms on the house we were living in, and drive a
pump for me. But he wouldn't listen, built another house, and drove a
pump there. I still had my water to carry from the spring under the
river bank. After he had done all this, he couldn't get a renter to suit
him, so for that year he got Will Paine and his cousin from the hills,
let them sleep in the back room of the new house, and let the schoolteacher have the front room to teach school in. The teacher slept in
his schoolhouse and boarded with us.

I didn't have much farm work to do that year. I just made and
tended the garden, did my housework, and cooked for those two boys,
the teacher, and my own family. Bruce was no trouble, and when he
got over that whooping cough, he went to growing. He was good-
natured, rolling and crawling all over the house, always finding something to play with, always smiling. He was quiet; he never had cried or
laughed out loud in his life, nor made a sound. Everyone said it was
because he was so good-natured, but I knew why it was. The teacher
called him "Happy" and every morning carried him down to the

schoolroom. Taking Bruce along was the only way Leslie got to go to school.

Life seemed to be running smoothly for us at last. Our little settlement was flourishing. We had a school and a good doctor, and we were all good friends. Someone even suggested getting a preacher and having church in our schoolhouse, but Mr. Potter said what we'd need would be a missionary, and Frank didn't think much of our Yankee preachers either, so we had to let things rock on, each family serving God in its own way.

That year ended and a new one came in. Frank was sure he was an experienced farmer now, as he had read all the farm papers he could get his hands on, so that year he got two Negro men to work for him. He let them farm their own way with the cotton, except three acres he measured off and worked himself. He said the newly cleared Delta land was the richest ground in the world, and that the Delta farmers only half-worked it. Mr. Lombard just laughed at him the way he kept his cotton field clean of weeds, and the way he worked his corn. But that fall Frank picked five bales of cotton off his three acres, and the Negroes' seven acres of cotton only made six bales. And Frank sold over a thousand bushels of corn to Mr. Lombard off thirty acres and had plenty to do on himself the coming year. We could easily have finished paying out our place and put ourselves straight with the world, our little home all our own, but in the following spring bad luck came in a new disguise.

When we bought our place, "seventy acres more or less," we took the old government survey. We joined Potter on one side, Millen on the other. Between us and Millen, but all on his land, was a broad brake. Millen was trying to buy up all the land around him. We knew he was going to buy the Potter place, and he had been after Frank to sell him ours, but of course Frank wouldn't think of it. So about the time crops were planted that spring, Millen came to Frank and told him he wasn't satisfied with the way the lines were run and insisted on running them over. He said he and Potter and others were all going in together and get the county surveyor, and as Frank was in the middle he must come in on it. He told Frank his share of the cost would be twenty dollars and boarding the surveyor while he was here. Frank had to consent.

I don't know all the law on it, but I know how he ruined us. He started a good hundred yards below the old government survey at the river, cut through our cultivated land, and took in part of our orchard. We got all of Millen's brake and were left with fifty acres instead of "seventy more or less." Our place was practically worthless. It was the end of my hopes, almost of my life. For days I doubted God's justice. What had we done to be beat on every turn we made? There wasn't a family in the state worked harder and tended to their own business more than we did. I don't believe there ever was a mother and wife wanted a home more or worked harder to get one than I did. Something was wrong. But what? I wished in my bitterness that our land that was taken from us would never do the one that took it any good, and it never did. But our home was gone. We knew it was a game of freeze-out, but we had no money to take it to court, and the man with money and power behind him, then as now, rode roughshod over the little fellow. So we sold out to Millen but were not to give possession until the first of the following year.

We were hopelessly beat, and it seemed I couldn't put any heart in anything. In July my last child was born. He should not have been born till the last of September, and he was a sorry-looking piece of humanity. He weighed less than three pounds. Young Dr. Smith rigged up a homemade incubator for him. He wrapped him first all over in medicated cotton. Then he took a soft flannel cloth and wrapped it all around him, cupping it up around his face. Then he took a big soft all-wool bed blanket and wrapped it round and round him, folding the two ends across and pinning them together. It was warm and soft, something like a cocoon. A roll or fall had no more effect on that tiny ugly little baby than it would have had on a young moth. Because the heavy blanket was held off his face a little, he got enough air. We never saw him except when we uncovered his face to feed him. We would have a spoonful of weakened milk in a medicine dropper, have a damp cloth ready, touch his face with it, and when he gaped open his mouth enough, squeeze a drop or two in it, and so on till he got a spoonful.

At feeding time the children could get a glimpse of him. He was two days old when the doctor was there helping us feed him, and he looked up at Leslie. She was standing looking at him with her hands clenched, her eyes blazing but full of tears. He said, "Why, Leslie, don't you like your little baby brother?"

"Baby brother, huh. Dr. Smith, I almost hate you. You just know how easy it is to beat Father, and you took advantage of him and passed that ugly thing off on him that you couldn't sell to anybody else. The very ugliest, littlest baby in heaven." She turned to me and said, "Mama, please, please, turn it back. You don't have to keep it. We don't need any more babies. I won't ever nurse it. Never."

I tried to explain, to comfort her, but she would not be comforted. Meantime Edie had crept up and was looking at it, and she said to Frankie, "That's no baby. It's a rat. Mama is trying to fool us."

Frankie said, "I don't know what it is, but God never made a baby that ugly."

Bruce we didn't dare even let see him. Bruce was then about eighteen months old and had never spoken a word, but he was full of mischief and harder to keep up with than four ordinary boys. He could run and play and climb like a monkey. As fast as he could be got out of one thing he was in another. Sometimes I thought it was because he never made any noise, and we never had any warning of what he was into. Leslie took care of him all the time. She loved him, petted him, helped him out of trouble and spanked him when nothing else would do. To be on the safe side we didn't let Bruce see the baby, but he understood what the others said, and we had to keep a constant guard over the carefully wrapped bundle. When the baby was a week old, and we began to believe he was going to live, the doctor told us we must name him. That day the old lady Potter came with the doctor and was taking on about him being so small. She slipped my engagement ring over his hand and up his arm almost to his shoulder. He was a wonderful small baby.

Frank said we would call him "Bob," as he was too small to carry anything more, but if he lived and got stronger, we would call him John Robert Hamilton. It was the first time he had ever given a double name to any of our children. I noticed it and wondered at it, but I had schooled myself never to think of his past any more, and in those days the duties and disappointments and pleasures of each day were as much as I could find time for. But I have wondered since if his giving Bob a double name wasn't because at last he had given up all hope of returning to whatever it was that waited for him in England. I believe that was it. I believe Nina's dying was a death blow to his dream of getting back whatever it was he had left behind him there.

Trouble very seldom kills, and when I got up after Bob was born I looked at our loss in a clearer light and felt it was partly our fault. That phrase "more or less" gave the man that beat us a chance to dispute the government survey. I was sure no one would try to beat me out of my children, and I did pray there would never be more nor less as long as I lived, and that we would get a chance to raise them right, for that is all parents can do under any circumstances, if they try. As my home was gone, I turned to my children as my one big job in life, and their father was with me in that. We agreed our children meant more to us than a home, and that we must be cheerful, happy, and contented, for they are great imitators.

All three of the oldest children were in school, but I had my hands full with all my work and taking care of Bruce, or "Happy," as everyone now called him. When he couldn't find anything else to do he would turn his attention to the baby. One day when the baby was a month old, I was busy getting dinner. It was almost noon and I was expecting Frank and the schoolteacher, Mr. Martin, for dinner. I had been watching Bruce play in front of the steps just a moment before the men stepped up on the porch. Bruce met them laughing, cutting all kinds of monkeyshines and talking with his bright, dancing eyes.

His father said, "What is it, Happy?"

When I saw how he was acting, my first thought was the baby. I ran into the room and saw that the bundle was gone off the bed. I grabbed Bruce. "Tell me what you have done with the baby."

Of course he couldn't tell, but he wouldn't even show me. In the meantime Frank and Mr. Martin had been all over the house and couldn't find the baby. I began losing my temper, shaking Bruce, and spanking him. Mr. Martin picked him up. "You can't tell her, Happy, but you will show me where he is, and I'll give you a nickel."

He set Bruce down, but Bruce held up his hand for the nickel before he took a step. Martin gave him the nickel, Bruce flew out of the house and motioned to Martin to follow. Down the front steps, around the house he ran so fast we could hardly follow. He stooped down and pointed under the house, and there, rolled back up under the front steps, was the bundle. Frank crawled under and brought him out. He wasn't hurt, but how Bruce ever got him down off the bed and down the steps, we could only guess. I wanted to spank him, but Frank wouldn't listen to it.

"You must show him the baby," he said. "Get him to loving it and make him understand he must help take care of it."

But I had lots of trouble with him even after that. Twice I came in, missed the baby from the bed, and found him stood up in a corner, where Bruce had propped him up; both times he was standing on his head. But he was so well-wrapped it never seemed even to disturb him. When he was three months old, he shed his covering, and he was the sweetest one of all my babies. Bruce turned all his attention to him then, and as Bob grew, Bruce's attention turned to worship and has lasted all their years.

Temporary Quarters

THE FIRST OF THE YEAR WE STARTED OUT AGAIN, homeless. Mrs. Lombard let us have their house, and we were to board Mr. Lombard and his agents, gin boss, and Mrs. Lombard and her little girl whenever they wanted to be there, which was pretty often. In all I had about ten boarders. Frank was renting some land on the Lombard place, working it with hired hands, and he was keeping books for Mr. Lombard. We were all right except that the children had to give up school. But between Frank and me we helped Leslie, and she helped the younger children.

Mr. and Mrs. Lombard were fine people, regular old southern aristocrats. Had been wealthy all their lives and so didn't feel like they had to make out like they were better than we were. They treated us as friends. They kept their rooms upstairs and had three horses, a steam yacht, and a small steamboat. The house stood at the top of the river bank, the edge of their front porch within six feet of the top of the steep bank where steps led down to the river. You could stand on the front porch and see up and down the Sunflower River for a mile or more. That was when phonographs first came out, and of course the Lombards had one. The music from that big tin horn carried up and down that river on still nights, so shrill and loud it almost deafened you, but it was heavenly music those days. Bruce loved music, and he was a privileged character among them all. He did just exactly as he pleased. But all my children were easy to get along with. I taught them if they did anything wrong during the day they must confess it before they went to bed by talking it over with Frank or me, whichever of us had time to hear them. They were not afraid of anything. We taught them they must have nothing to hide; then they could say their prayers, go to bed with a clear conscience, and sleep good.

Frankie was the one we had the most trouble with. He would tell a lie to get out of trouble, but I don't believe he ever got away with it. My severest test with him and greatest victory was one fall day when everything was dry. They had a fine alfalfa field that had been mowed and was curing, and just on the far side our cotton field joined it, but there was a wide strip of dead sage grass between the fields, and a good many quail used it. Frankie wanted to set some bird traps and deadfalls to catch them. Frank had made him some traps and showed him how to set them, but every time he looked in them the corn was gone and the traps thrown. The grass was so thick the traps couldn't fall flat enough on the ground to hold the birds. I can just see him trying to think out a way to get rid of that grass, and at last he hit on an idea. He carried his traps over and put them in the cotton. Never thinking that the grass grew to the very edge of the alfalfa, or that the wind was just right to sweep a fire right through the alfalfa and ruin a ten-acre field of it, he set that grass afire and started to run to the house to get corn to set his traps.

Mr. Lombard's agent came along just then, jumped off his horse, and began stamping the fire out. Frank was working near by, saw the fire, and hurried over and helped. They soon got it out. Frank saw the boy's head bobbing up and down going around the corner of the barn, all unconscious of what he had done, till something made him turn and look back. He trotted out across the road to think what was best to do, then he ran to the house.

I saw the fire but didn't know how it had started until Frank came in to dinner. He told me. He said the agent told him not to say anything to Frankie about it, that he was too little to understand what he had done, but Frank and I felt he should be made to realize. So when Frankie came in I called him to me and said, "Frankie, do you realize the harm you did in setting that grass afire? It came near getting in the field and would have burned all the hay that was curing, besides ruining the young alfalfa and causing big damage that Father would have had to make good. All that saved it was Father and Mr. Scruggs."

"But Mama, I never—," he began, his big eyes wide and innocent.

I stopped him before he could tell the lie he was ready to tell. I said, "Now, Frankie, we will say no more about it till you can say you did it, and if you are sorry for it, tell Mr. Scruggs so. You see, Frankie, if you deny it you will be telling a lie, for God saw you do it. So did Mr. Scruggs. Now you run and play, have all the fun you can, but until you acknowledge what you did, you can't say your prayers to God, you know, and you can't kiss me goodnight."

He tried to play, got through the day, that night got ready for bed and came to me to say his prayers. I asked him if he was ready to own to what he did. He shook his head and said "No." I told him to run on to bed then and to sleep. He wanted to kiss me goodnight. I turned my head and told him I couldn't kiss a little boy with a lie on his lips, a little boy that was afraid to tell the truth. The next night was the same. But the third night he came, put his arms around me and said, "Mama, I did set the grass afire. I couldn't hold the birds in my traps. I didn't think about that hay till I turned and saw Father and Mr. Scruggs putting it out, and then I was scared. I am sorry. I want to say my prayers. I am so sleepy."

I asked him if he would tell Mr. Scruggs the first time he saw him, and he nodded his curly head. So he said his prayers and kissed me goodnight.

The next morning Mr. Scruggs was late for breakfast. Everyone else was gone. After he ate, he said he had some work to do and started back upstairs. I told him he would have a visitor up there presently, and when the children came running in for their breakfast I motioned upstairs and told Frankie Mr. Scruggs was up there alone if he wanted to see him. He hesitated a minute, then squared his shoulders and darted upstairs. When he came down he ate his breakfast and ran out to play.

When Mr. Scruggs came down a little later he laughed and shook his fist at me and said, "I thought you had forgot all about that grass fire, and here you have been putting that little fellow through the third degree. You didn't whip him, did you?"

I said, "No, that isn't our way of handling a thing like that. Frankie is a fine boy, but stubborn, and would grow up into a first-class liar if I would let him. So I use other methods than whipping. I whip him for something mean I catch him in, but not for lying."

Mr. Scruggs said, "You know, when he came upstairs and looked so straight at me, owned to setting the fire, told me he was sorry and how he hadn't been able to say his prayers to God or kiss his mother goodnight since he'd done it, well, I tell you Mrs. Hamilton—," and there were tears in his eyes, "—I lost my mother when I was a small boy, but I missed her more right then than ever before."

I could shield my children from sin and from growing into coarse men and women, but they were often subjected to embarrassment that I could not help them with. Like one time when Mrs. Lombard was spending the weekend with us and had brought some wealthy friends and relations with her. The Lombards' little girl, Minna, was a lovely child, loved by all. When she came out in the country after living cooped up in town, she would run and play out of doors with my children all day long. Their greatest sport was throwing mudballs stuck on long canes across the river, seeing whose mudball would go the farthest. This particular day they were having great sport, laughing and shouting with joy. But there was another little girl in the crowd of visitors besides Minna. She would take no part in their game but kept begging Minna to come go upstairs and play post office with her. Minna told her she wouldn't and tried to get her to come play mudballs with them. The little girl turned away with a pout and said in an ugly voice, "Minna, I can't see how you can play with those poor children. I won't." And she went in the house.

Frankie and Edie took the snub for what it was worth and went on playing, but Leslie was always sensitive. She dropped her cane and started to the house. Minna called after her to pay no attention to the little girl, but come on and play.

Leslie said, "No, thank you, Minna, I am going to the house."

So the three of them went on with their game, and Leslie came to me, heartbroken, sobbing out her story. "Mama, you know we don't want to be rich, but in some way from what Father has said at different times in telling us stories of his life as a child . . . " Just then Frank came in, and, seeing Leslie's tears, asked what was wrong.

She turned on him with fists clenched and her eyes blazing, told him what had happened, then said, "Why don't you come out and tell us why we are not good enough to play with that little girl?"

Frank walked up and down the room for a moment, as though he couldn't face her, then he whirled as quick, and said, "My children are as good as any in America if blood counts, and it does. Money doesn't count, Leslie. You children have blood in your veins that many an American has traded name and fortune for. Hold up your head, child. You don't have to stoop to anyone."

Mrs. Lombard had come in unobserved and heard part of what he said. He turned to leave the room, but she stopped him, saying, "I came to apologize for what that little girl said. Mr. Hamilton, I heard what you told Leslie and am not one bit surprised. I always knew you were hiding something, but you can't hide it. Blood will tell. It shows in your face, your carriage, your speech, in every move you make."

He bowed to her, polite but cold, and said, "I don't deserve the compliment, Mrs. Lombard, and I hope what you heard a moment ago you will forget as just a slip of the tongue to pacify a little hurt child."

And he went out. Leslie had already slipped out and didn't hear her father's excuse, or there might have been another scene.

One day Mrs. Lombard was playing with Bruce, and he was talking to her with his head and his eyes like he always did. She took up a lot of time with him, and this day after he ran out, she said to me, "That child can almost speak with his eyes. They are beautiful eyes with such a wistful look in them you have to understand him. They remind me so strangely of someone, and I can't figure out who it is."

I said, after a minute, "Is it Leila Whitforth?"

She called him in to her and looked long at him, then looked at me so queer and said, "Why have I never seen it was her eyes? But how in the world . . .?"

Then I told her all about Leila's dying, and how I believed it had been the cause of Bruce's dumbness, and from that day she took an even greater interest in him. Nothing was too good for Bruce after that, for, you see, Leila had been related to her. It was Mrs. Lombard who finally helped us to get Bruce to a throat specialist in Memphis. He told us Bruce was not dumb as we thought; he only had a partial paralysis of some throat muscle. He said the only way to get him to talk was to put him in school and let him mix with strange children in strange surroundings, with a kind teacher. He said Bruce made such a go of using his eyes, hands, and feet and nodding his head that we had quit trying to make him talk, and that was true, for we believed him dumb. That doctor, and the fact that we were losing money every day where we were, made us decide to leave the Lombard place and go where we could get Bruce, and the other children, too, in school.

God and All the Angels Laughing

WE MOVED OVER ON LUCY'S HUSBAND'S PLACE near Parchman. The country around the state farm was so changed from when we had left there six years before. The state farm had nearly all been cleared up and the roads graded, though not yet graveled. The old "Cyclone" was all great fields and gardens. Every camp looked like a little town, with nice dwelling houses for the officers, great big barns, fine cattle, mules, and stock of all kinds. Even the "cages" themselves, where the convicts were housed for the night, looked nice on the outside. I couldn't say about the insides, but from the way the convicts would sing and yell going in from work in gangs of fifty, they must not have been bad. It was always a treat for us to hear the twelve o'clock train blow for Parchman, to hear the fifty mules throw up their heads and bray, and the plough boys and the hoe gang yell. They would plough out to the turnrow, then all unhitch, and go stringing along with their mules into camp. Hoe hands were the same, working side by side strung out across the field all in a straight line guarded by "trusties" with guns on their shoulders, a white driver with each gang.

We lived right where we could see almost all over either No. 1 or No. 2 Camp. The convicts were worked hard but were well fed and clothed. Most of the Negroes, anyway, were treated better as prisoners on the Parchman farm than as free men and women before they came there. They were treated according to the way they behaved, unless they had a mean driver, and a mean driver never stayed long. We had heard so much before we moved there of the cruel treatment the poor convicts got and of the danger in living close by, but we never saw any of it unless one of the convicts ran away. Then when they caught him, if he surrendered peaceable, he only got a flogging with a strap, and fifty lashes was the limit. Of course, if he resisted and fought, he was generally wounded or killed outright, and nearly always by a convict guard who got a pardon as a reward.

We lived there for three years and farmed every year. We made good crops but had to work so hard. Frank was determined to master the cotton-growing business, and working fifteen acres he worked it as he would a garden. He would allow very little ploughing, and that meant so much hoeing to keep the weeds out. He flatweeded it up one side of the row; then when the weeds and grass were cut and scraped all back to the middle, then and only then would he let the cotton be thinned down to two stalks to the hill, eighteen inches apart. If it got too rank, we would have to go in along in August and pull one stalk out of every hill and top the other.

Besides our cotton we had a big garden: all kinds of truck patches, such as watermelon, canteloupe, popcorn and peanuts. How those children had to work to have them. They insisted on having such, though, so Frank would have the ground broken for them and help them get it planted; then he would tell them to go to work and see they didn't let any grass or weeds grow. Frankie was the one who always proposed some new truck patch, but Leslie and Edie had to help carry it out. Not that Frankie shirked his part, but as Leslie and he were large enough now to hoe in the cotton some, they had to do the other work on the side.

Frankie got lots of work out of the trusties off the state farm. He made friends of them all by always being kind to them, never jeering or making light of them. Then, too, he would shoot birds for them. He had a twelve-gauge shotgun and was a fine shot. Blackbirds were thick around there; they roosted in a big canebrake near the farm and about sundown would fly over in droves. Frankie would take his gun and go to the post office. No one was allowed to carry a gun through the farm, so Frankie would walk on the railroad when the convicts would be going in at quitting time. He would wait till a cloud of blackbirds was going over the convicts, then shoot both barrels of the gun. How they would scramble and grab for the birds! Of course they weren't allowed very far out of line, but they managed to get all the birds that fell. That way Frankie made lots of friends among them.

The trusties were all over the country, hunting, fishing, and gathering wild plums, blackberries, and muscadines for the sergeants, as they all had lots of convict servants. There wasn't a day that from one to three trusties didn't come by where Frankie was working, and for a nickel or a piece of pie or cake, he would hire them to go work for an hour in his melon patch. He got most of his work done that way, but we warned him never to take anything any of them offered him; we gave him to understand that he as well as the convict would be a criminal, guilty of taking stolen goods.

You see, there were hundreds of people scattered over that country that almost depended on those Negro convicts to keep them up, and they weren't all Negroes either. When we lived near No. 2 Camp there was just a line fence between us and the farm. They had a ditch running close against the fence on their side, about three feet wide and four feet deep. There never was a morning we wouldn't see a convict slipping down that ditch with a big load on his back, slipping it to someone in the woods that grew at each end of that ditch. They would pay the convict maybe a dime or fifteen cents for five dollars worth of stuff stolen from the camp storeroom.

Back of our place was a low, flat, swampy piece of land, maybe a hundred acres, belonging to the state. We had a potato patch down near the back of our field and I went one day with Frankie to get some potatoes. A bunch of buzzards flew up over in those woods near our fence. We had lost a calf a few days before, and Frankie went over to see if it was the calf the buzzards were eating. It was about a two-year-old calf with the state mark on it; it had been killed and one quarter skinned and cut off, hacked off with an ax. Some convict had killed and sold that quarter for maybe fifty cents or less.

Another time Frankie was rabbit hunting near there and his dog ran a rabbit right into a hollow log. He ran to the mouth of the log to get it out, and there in the mouth was a big ham, about ten pounds of coffee and ten of sugar. Frankie called his dog and got out of there as quick as he could. Most of those trusties were "lifers" who never expected to get free and just wanted a little change in their pockets. I don't believe they ever stole from outsiders, though there was lots of stealing done outside and laid to the trusties. But I never could see why they would need to go outside to steal, as easy as it seemed to be to do inside.

Several plantation owners living near the farm bought all their
supplies, groceries, plough tools, seed, and even mules from trusties,
guards, or sergeants, whoever it happened to be, off the state farm at
the rate of about one dollar for ten dollars worth. Frank ran a gin one
fall for a man whose place joined the farm, and I could tell about lots
of crookedness and stealing that went on off the farm. Frank could
have made himself rich if he had been willing to stoop to that petty
thievery, but he wasn't. Of course we never talked of the stealing
before the children. But I am not writing a history of the state farm,
nor of the men who made their fortunes stealing from it, but of my
own life, which was not all work and no play.

When we moved to Parchman, Bruce was going on five, and we put
him in school with a Miss Gwynn, a kind woman who took lots of
pains with him. He hadn't been going to her a month when he came
home one night the happiest, most excited little boy. He opened his
book for me, pointed to an A, and said "Ahh." Through the whole
alphabet he went making the same sound, no more than a grunt, but it
was a sound. When his father came in, he repeated the performance
for him. Of course we were all delighted. The greatest thing in his
favor was that he paid no attention to ridicule. He started out to learn
to talk, and nothing could stop him.

A night or two after that the children were undressing for bed, and I
was getting the baby ready for bed, waiting for the others to come to
me and say their prayers. That was the sweetest hour in the day for
me, sitting and resting and having them come in their little nighties,
kneel down by me and say their prayers, kiss us goodnight, and go to
bed. Bruce had never taken part in that but had always stood and
looked longingly at the rest. That night without any warning he
dropped down by my side, too, folded his hands, shut his eyes, and
began grunting, making the only sound he could. His father, reading
the paper nearby, looked over the top of it, then raised it to keep me
from seeing him laugh. Just then in walked Edie ready for bed. She
stopped short, her eyes almost popping out with surprise. She stood
just behind Bruce for a minute, than raised her foot and kicked him,
none too gently, saying, "Bruce, don't you know better than that?
What does God know about that grunting? You will have God and all
the angels laughing at you."

Bruce jumped up furious, his fists doubled up, and waded into her for a fight. Leslie stood by, taking it all in, and now she spoke up. "That's right, Bruce. Maybe you can't pray yet, but you can fight."

The only thing that kept that praying time from turning into a child's fight was Frank gathering Bruce up in his arms and carrying him off to bed. When he came back, he said, "Edie, from now on Bruce says his prayers if he wants to, and no remarks from anyone. God understands him the same as He does you. And when Bruce starts talking to any of you, stop and listen to him. He is going to talk. He is so determined he is bound to succeed, and when he does he will make up for lost time."

Frank's prophecy proved true. Bruce followed anyone around that would listen to him continually talking, talking. It was a long time before he formed words clear enough so we could understand him, but in time he came to speak as plain as anyone, unless he got a scare or a severe shock, when he would lose all power of speech for as long as twenty-four hours at a time. But he never lost the use of his other senses; he could run, play, work, and fight as hard as anyone, and his mind was sharp and clear always.

When he got to talking plain enough that we could understand him at all, Leslie would include him in the spelling lessons she would give out at night to Frankie and Edie. He would talk as hard as he could while waiting for his word. It really seemed those first few months his tongue was hung in the middle and working both ends. One night Leslie gave him a word, and he was busy jabbering to his father. When she called his name, he started, and said just as quick, "t-o-e."

She looked so disgusted and said, "Bruce, you know better. You don't even know what word I gave you."

"And I don't care," Bruce came back at her. "I can spell anything I want with 't-o-e'."

I often think, when I turn back to read over the pages I have written here, that I am like Bruce—I can spell anything I want with "t-o-e"; for these forty-five years of reading very little and writing nothing except maybe a few lines of a letter now and then don't seem to have left me much of a speller.

Two families lived close enough to us to be real neighbors. Our nearest church was at Rome, and the roads were so bad we couldn't get there, so those that could and wanted to had their church at home, as Christ taught his disciples to pray, in secret. God smiles on a church of that kind when he knows people can't do any better. Our recreation and amusement was watching over our children, helping them find life and fun when they weren't at work, and making play out of their work, knowing they were working harder than any children in the country their size and age. And they weren't alone, for every moment I was away from my sewing and housework, I was helping them hoe, hoe. Frankie said one day when we were all so tired from work in the field, "If Father was in heaven, he wouldn't be content unless he could get a crew out flatweeding the golden streets."

Frankie was always telling us how easy Mr. Allen, the sergeant of No. 2 Camp, was making work of the same kind we were doing. "You just wait, Mama, till I get to be a big boy, big enough to plough. This old hoeing that's breaking all our backs will be cut out."

But except for making them work so hard, their father was perfect in their eyes. Not one of them would have allowed me to hint anything else, if I had wanted to, which I didn't. I knew they were right. I knew Frank worked far too hard himself, did his work better than anyone else, and expected his children to do the same. When Frankie would tell him of some easy way he had learned at the state farm, Frank would just say, "That's right, son. Pick up all the information you can over there, but be sure you don't pick up anything else."

He saw to it his children were raised to be honest in everything.

I worried about the children not getting to go to school, for some meddlesome, gossipy people had broken up our school of that first year. Frank said, when I would fret about it, "That don't bother me, Mary, for I prefer teaching them at home. Then they won't learn anything but what I want them to. My education has been my greatest handicap ever since I came to America. If I thought they would ever get to England to live—but what is the use of talking? I will teach them when they can't get to a school."

And he did, making it up to them in many ways: got them good books and also trained them, girls and boys alike, to box, to keep their bodies straight and supple and athletic, and to shoot a gun. We weren't afraid of the convicts, but one never knows, and to be on the safe side he taught both little girls to shoot a gun by the time they were six years old. Frankie could shoot when he was five years old, and by the time he was seven and eight, it was hard for a grown man to beat him. They practiced shooting Frankie's .22 rifle. They were all good; Edie was a close second to Frankie in hitting a mark or killing a squirrel, rabbit, bird, or fish. She would go hunting with Frankie, she with his .22 rifle, he with a shotgun, and they never failed to bring back some game. Leslie never cared to hunt but liked to stay at home and help me.

After my morning work of milking, churning, cleaning house, getting dinner and supper at one time, and cutting a dress for someone, I would help the children in the field all afternoon. Then I would come in at sundown and milk, while Leslie finished supper. Bruce always had the wood and kindling in and water pumped for the stock and the house. After we ate supper—which was always a happy meal, to know our day's work was over—while the children did the dishes, I started making the dress I had cut out that morning, and I never got up from the machine till that dress was finished. Every one I made meant a dollar cash, and that was mine. I wasn't supposed to put that in the living fund, but to do as I pleased with it. While we were making those crops I would make a dollar sewing almost every day.

Every Saturday night each child got some money for every little extra piece of work they did over their regular work. If they did it for me, I paid them out of my money; if for their father, he paid them. They spent their money for what they pleased, but we never were afraid of their spending it foolishly. We got them good comfortable clothes, and they had nowhere to wear fine clothes.

Now that I had given up ever owning a home of our own, I had nothing to live for but to make every house we lived in home. That was my one thought all day long and every waking moment at night. I had more time to study my children than ever before. The country was new, and there were few people and no amusements except what we made ourselves. I didn't want my children to remember me with hope gone, seeming to be worn out with work, and in an ugly mood. As they grew, each one so different and to my selfish mind so sweet, I had a job keeping up with them. Whether I was sewing, working in the garden, cooking, milking, tending my chickens, or helping the children hoe, my mind was always with them. And watching them at times like that gave me a thrill. They were my flower garden in my hard years of toil and work and loneliness. As each child was born it was a flower added to my garden, each a new kind, each needing different care and cultivation. I had nothing the modern mother has to help me. I just had to depend on my common sense, believing that as we sowed, so we would reap.

Frankie and Leslie had twenty-five pounds of cotton a day to pick, which went in the family funds; all they picked over that was their own at the regular price. They averaged about a dollar a week of spending money that fall. A Negro woman, Aunt Lizzie, and her children helped Frankie and Leslie pick. Leslie weighed the cotton or saw that it was weighed right and turned the weights over to her father at night. Edie's share was fifteen pounds a day. She went behind every day, but what did she care? She didn't need money anyway for anything but shells, and she could always borrow those from Frankie whether he was willing or not. What little time the children weren't working, Frankie and Edie were off hunting. Bob, as he grew older, never cared to hunt much; he would rather model in clay, like Leslie did.

Through one side of our field a little bayou ran, and beyond it the woods began, with just a pole or small log to cross the bayou on. Frankie had a little dog, a great hunter, the children thought; it would run anything from a chipmunk to a bear, but it liked to run wild hogs best of all. There were lots of them all through those woods—domestic hogs that had strayed off from home and gone wild and raised young. All of them were big, fat, and very, very dangerous. They would come under our wire fence into the corn and do lots of damage. Frankie's dog liked to run in among them and get them chasing him; he could easily outrun them. But the trouble was he would always run straight to the children, and several times they had had to run for their lives from a drove of wild hogs.

One time these hogs, about ten of them, came charging right after the children. They got so close Frankie yelled, "Climb a tree, Edie." She dropped her rifle and climbed a tree just in time to save her life. She would have been torn to pieces in an instant. Frankie managed to get up another tree, and those hogs surrounded them, champing, foaming at the mouth. They thought their time had come, and Edie began to cry. Frankie called his dog. It came back close enough to see and seemed to understand what a scrape it had got them in and what it must do. It charged in among the hogs, and when it got their attention, started off at a swift run, all the hogs after it, straight away from home. The children slid down out of their trees and started for home. At the fence Frankie gave Edie the shotgun, and he took the rifle. He told her to go in the field where Aunt Lizzie and her children were picking cotton, saying, "If the hogs follow the dog back, or catch him, I'll kill some of them." He thought there at the fence he was out of danger.

The dog came racing back in a little bit, having left the hogs all behind but one great big one that he was easily outrunning. But when the dog got within a few feet of Frankie, he called to it. It changed its course and darted off in another direction, but the hog saw Frankie and came straight for him. Instead of shooting as he said he would, he turned and ran as hard as he could, yelling every jump. The hog was gaining on him, and by the time he reached the footlog across the bayou, the hog was right at his heels in the water, which wasn't over a foot deep. Leslie and Edie began to scream and little niggers to run from the field. Aunt Lizzie saw he was going to be killed. In her excitement she yelled, "Shoot, Frankie. If you let dat hawg kill you I'm gwine beat you, boy. Shoot."

She saved him. For he turned and shot the hog in the head. It fell, wounded and squealing. Aunt Lizzie knew the danger of that squealing if any of the others heard it, so she hollered, "Kill hit."

He did. Put a bullet through its brain. They all came to the house, Lizzie sent for her man, and they dressed it. It weighed 150 pounds dressed. I gave them half, for those hogs belonged to no one except the man that killed them.

You would think that would have given those children a scare, but it didn't. Some would think we were wrong for letting them run such risks, be in so much danger, but we couldn't see it that way; we thought it not half as dangerous as running around over the country with bad companions, getting into trouble that they couldn't get out of by climbing a tree.

All my children were truthful and honest and full of fun. But Bruce stood alone among them. He was the best worker of them all, determined in everything he undertook. Bob was the only one that could turn Bruce's mind once he set his head, and Bob could mold him as he could clay. Bob did the planning, and Bruce did all the work for both of them, and all the fighting. For Bob could do no wrong in Bruce's eyes. As Bruce grew older, he was deeper; there was always some surprising trait popping out at unexpected times. He reminded me of a walnut—rough on the outside but fine and sweet on the inside. But he was always nervous.

Edie was made up of laughter, fun, and pure joy of living, happy under all circumstances. Nothing ever worried her and she could see a funny side to everything and everybody. She wouldn't do any housework if she could help it but would work outdoors, milk, tend the stock, ride, hunt, fish, do everything the boys could. At drawing she could beat them all, but she wouldn't draw anything but comic pictures.

Leslie was my standby. She was taking most of the housework off my hands now, and that left me more time to sew. I was getting more than I could do, and I sewed day and night. I would rather sew for the colored people than the white; I could make two dresses for the colored women as quick and easy as one for the white, and all paid me the same price. All a Negro asked was to make a dress fit. I had lots of Negro customers, mostly wives, mothers, sisters, or just plain "women" of the convicts or trusties. They were all sure pay and never came for their dress without the cash. They all liked to primp and strut before my looking glass. If Edie was around she would get her pencil and cardboard and draw their picture. She would catch every little comical thing about them, every expression. One day a woman caught her at it, and instead of getting mad, gave her a quarter for it. After that most everyone that came wanted her picture made at two bits apiece, and I think Edie brought me more work that way. At any rate, from cotton-picking time till after Christmas I made an average of forty dollars a month sewing, at the rate of one dollar a dress; but in order to make my two dresses a day I would have to sew till ten o'clock every night.

One Saturday late that fall a colored woman named Rose brought me two dresses to make for her. She was one-eyed but healthy and good-looking. She brought two other women with her, and they each had a dress for me to make. They were to come the following Saturday to get them. It was six months before I saw those two girls again, and I never did see Rose again.

I heard that she met a horrible fate. I cannot vouch for it as truth since I didn't see it, but I was told on good authority the reason she never came for the dresses she left with me. It seems she was one of several Negro women living around Parchman that bothered around the convict cages a good deal. They had all been notified time after time to stay away, and Rose, the most persistent of them, had been given a few lashes the last time they caught her there. But nothing did any good. Of course the women couldn't get to the men inside the cages, but the men as they passed in and out would slip them money, and their being there kept the men stirred up. Rose was told the next time she came bothering around she would be thrown in the bull pen. She told them, "Dat jest suit me exactly, kaze dat's whar my man is at."

That happened just a few days before the Saturday she brought me her dresses to make. The next day, Sunday, we heard that Rose was sent to the hospital at Jackson but died before she got there. It seems the three of those women went from my house that day straight to the convict camp and were bothering around the convicts, begging money, getting the men all stirred up as that class of women will. The two girls with her were whipped and run off and told never to come through the farm again or they would get the same treatment Rose was getting.

Rose they threw in the bull pen, among fifty or a hundred Negroes that had been penned up for months or years. Of course one night with those fiends was enough. She must have died, as we heard, for she was never seen in those parts again. Six months later the other two girls got off the train at Minot and came for their dresses, but they didn't mention Rose. You may think Rose's treatment was cruel, but people like us, who lived close enough to know the trouble such characters cause among those convict camp gangs, know she got her just dues. I never knew she was one of those chippies till I heard of her fate.

We lived there close to Parchman for over three years; after the first year we moved off Charlie Lawlor's land and leased forty acres of our own joining the state farm on one side, with the line fence only about a hundred yards from our house. On the front our forty joined the Minot place and the railroad, and on the other side and the back was woods, cane, sage grass, and bayou. This sage grass was almost as tall as a man and grew all around the edge of the woods. Whenever a convict would break, he would try and make it to this woods through our field, and if he could get into the sage grass and cane, he stood a good chance to get away.

It was always hard for us to tell whether a convict had broken away or whether they were just training the bloodhounds. Sometimes a convict would come slipping, running zigzag, climbing a sapling, then down again, doubling back on his track; then here came the dogs, always ten of them or more, in full cry, with drivers, trusties, and sometimes a sergeant coming through our fields, cutting fences, running over ploughs, and smashing everything in the way—almost as bad in training the dogs as when they were really after an escaped convict. But they always came back, checked up on all the damage, paid in full, and sent men to fix up all the fences they cut. It always made me shudder to see those dogs. I couldn't help but feel it was cruel and cold-blooded, but it was just.

One time I am thinking of, a Negro came rushing by the house. I was on the porch sewing; Frankie, Edie, and Leslie were just above the house, between the house and the woods, picking cotton. The Negro man darted by the house and ran straight to the children, jumping in the row where they were picking, running, slipping, crawling through the weeds. He didn't speak to them, and they thought him a trainer, for the dogs were already coming, men on horseback, a bigger crowd than usual. They cut the fence and ran over some ploughs, so the children came to the house. As they came, someone asked them if we had seen a Negro. Frankie told them, but the dogs were already on his track and going out of sight in the woods. We were sure they would get him right there, but they turned and were going down next the bayou. Frankie said, "Father, can I take your rifle and run down to the slough? I know where he is headed, and I might as well have that fifty dollars as anyone."

Frank said, "Yes, son, but don't shoot him more than once with that gun, for you might hurt him."

He went out so excited, and I said, "Frank, what did you let him go for? The idea of that child killing for money."

Frank said, "Don't worry. He won't shoot, but if I had told him not to go he would think I was trying to beat him out of getting fifty dollars."

And while we were still talking, he came running back, his eyes so big and nearly popping out of his head. "I couldn't shoot him, Father.

I was standing on the bank and saw something coming towards me, only the head sticking out of the water. I thought it was a dog, but when it got almost to my feet, it jumped up and it was that nigger. He ran at me, and I ran. I was so sorry for him. He was crawling on the bottom, Father."

My! We both knew what that nigger was fixing to do. Take that gun from Frankie and maybe kill him. Before the boy got through talking good we heard the guns, eight or ten shots. Someone screamed, and in about twenty minutes they came back by our house, one trusty carrying the man across his saddle. The crowd wasn't quite as noisy as when they were going, but they were all laughing and talking like they were coming home from a hunt. I don't know whether the man was dead or not, but he was all wet and covered with blood and mud. But such things had to be. It was all in the day's work. As long as there is a prison for criminals, there has to be discipline, and a prisoner that is dangerous and daring enough to run from under the guns is dangerous enough to kill anyone that stands between him and freedom.

One day that fall I sent Bruce to Parchman to the store to get several little things that I must have in a hurry. He wasn't six years old yet, but he was quick and reliable and never forgot one thing. He was gone longer than usual, and when he came in, I could tell something was wrong. I had heard guns, but as there was always so much shooting, Negroes killing rabbits and birds, I had thought nothing of it. I asked Bruce if he was sick, or what had happened to him. He went to the door, pointed down the road, and made the awfullest face of fear and anger. I knew then whatever it was had caused him to lose his speech again. I tried to get him to go lie down, and I went out of the room so he would be quiet.

But as soon as I left the room he must have jumped up, got an old army gun of Frank's, and started off down the road. The first I knew I heard someone talking to him just outside the gate, saying, "Bruce, you can't carry that big gun, let alone shoot it. Besides that nigger is back at work. And there is your mother. Tell her how much you enjoyed seeing him whipped."

It was the driver of one of the hoe gangs and a friend of ours. I said, "What happened to the boy? He can't or won't talk."

He said, "I guess you couldn't talk either, Mrs. Hamilton, if you had just gone through what he has," and he told me.

To get to the store Bruce had to go through the state farm where the highway ran one mile along the railroad, which was graded almost all the way, and in the lowest part was about seven feet high with a culvert about three feet in diameter running under to let the water through. Bruce was coming home and was just opposite this culvert, when a convict jumped from under the guns of a shovel gang, ran straight to Bruce, grabbed him up, and held him in front of him while he backed into that culvert. Guns were popping all round Bruce, while the nigger, who had dropped the boy when he got into the culvert safely, ran down the other side of that high dump and made the woods.

"If there had been one good shot among those crazy trusties, Mrs. Hamilton, that boy would have been killed, for they were so rattled they didn't have sense enough to stop shooting till I stopped them. I was scared so bad myself I could hardly go to the boy when I did get the shooting stopped. I expected to find him shot to pieces, but when I got to him I found him standing against the railroad bank, holding his packages, not hurt, but pale, and the maddest-looking little boy I ever saw. I wanted to bring him home, but he wouldn't let me. He kept listening and pointing up the road to where they had caught the nigger and were bringing him back. I couldn't get him to leave. So when they threw the nigger, he calmly folded his arms and watched the whipping. When it was over, he started for home."

Bruce seemed all right after everything was explained to me, but he was nervous still and couldn't speak. He was restless all night. Next morning he got up as usual, did his work, played, but he still couldn't speak. We knew there was nothing to do but wait till something happened to loosen his tongue. That afternoon Frankie said, "Bruce, I can't see why you didn't ruin those nice new pants while that convict had you backed up against that culvert and all those shots flying around you."

Bruce was awful proud. He jumped up, whirled around, and said, "You shut up. My pants is all right."

His pride had been touched and his voice was back.

But such things as I have just told began to make Frank and me see that that was no place to raise a family, especially as there was no school. About that time the Davises, old neighbors of ours on the Sunflower River, who had sold out to Millen the same time we did and gone to Memphis to live, wrote us making us an offer of a good home in Arkansas, not far from where we lived when we were first married. Mrs. Davis and I had been writing to each other all this time, and she thought it a shame to bring up our children so near the state farm, with no chance to educate them. It seemed Mr. Davis was now a concrete contractor, and while doing some work in Black Rock, Arkansas, had seen a farm, taken a fancy to it, bought it, and now that he had it, didn't know what to do with it. They told us we could have it as long as we wanted it if we would pay the taxes and keep up repairs. It was six miles from Pocohontas, close to a good school and churches, and had a fine orchard, nice dwelling house, and barn. The land, about forty acres in cultivation, was part river bottom, part hill land.

The children were crazy to go. I had never told them much of our life in that country, of their father's bad health there. Frank's health had improved so there didn't seem any chance for his old trouble to come back on him. We both felt we owed it to the children to go. We couldn't dampen their hopes by telling them their father was an invalid when we lived there before. We would be away from a sawmill town and in the country, and maybe his health would stay all right.

The children talked of nothing else after we decided to go. Bob asked me question after question one day when I was busy getting ready to go and trying to get all my sewing done that I had on hand, for we needed the money and I knew money would be scarce in those hills. My mind was running on everything except what Bob was talking about, when he asked me if people living in Arkansas really did have moss on their backs. I said, "I think so, yes," not realizing what he had asked me. But I did later.

I had a shadowy misgiving we were doing wrong to go, but Frank wanted to. So we shipped the things we needed most, enough to keep house with, then sold the rest—cows, calves, horses, corn, and farm tools. We took our baggage, and one fine morning in February, when the country was humming with life—birds singing, Negroes yelling and singing—we bid farewell to our few friends, and to Lucy and her family, and left dear old Mississippi, we thought, forever. It was like burying an old friend to me. I had found my first real happiness here through Frank's health. I wouldn't think of the work, struggles, and fighting our way through this wilderness, for there was so much more happiness than trouble. I hated to leave, but no one, not even Leslie, knew that. My children that were living, all but one, were born there. I remembered our coming to this country, how we had looked on it as an adventure. Going back must just be another adventure. So when we neared Memphis, leaving Mississippi behind forever, I thought then, I quit looking back in my mind and looked forward.

PART THREE

THE END OF THE TRAIL

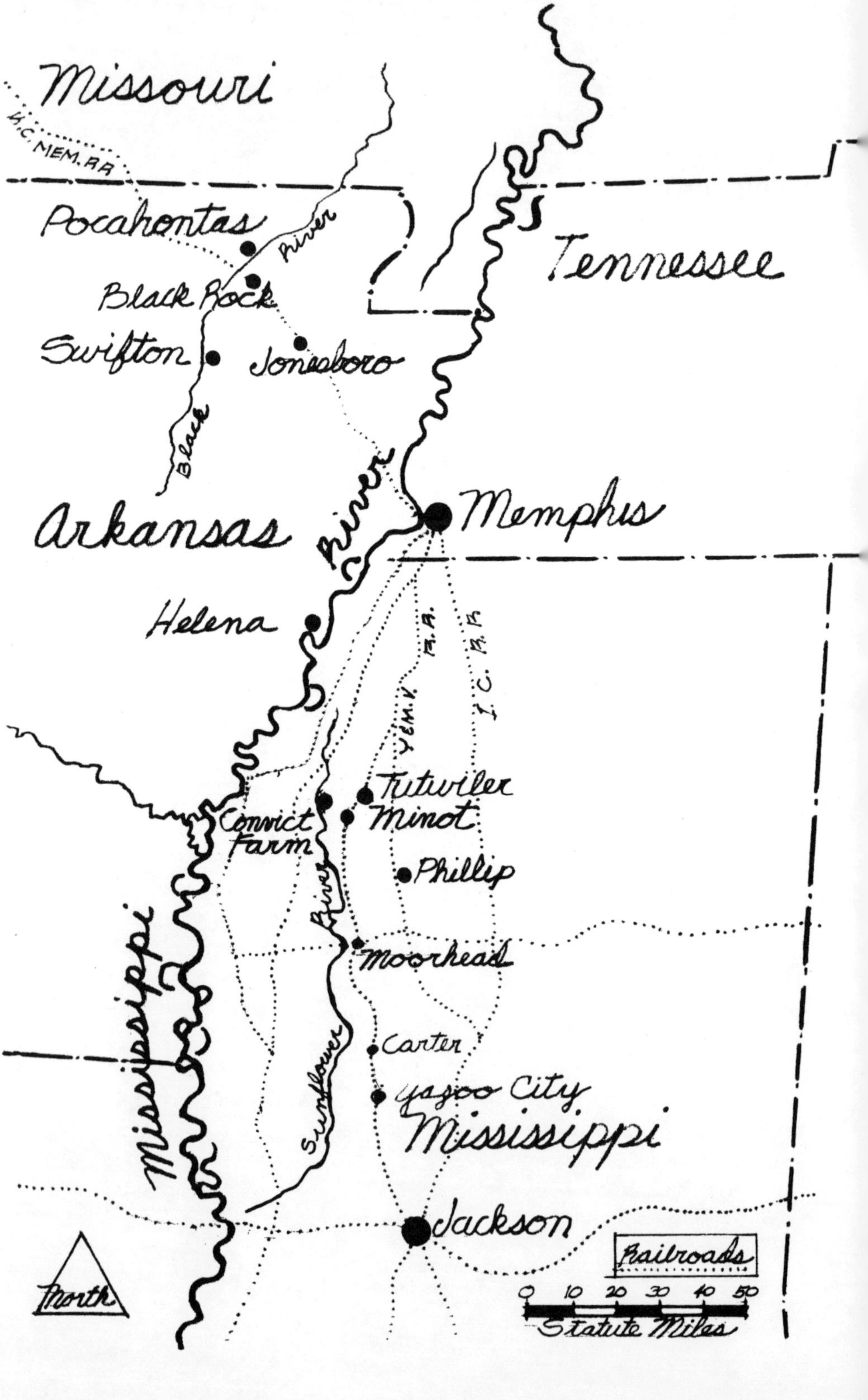

Missouri
K.C. MEM. RR
Pocahontas
River
Black Rock
Swifton
Jonesboro
Black
Tennessee
Arkansas
River
Memphis
Helena
Y & M.V. R.R.
I. C. R.R.
Tutwiler
Minot
Convict Farm
Phillip
River
Moorhead
Mississippi
Carter
Sunflower
Yazoo City
Mississippi
Jackson
Railroads
0 10 20 30 40 50
Statute Miles
North

Arkansas Again

WHEN WE ARRIVED IN POCOHONTAS IN THE WINTER OF 1911, it was cold and there was just enough snow on the ground to make sleighing good. Frank had shipped our goods to a man named John Slayton, and he was at the depot with a good team and sleigh, waiting to take us out to our new home. We were in the foothills of the Ozarks, and the wind came howling and whistling around those hills something fierce. John Slayton wouldn't let us get out when we got to our house; he just stopped there long enough to take in our trunk and suitcases, then insisted on us going to his house for the night. Said it wasn't but a half-mile further, and his wife was expecting us.

They were well-fixed, prosperous farmers, thrifty and shrewd, and were the kindest-hearted people we ever met. We thought so then, and all the time we knew them never had reason to change our minds. We knew the Davises had written them about us, but we never expected such a warm welcome as they gave us. They treated us like old friends. We hadn't been in the house over thirty minutes, when Bob and Bruce, who had been out in the yard playing with Slayton's little boy, Lester, came in, and Lester walked up to his father and said, pointing to Bob, "Papa, that little boy told me to please show him the moss on my back."

I wanted to sink through the floor I was so surprised and embarrassed. I was so afraid it would offend them, but we all laughed it off, and when I got Bob off to myself I gave him a good talking to, explaining what I should have explained to him before, that "mossback" was just a joke, and that he was one himself now that we were living in Arkansas.

That afternoon Frank took the boys, went to our house, and put up stoves, and next morning we all moved into our new home. We found the fires going, the house warm and cozy, and a fine pump of water near. There was a big barn just under the hill and a nice servant's house in the yard—and what a yard! A half-acre, smooth and grassy, never any mud, little shade trees scattered all over it. From our barn on to the Black River was level land, but the strange part to us was that the river bottomland was not very rich, was hard to work and didn't make very good crops of any kind. From the barn up to the house was a steep slope, and on top of that little hill where the house and outbuildings stood, the ground was level again. Then straight away from the house rose a gradual slope up for a mile to the Cherry Hill schoolhouse.

When spring opened up more, with trees putting out their leaves and the orchards blooming, then I loved it; but before the leaves put out we were acquainted with every man, woman, and child for five miles around and liked them all. When you move to the hill country of Arkansas, if you make a good impression on the first family you meet and make friends with them, you are looked on as a friend and neighbor by the whole community. Besides we were half Arkansans already. I had lived there when a girl, and my father, mother, and brother were all buried there on Crowley's Ridge, which we could see from the schoolhouse on top of Cherry Hill. I never was one who could go and visit the graves of loved ones, but someway it comforted me to be nearer them.

The first year we didn't farm much, as most of the cultivated land was just meadowland, but everybody worked hard and played hard, too. The children did the farming with Frankie ploughing that first year, and Frank went to work in the timber. That fall we had some corn, and we made 200 gallons of syrup from our sugar cane. It didn't cost half as much to live as in the Delta. We could get all the cows we wanted to milk, just for feeding them; all we were asked to do was to mark the calves with the owner's mark when we turned them out.

Here every boy and girl in the country worked out, hoeing, picking cotton and peas; so ours did, too. Every day they weren't in their own crop or in school, they were working for our nearest neighbor, John Slayton. How can I go ahead writing of those three happy years in Arkansas, of all the good people? They were all good and fun-loving, but this man Slayton and his wife stood head and shoulders above them all to us. They treated Frank like he was their father. From the start he was Uncle Frank to them, and to my three oldest children they were as a big brother and sister. I think they thought that Frankie and Leslie were hustlers. Also, like I did, they saw that Frank's age was beginning to tell on him. He was working too hard, and the climate wasn't agreeing with him as I had been so afraid it wouldn't. Still, that first year we enjoyed every minute of our lives.

The Cherry Hill school was a fine large school, and all the pupils played baseball. On clear still days when the wind was right, we could hear them hollering on the top of that hill a full mile away. We always believed in having the children's playmates come to our house to play rather than have our children running around over the country hunting amusement, so we made them all welcome. Our yard made the finest baseball diamond, and it was nothing to have from ten to twenty children of all sizes there all day Sunday. No, oh no, I didn't have them all for dinner, but I always made a large dish of cookies, and they would stop their play for a lunch outside under the trees.

But nights were our happiest times, when our family was all alone. We had good books and took several good magazines. Leslie was a fine reader. Her father would select something for her to read to the rest of us, then he would sit reading or writing himself. But if she miscalled a word, which she got so she would do sometimes just to see if she could catch him so deep in his own book he wouldn't notice, he never failed to stop her, pronounce the word correctly and tell them the meaning of it. Sometimes she would be reading of some foreign country they did not understand and would stop and ask him about it. Often as not it would be some place he had been, as he had traveled all over the world it seemed, and he would make it so interesting and plain to us that it made our reading hour a very happy one.

He got so he talked more freely of his nine years in India in the army, of his life in the barracks at the foot of the Himalayan mountains, the wild boar hunting, the soldiers horseback with their carbines; of the green parrots, the magpies, the jackdaws and their pranks, the peacocks that were considered a sacred bird there; and (what the children liked best of all) tales of the thousands of little white-collared monkeys that were thicker there, he said, than squirrels were here. When at last he would stop, and their eager faces and questions could get no more out of him, he would stare into the fire with the strangest look on his face, seeing, I knew, many things he would not tell us. And it made me oh, so sad to see that look, him grieving over something he could not let me share. After the reading was over, then there were lessons. Frank would help the larger ones, I the smaller ones.

Frank's partner in all his timber work was a man named Collins, a widower living alone with his two boys. Will, the youngest, was fourteen, shy and mannerly, and he and Frankie took to each other. Will used to come to our house two or three nights a week and stay till bedtime. We treated him like one of the family, and one day when I asked him if he could remember his mother, he said, "No, for I wasn't but two when she died. I never missed her until you all came here, but now I think it great for a fellow to have a mother."

And I on my part thought it great to be able to be a friend to a boy like that, to make life happier for him. It eases many an ache and rests you when tired to know you can help some lonely child besides your own.

On the sixteenth of November of our second year, Frank's birthday, I was fixing his usual birthday dinner. All the children were doing their part, each in his way. Frankie told Will he was going to go duck hunting to kill his father some ducks, and Will said he would go squirrel hunting. He asked me if I would cook all he and Frankie killed, and I said "Yes, but to be safe I'll roast a couple of chickens."

Just as I got my chickens in the roaster the boys came back. Frankie had four ducks, Will six squirrels. How we did work to get them on. Dinner was late of course, but such a dinner when it was ready! Will and his father took dinner with us.

Every day was crowded with some new pleasure. What I liked about that country was you seldom ever heard of clashing, fighting, or quarreling among neighbors. I remember one time though, a hotheaded neighbor of ours named Jones got mad at Frank over some trifle. Frank knew nothing about it. We were just sitting down to the breakfast table one cold morning when Jones hollered outside. Frank stepped to the door and invited him in, when to Frank's surprise, Jones said, "No, I won't come in. I came up here to give you a damned good licking. Come on out."

Frank saw he was drinking, and he said, "I am surprised at you,

Jones, wanting to fight before breakfast. Come on in and eat breakfast, drink a good hot cup of coffee with me and that will warm you up so you can fight better. You're cold and numb and I could step out there and easily whip you now, but with a good hot breakfast under your belt you might whip me."

I stepped to the door then and invited him in, too. He came in, ate a hearty breakfast, and drank two cups of coffee. He seemed to enjoy it, and before the meal was over he was the merriest one of us all and seemed to have forgot he came to fight. They all went over to the fire together after breakfast and when Frank asked him if he wanted to step outside now and fight, he stuck out his hand and Frank shook hands with him.

"That's better," Frank said. "Fighting is hard on old clothes and nerves, and besides, I'd hate to have my wife and children see me get licked."

After he left Frankie said, "Father, why didn't you whip him?"

Frank laughed. "Yes, son, I could whip him easy, for he was too cold and hungry and mad to fight. But there's no honor and nothing brave about whipping a man in that condition. But I would like to know what he was mad about." But he never did find out, and probably the man didn't know himself when he got sober.

The second year we were there Frank bought two fine big fat horses but was still doing timber work himself, the children just making a small crop of our own. Those horses were running in the pasture with nothing to do over half the time. So Frankie and Leslie put their heads together to study some plan besides working out by the day to make some money, as their own crop didn't keep them busy half the time. They went to a man living near us that had more land than he could work, and he told them they could have all the land they would work. Then they went to John Slayton for advice. He asked them what their father thought about it, and Leslie said, "He doesn't know about it; if he did he wouldn't allow us to do it, but if we can make the trade, get a contract made and signed, he won't let us fall down on our contract. We are a little uneasy about his letting us have the horses, is all."

It tickled Slayton to see how gritty they were, and he said, "Go ahead, and make your trade. I will back you and lend you horses free of charge, or feed, any time you can't get your father's."

They made their trade and drew up a contract, all signed. Even the man that let them have the land looked on it as a joke. He couldn't work the land himself so didn't care. Of course I knew all about it and approved of it. Then one night they showed their father the contract. He looked at it. It was for fifteen acres of land.

He said, "You two think you are smart, don't you?"

Leslie said, "No, but we are not lazy, if that is what you mean. We're tired of working out by the day, and we are getting big enough now to help make the living, and we want to make money enough to get our school clothes, and why not let us make it the easiest way, and put those lazy horses to work?"

Frank said, "All right. You can have the horses every day I am not using them; but our crop at home must not suffer for the want of work."

Next morning they took their dinner and a jug of water, put their plough and hoes in the wagon, and were off by daylight, all five of them, the happiest, most important-feeling kids. They were real farmers now. Frankie went to breaking his land for peas, while the rest got the cotton land cleaned up. Well, they made their crop, worked the crop at home, and gathered it all; and that extra came in so handy, for Frank had bad luck over some timber and lost more than we could afford—in fact, so much that it cut out Frankie's going to school that fall altogether. When the children sold their cotton, they were able to get good clothes to do them all winter, and they turned the rest, better than a hundred dollars, over to their father.

This was before the world war, when people in that country were plain; rich and poor lived alike, worked, and went to church on horseback or in a wagon or walking. They didn't put on style, just dressed neat and nice, and they were the healthiest people I believe I ever saw. When there was sickness it was generally among people that had moved in from other parts of the country for amusement or profit.

Pearling on the Black River was at its height. The mussels were opened, washed, dried, and sold by the hundred pound for button makings. Sometimes one of them would have a pearl, some worth a dollar, some worth several hundred dollars. I believe those pearl buyers could smell a pearl a hundred miles, and here would come motorboats, three or four. The news would spread, and the youngsters would collect up and go swimming, feeling with their feet for the mussels. When they found one, they would hold their hand over their nose and duck or dive for it. They could tell by looking at the outside whether they had a pearl and whether it was a valuable one or a cheap one, which they called a "rosebud," far prettier, I thought, than the real pearls. Most of the pearls were found in mussels they called "washboards."

I went often with the children all through that summer, to watch them play in the clear, shallow, rock-bottomed water and on the sand bars. I was afraid they would get drowned unless I was along to save them if they got in deep water. How I was to save them was a mystery even to me, as I couldn't swim a stroke.

At last, through all the family working hard, we were putting away some money against a rainy day. I was worrying a good deal about Frank. His old trouble was coming back on him in a mild form of Bright's disease. He was gradually getting worse, but he went ahead. The children all knew he was far from well that third year, but he seemed more cheerful than ever and took a more active part in his neighbors' lives, his friends, his work. Nearly everyone around there belonged to a farmers union. Frank joined. But most of the Arkansas people didn't need any kind of union or anything else except their natural goodness to be neighborly and kind to each other and strangers.

As fall drew nearer so we could have a fire nights, how we enjoyed gathering around the fireplace, reading and talking over the day's affairs! The girls were going to school. One night Leslie said, "Father, we have some questions to answer tomorrow and I am puzzled. Maybe you can help me."

He laid his book down and said, "Let's hear them."

She said, "One is, 'Who are your ancestors? Where were your father and your mother born and of what nationality are they?' I have written that Mama was born in Illinois, and her father and mother as well; that her parents on both sides were Scotch and Dutch. Father never had any ancestors, not even a father or mother. He just came up overnight like a mushroom. He thinks that happened in England, as his passport to America was made out in England. What do you think of my answers?"

He laughed and said, "I think you are just plain lying, or that teacher is fishing for information, and I won't answer. But I have been thinking lately a good deal. If we don't have any more bad luck and can keep putting by some more money, by March I would like to go back to England. You children are getting large enough to go ahead now for a while. I would be gone about four months. Then when I got back I could bring you all proof to show you you have a right to be proud of your father's blood."

They all spoke up, telling him they were proud of him anyway and couldn't love him more if he was the king of England. But he saw how eager they were for him to talk, and he knew that was why Leslie had spoken as she did. He talked to us more that night than he ever had before—of his home, his church, his old schooldays; of a bell in his school that had one boy's name carved in it in one direct line of his family for over six hundred years; of the church register with all their names, all belonging to that church, christened as babies for over six hundred years. Then he turned to Leslie.

"So when your teacher asks you if your father wasn't an infidel, you'll know what to tell him. I can think of no greater joy than to know all your names would be entered in the same book."

But with all his talk we were as much in the dark as ever. And I think the children as well as I had a feeling of some shadow hanging over us, that these sweet family talks couldn't last.

Just a few days after this, Frank got a letter from Black Rock, offering him a job. It wouldn't last but a month, grading and shipping lumber. I was so glad for him, for it meant that the trip to England, which I could see he was counting on so much, was nearer. He went to Black Rock, and the children and I finished picking the cotton. We had a pretty good hill crop that year. School was out till after Christmas.

We got every bit of our farm work done—corn gathered, cotton all picked. Made our regular two hundred gallons of syrup that fall. I had put by plenty of fruit, canned and dried, and had stored and canned vegetables enough to do us all winter. Our winter work all done, we looked forward to a winter rest. At least I did. I had not had much rest since I was married, and now as the children were getting large enough to go ahead, I felt I needed some. Must have some so I could go ahead and take Frank's place as well as my own, if he got to go to England in the spring as he was planning. I had got over wondering about his past, or feeling that it would ever concern me; but when I saw how anxious he was to go, how his face lit up at the thought of his home, why, then for his sake, and for the children's, I was anxious. They had a right to know who their father was, what blood flowed in their veins. I must do everything to help them. We could live some way while he was gone. He must go. So my thoughts ran every wakeful moment.

But Death—

Frank wrote me from Black Rock that he would be home in a few days, and that he and Collins were to go to Swifton to look at some more timber. He wrote that if the children and some of their schoolmates wanted to go along, he would take the wagon. Of course they soon had a load anxious to go.

When Frank got home, he told me he had been hurt that morning loading their last carload of lumber. He was standing with his book checking the lumber as they shoved it into the car, and a careless Negro let a heavy plank slip. It struck Frank in the lower part of his bowels. He said it made him so sick and dizzy all day, and that he didn't feel like making the trip to Swifton next day. I urged him not to try it, but when morning came he said he couldn't disappoint the children, and that he would be all right, except he was so stiff and sore. He wouldn't let me tell the children about his hurt, and so they started off.

I was a little uneasy about Frank, but not enough to dampen Bob's and Bruce's high spirits. They were the only ones left behind, and they had thought of a thousand things to do while their father and the older children were gone. First they wanted to go to the orchard and gather the late apples. It was a beautiful day for late fall. The hills were all red and gold leaves blowing, falling to the earth. Bob asked me if I believed those leaves dying meant people dying, and I told him, "No, oh no. It means winter is coming, bringing rest, peace, and happiness to those whose work has been well done."

Bob said, "Yes, and Thanksgiving, and Father home for dinner. But how can we have a Thanksgiving dinner with Leslie and Edie and Frankie gone?"

Bruce said, "Don't you worry about them. They are all right. You hurry and help with these apples."

They climbed the tree, picked, and put the apples in baskets. I picked all I could reach from the lower branches. When we got all we could get that way, we shook all the rest off for early use. That night we sat by the fire and wrapped the hand-picked ones in paper, like oranges, to put away for Christmas. As we worked I was so happy and contented. I felt as if all my life I had been struggling through a dark woods, with just glimpses of sunshine along the way, and now here in Arkansas we had at last broken through the woods to a great bright sunlit clearing. We were busy talking and planning our Thanksgiving dinner, for Frank would be back for Thanksgiving but was going to leave the children in Swifton for a few days. Bob and Bruce wanted to surprise their father by buying the Thanksgiving dinner things themselves.

"But where will we get the money?" Bob asked.

Bruce as usual had an answer. "We will go over to Brown's and pick cotton if Mama will go with us."

Of course I went. We took our dinner and I helped them some. How they did work and plan! They wanted to earn enough to buy a small turkey if they could just pick fast enough. Their little hands flew and their tongues, too. When we went home Wednesday night before Thanksgiving, they were the happiest little boys you ever saw, with two dollars and a half in their pockets. As we walked home they decided they would go straight on up the road and get their turkey, and I would start baking and getting things ready for dinner the next day.

But before we got in the house Mr. Collins drove up in the wagon with Frank. He helped Frank out of the wagon and into the house, and then either because he was scared or didn't think Frank was bad off, he went right on. I got Frank's clothes off, and Bruce and I got him in bed. He could walk by himself and I couldn't think he was dangerously sick, but when he went to lie down he fainted. That scared me and I sent Bruce for John Slayton. It didn't take him long to come and Collins was with him. Slayton went for a doctor, and Collins told me what had happened.

Instead of Frank's getting better after they left that morning, he got worse and worse, as the jolting of the wagon over those rough roads was terrible. He suffered all day and all night, and as the children were planning on staying in Swifton anyway, he managed to keep them from knowing how sick he was, bid them all good-bye, and got Collins to bring him back home. On the way he got worse, was delirious and so bad off that Collins stopped and got him to a doctor. The doctor said that hurt with the plank had caused his suffering and nothing but an immediate operation would save him. Frank was out of his head, and Collins didn't know any better than to let that doctor go ahead. The doctor made an incision that punctured his bladder and intestines and left him in that condition. Mr. Collins brought him on home in the wagon, over twelve miles.

As Collins finished telling me this, Slayton came in with our doctor. The doctor came in, looked Frank over, and didn't say anything except to send me to the kitchen for warm water. But I could still hear them. Frank said, "I've been left in bad shape, haven't I, Doctor?"

The doctor said, "Bad? You may as well know the truth, Hamilton. You can place a murder charge against the butcher that did that work. I can do you no good, and nobody else can."

When I heard him say that, I ran back into the room. Surely he was joking, but when I saw Frank's poor face, I knew. He had jumped straight up out of the bed and was standing on the floor, and oh, such a look on his face—despair, and anger, too. He said, "That is not news to me, but for God's sake, break it more gently to my wife."

Then he saw me. I don't know how I managed to get across the room to him. "Frank, Frank," I cried, "you know it's not true. You know you're not going to die."

It was too sudden. I couldn't think it was true. The room was still. It was a shock to everybody. I could hear little Bob and Bruce crying. Frank was the first of us to speak again. He said, "Doctor, you may as well get it over with. At least you can tell her it won't be soon."

The doctor said, "I wish I could, but you can't live twenty-four hours, Hamilton."

Frank was back on the bed now, and so white. He said, "Yes, I will live a week or more, but I want the children."

Oh, my God. Twenty-four hours. How could I bear it? He looked so pitiful, so helpless. Hundreds of times before I had seen him sick, suffering, but I could always help him. Now I could do nothing. I never once had dreamed the time would ever come when I couldn't shield him. But death . . . I was helpless. I remembered how when I first saw his face white with pain, many years ago, I wondered if the strange feeling I had for him could be love, and now that we were coming to the end of our trail, I knew that it was love. Oh, how I loved him, always had loved him—better than all my children—but what could I do to make him know it in twenty-four hours?

I heard the doctor ask him if he had all his affairs straight, if he had any insurance to leave his wife.

"No insurance but my children, the best on earth. They will take care of her as long as she lives. They are worth more than all the money on earth would be to her." Then he looked at the doctor and smiled and said, "Sir, how many men have you given twenty-four hours to live and then asked them if they have their worldly affairs straight? You don't give a man much notice. When you go back to town, I will have you send a wire to my children."

He asked for pencil and paper and wrote out a telegram to the children, saying, "Come at once. Father dangerously ill." He gave it to the doctor and told me to give him money to pay for it. The doctor gave me a lot of medicine to be given him every half-hour day and night, inserted a rubber tube in that incision to carry off the poison, shook hands with him, and left.

News flies fast and everyone in the country came next day, all so kind and good, offering every assistance and sympathy. Frank told us all that the doctor had alarmed us unnecessarily. "I can never get well. I knew that as soon as I came to myself and found out what that doctor had done, but I will last for days, maybe weeks. But to be on the safe side, I want you, Slayton, and Collins, my best friends, to help me. I owe a few dollars around here, and I want to settle up with everyone and get that off my hands in case something does happen."

He asked for writing material, made out a complete statement of every dollar he owed, and gave it to them with the money to settle up. Everyone wanted to help sit up nights with him, but he told them all he would rather they go home and get their rest.

"Mary can sit by me," he said. "She is used to waiting on me. She can rest in a rocking chair and sleep. She can do everything that is needed. The children will be close, and she can wake them if anything happens."

He felt like me, he didn't want them; good friends as they were, he would rather we be by ourselves. He was going about his preparations so calmly that the shock, the horror of it all, had kind of worn off, but when we were alone at last, with everyone out in the yard, we had a chance to talk. I could do nothing but cry, hard as I tried not to. He put his arms around me and told me not to cry, as it would only make it harder; we must face it for the children's sake without flinching.

"We must both be cheerful, Mary. They must look on this as something that comes to all, to be met calmly. I am so thankful I was called first, so you will be able to take care of me and be with the children when I am gone. They will need you."

I said, "Frank, tell me if I have ever done anything to you so wrong you can't forgive me. If I have to lose you, it must be with a clear conscience."

He laughed, and said, "The idea of you thinking of a thing like that, Mary. Of course we have had our little spats, as all people who live together do, but I have never for one moment been anything but glad that I married you—but time is too short to talk about things like that. In case the children don't get here, or I should be unconscious when they come, I have so much to tell them."

And he gave me messages for them, mostly to Frank, how he must go ahead, as the responsibility for the family would rest now on his sixteen-year-old shoulders.

"But he knows," Frank said. "We have talked together so much he knows what is expected of him. He is honest and a good worker; he has a head of his own that will be hard to lead off. He must take my place with Bob and Bruce. He has but one fault; he is going to expect too much of them. He must be patient with them."

He was so still for a few minutes that I thought he had dropped off to sleep; then he opened his eyes and said, "Mary, there is something else I have always promised you I would straighten out, but I am afraid now I won't have time. To explain it all now would only make the children discontented, because they couldn't claim their right to something they can't prove when I am gone. It would take money and influence, and you won't have either. If I had got to take that trip home instead of the one that I am about to take . . . I wonder if it is a judgment sent on me, Mary. God help me. It is too late."

Then he asked for Bob and Bruce and for something to eat. He ate to the last, but every drop of water, coffee, milk, and all medicine worked out through that tube as fast as he drank it. The children came home the next day, heartbroken; but he met them all with a smile, telling them they mustn't take it so hard, it only unnerved him and them, and they must help him fight for life, for if he was to stay with us a few weeks he must keep every ounce of strength he had. But as the days passed, he lost weight and strength so fast he was just a shadow of himself.

For five weeks I sat by him all night long, never taking my clothes off, except to change them twice a week. The weather was cold but we managed to keep the house around seventy degrees. I would put a large quilt in a big rocking chair and fold it all around me except for one hand. I kept one hand always on his bed, so at his least move I could be up. I never missed giving him a dose of medicine. Some nights he was restless. Then we would talk. Maybe he would wake me up to tell me of some little thing he had forgotten to be looked after after he was gone. Always he made it seem like he was going off on a trip and wasn't taking it any more seriously than that. The neighbors all humored him in this. Every time anyone came in they would bring him something—an apple, a choice bit of meat, some little gift. How his eyes would light with pleasure! Leslie or Edie stayed with him daytimes while I washed and sterilized everything about him.

If he suffered, and I know now he must have suffered terribly, he never let us know it. Sometimes he would sort of faint away, but when he came to himself he would always say it wasn't any pain, just his medicine made him swoon like that. His mind was clear, except for once in a while when the medicine would make it wander. Then he would ramble and talk of his soldier days in India. All at once he would salute some superior officer or would call Mr. Slayton or Mr. Collins his bodyguard and give him orders in Hindustani. He would sing his old war songs, sometimes snatches of hymns, but he always ended by trailing off in Hindustani.

When the family was all alone we would talk and read as usual. He insisted on that. To everyone but me he seemed better. My brother-in-law, Charlie Lawlor, came from Mississippi to see him. Charlie was so sure he stood a chance to live if he could just get to Dr. Johnson in Memphis. Why he thought so I don't know, for he knew Frank's bladder had been severed and since his arrival home had been removed entirely. How could Charlie think there was a chance for him to get well? It was just talk, and I knew it. I knew nothing but pure grit and determination had kept Frank alive this long. I told Charlie that Frank couldn't stand the trip, but the rest of them persuaded him to go. The children all talked to him, telling him just to live, to stay with them as long as he could, even if he never walked another step.

"We will work for you, Father," they cried, and I said, "Yes, Frank, yes, we want you. I don't see how we can live without you. But do what you think best about trying the trip to Memphis."

Frank said, "Charlie thinks we could get along better in Mississippi. The land is better there and it won't be so hard on the children to make a living. I think it best for us to go. You can take me to Memphis and go on to Charlie's. He is leasing a place at Minot for you. Yes, it is best; Charlie convinced me before he went back, and we must go. Whichever way Dr. Johnson decides, it is best for you and the children to be in Mississippi, and if I die I want to be laid to rest in Mississippi. This doctor here will go with me to Memphis."

So we made arrangements to go, but my heart was heavy and I couldn't see it as anything but wrong to leave our home and friends there, with Frank in the shape he was in. If I could just have known how to get in touch with Jim Thompson. But we had never heard from him since the day we told him good-bye at Concordia Island and started our circling around in the wilderness of the Delta. I believe he wrote us, but we never got the letters. I had no choice but to let Charlie Lawlor take the reins as he so clearly wanted to do.

We were to start the following Sunday morning. The neighbors all came and offered their help. Some of them would stay with the children till we sent for them, and if Frankie took the team and wagon through by land, Will Collins would go with him. I will never forget the goodness of a single one of those people. It was hard to tell who was the best, they were all so good.

Sunday morning came, and everyone came to see us off. John Slayton brought his buggy to take Frank to the river, a mile away. There we were met with a boat to take us to Black Rock to catch the train to Memphis. Slayton and Collins went with us to take care of Frank. They stayed with us all night at the hotel, helped him on the train, bid him good-bye and Godspeed to health and happiness, and told us again not to worry one moment about the children, for they would be seen to. After they left Frank said, "I am wondering which of those two men I like best. They have both been the best of friends in all things."

Yes, everyone had been good to us, but John Slayton and his wife stood by us through sickness, trouble, and happiness. Not because we had money, but just because they were good.

To leave our friends and our children saddened us both. I thought Frank was going to break down. The doctor came and sat down by him to see how he was standing the trip, and he cheered up and began to look around. There was a bunch of college boys in the train, going back to school, shouting and singing. He brightened up and seemed to enjoy it so much. They sang snatches of every silly song they could think of, ending up every one with "Three Blind Mice," one of the songs Frank used to sing for the children when they were small. I almost prayed they would sing some of Frank's favorite hymns, and just before we got to Memphis, they did, one after another. Just as the train was slowing up for Memphis they began singing "Abide with me, Fast falls the eventide," his old Church of England song. His eyes filled with tears; mine did, too, but I kept my head turned away. I wondered if those foolish boys would ever know they had entertained a dying man with his own college songs and church hymns and what pleasure they had given him.

Charlie met us and took us to Dr. Johnson. Of course he could do nothing. He gave Frank hopes of a later operation, if he would go down to Mississippi, rest, drink plenty of milk, and eat anything he wanted, as nothing would hurt him. But when Dr. Johnson removed from his side the tube that was carrying off the poison, I couldn't help crying out. I knew that meant the end. But Frank thought the doctor knew best. He was like a man waiting to be sentenced to death. And after he had begun to hope a little, it was more pitiful than the first time the doctor told him he would die.

I wrote the children to sell out all except what we needed, for I must get Frank started to Mississippi. I thought they would have enough to pay their way and for Frankie to drive through on. After posting the letter, I determined to devote every moment of my time, every thought, to Frank. I paid our hotel bill (Dr. Johnson refused to take one cent for his examination) and our train fare to Tutwiler, kept back ten dollars, and turned the rest over to Charlie, eighty dollars, to bear all expenses. It was all we had in the world, and Frank's lodge friends had furnished some of that.

"Abide with Me"

EVERY HOPE WAS GONE. I could only pray the children would get to us in time. Lucy and Charlie did everything they could to make Frank comfortable, but he was in low spirits. He was bothered about the children, about Frankie more than all. He knew Frankie had a bad trip ahead of him driving through the country, and he knew, now that it was too late, that we had made a great mistake in leaving Arkansas. The friends we had left in Mississippi were gone now, or dead, all but my sister's people, and a Mr. and Mrs. Owens. They were the same good friends, but Frank missed people coming in every hour through the day to see him, and he missed the children.

I would read to him and talk to him, but the one really bright spot in those weeks there was a Mr. Ferguson of Rome, a Baptist preacher, who came every day to see him. Frank enjoyed that man and their talks, sometimes about religion, sometimes about travels, sometimes just about ordinary everyday affairs. He would read to Frank from the Bible and from other good books. One day after he left, Frank said to me, "Mary, have you ever thought of my trouble with the Baptist Church in Missouri causing me to come to Mississippi in the beginning and now this Baptist preacher trying to put me right for my last trip? He is a fine fellow, and his church is all right. I can see how the fault was mine in not sizing up the men rather than the church."

I asked him if he had thought of joining the church, if he would feel better satisfied, but he answered me right quick. "No, I belong to the Church of England. Once a member of that church, always a member. I have lived and I expect to die in it. I know I have not always lived right, but who does? One thing, I won't hide behind a church. I believe I have atoned for my sins right here on earth. I will face my Maker with a clean slate in not leading others astray. I have been as virtuous as any woman. My only sin has been to myself, and I have been honest and straight with everyone else."

I commenced to cry. I couldn't help it. I went to him and said, "Frank, have you been honest with me and your children? I don't care for myself any longer; life is too near over for me, but how can you leave them with a cloud hanging over them? You say you are going to test Mr. Ferguson's religion; why not test his friendship, too? Tell me everything before him; so if the children need help he can help them go to the right one; or better still, just tell the children and me. You can trust us. Tell the children just for their own satisfaction and peace of mind. You don't need to tell me. I have not asked you for myself, but just for them."

Just then Lucy came in, and that stopped all talk for the time.

I was sorry I spoke as I did, for he was restless afterwards and seemed worse, but the children came in on the four o'clock train and that cheered him. They had so much to tell; he asked so many questions. We got a letter from Frankie the next day. Frank was so glad, and he kept the letter under his pillow. I don't know how many times he read it, always with tears in his eyes. One time he murmured, "God help my boy to get here in time, and I will make it all right."

The next day Mr. Ferguson came to see him and Frank talked more than ever before, describing more of his travels and his life as a soldier; then he brought the talk around to his beliefs, telling something of our life and how he had helped to bring up his children to be honest, clean, and truthful and to serve God in their own way, to believe, to have faith in prayer. He ended up, "I have tried to see my children were brought up in faith as I was, and now I want to ask you, sir, if I was to give up my church and join yours, let you baptize me, do you think I would stand a better chance of heaven?"

"No, indeed," Mr. Ferguson said quickly. "One church is as good as another. You have been baptized; confess your sins to God alone. He alone can save you."

Frank said, "Thank you, sir. That is the way I feel about it."

I have wondered many times since then if Mr. Ferguson didn't, with those words, seal Frank's lips. For the next day he spoke to me again and for the last time of his past life and asked me to release him from his promise to tell me who he was before he died. It was after we had got through bathing and dressing him as usual. He was so weak and frail, but still brave, and it wrung our hearts to see him so.

He turned to me and said, "Mary, I am worse. I can't live to see Frankie. I want to ask you something and I will abide by your answer. If I tell you, and a dying man won't lie, that you are my lawful wife and my only one, and swear to it as a dying man, can you be satisfied? If Frankie had got here, I had determined to tell all, but what I could tell would benefit none of our children but Frankie. Our property in England is entailed and would go to the oldest boy. I am the youngest of four boys; everything is in my oldest brother Robert's name. We are an old family, with a good old name, but no longer rich, and there are too many between the property and me. Bob's wife never had any children. My second brother was an old bachelor, my third was in Australia. He and I had some money left to us by my mother. It was invested in Australia, but Bob claimed I ran through my part in the military school and the army. We had some trouble when I came to America, nothing dishonest on either part, but I left, angry at them all, and swore I was dead to them all." He squared his jaw and said, "Yes, dead, buried long ago, and I can do no good to anyone by opening that grave; when this body is buried now that secret is safe forever."

He laughed. "I cheated them, didn't I, Mary? Dead to them all and living thirty happy years of married life with you." Then with another laugh more pitiful than a cry would have been, he said, "I will be the first of my family to be laid outside the family vault. I will be glad to rest in America, near my American children. What do you say, Mary? May I go in peace?"

"Oh yes, yes," I cried. "What does it matter to us, if it matters so much to you?" Leslie had come in, and Edie, and they both said, like me, that all we wanted was to see him contented.

Just then Bob came in, and Frank laid his hand on Bob's head and said, "As long as Bob lives, you have me with you. Even after I am gone, if they ever send anyone from home trying to trace me, they will know they are on the right track if they run across Bob. But the family likeness runs through all my children. May God do better by them than I have."

That was the last he ever spoke to us, for after that he grew steadily worse. He talked, rambling most all the time, and when he talked it was always in Hindustani, except for one time. One time he cried out, his eyes shining, "Yes, Mother, I can see you up there at the top of those glorious old Himalaya Mountains in the sky; yes, up, up there, flowers as high as the eye can see." Then he wandered off into Hindustani again. He was with his soldier friends, talking a language strange to us—sometimes singing, giving orders, or storming out at his bodyguards. Was it to guard his secret to the end that even when his mind was rambling, he talked in a language we couldn't understand? I think it was. I know it wasn't because his memory of that country and his soldier life was sweeter than his life with us.

He lived on, unconscious part of the time and delirious the rest, till the evening of January the twenty-eighth. Blood poisoning had set up, and we knew he couldn't last many more hours. I asked Mr. and Mrs. Owens to sing something, see if they couldn't soothe him that way. They began singing, "Abide with me, Fast falls the eventide." He lay so quiet for a moment, smiled, and was gone.

Oh God, how could I stand it? We thought we were prepared to meet it, but we weren't. He was so peaceful, so sweet. I was so lonely. We all went out under the stars that he loved so well. I was half-crazy with grief. I told them, "I want to bathe and dress him. He would want me to. If I could know he would be taken care of, if I could know he would be as happy in heaven as he was here with us."

We tried to comfort each other, widow and orphaned children, with one of us not here but somewhere between Arkansas and Mississippi trying to get to his father. Frankie was the only Frank Hamilton left on earth to me now. "Oh, if Frankie had been with us," I cried.

Loving, practical Leslie spoke up and said, "I am glad he was spared."

A telephone message from Frankie called me back into the house. He was in Helena and had run out of money. It would cost five dollars to stand some kind of inspection to get his team across the river. I had seven of my ten dollars left. I gave it to Charlie and he said he would go and see about getting Frankie across the river, but when he got there Will Collins, who was with Frankie, had sold some pearls he had in his pocket, and they were on this side in Mississippi. I begged Charlie to put off Frank's funeral till Frankie could get here, but he said, "No, I have made all arrangements. It can't be put off."

I could do nothing. We understood we were alone. Poor little Frankie got there just after we got home from the funeral and never even saw his father again. But he got his father's dying message, and he knew his father depended on him. That was enough. He squared his sixteen-year-old shoulders and said, "Mama, we will move tomorrow."

Neither the Red Silk

WE HAD BROUGHT FRANK BACK TO A LONG REST in his beloved Delta, the place where he worked so hard to open up the country and make homes for hundreds of other people, yet owned nothing himself but the six feet of earth where his poor little body will rest till the end of time. We, his wife and five children, were left to carry on the home, with nothing to go ahead with but good health for the children and a sweet memory of their father. Our love for him outweighed the mystery of his life, and we all felt it was right and honorable for him to carry his secret to the grave with him if he wished. Whatever it was, he was now forgotten by all but his wife and children, who would believe in him and love the memory of him forever.

The next day, the lonely day after his death, we moved to Minot, onto land leased by Frank just a week before he died, from a son-in-law of Frank's old friend, Captain Thomas. We took up our new life, all mystery forgotten, all wrong, if any there was, forgiven. Minot was our old home, and we had been gone from there only three years, but all of our old neighbors were either dead or moved away, and we were among strangers in a strange country.

After we got moved and paid the freight on our goods, we had one dollar among us. We spent it for a broom for me and some nails for Frank to repair the barn. But those children had $10,000 worth of grit and determination. By Frank buying up scrap cotton and picking it out, by trapping, by raising our own corn and meat, and by all hands, even the little boys and me, working our own crop early and late with every ounce of strength we had, we managed not to starve that year.

Bob was so little Frank had to saw off his hoe handle, and Bruce did his first ploughing when he was so small he had to stand on his tiptoes to reach the plough handles. Edie was willing and a good worker, but Leslie took sick soon after we moved, and the doctor said it was tuberculosis. I was sure it was just a general breakdown from the worry and strain that had been on her small shoulders the past months, all her life in fact, but she needed a rest, so she took the treatment at home. It wasn't a complete rest either, for she helped the children with their lessons when they had time for lessons, and nothing changed her from a sweet, steady little girl, always ready to help anyone in trouble. She was a steadfast Christian and made us all listen to her read a full chapter from the Bible every night, in spite of the children's fidgeting at the long ones. Frank's death had brought us all nearer to God. Made us all feel we had more to live for and far more to die for.

I don't know how I could have done without Leslie that first year. I had nursed Frank, worked day and night for him and my children and home, and even a work of pleasure and love kept up for thirty years will break the stoutest one. I missed Frank. I could see no way to live. It is strange that the more our loved ones depend on us the harder it is to give them up. I would never break down before the children, or give way to my feelings, and they were the same. We talked as little as possible, but he was never far from our thoughts. It was a hard and lonely year. My health was breaking fast, but I managed to do most of the cooking, helped in the garden, raised chickens, and took in sewing to bring in a little extra money, and as Leslie grew stronger, she helped me more with the housework.

Our work was steady as clockwork, and by all doing our share we made a good crop; fifteen bales of cotton, four hundred bushels of corn, plenty of syrup and potatoes, and our own meat and lard. This Delta land is so rich, and there was no boll weevil then; but that was 1914 and cotton dropped to five and six cents a pound. So at the end of the year, after we had paid our rent, we had less than one dollar left for our year's work.

The second year we made a bigger crop, Bob and Bruce went to school till hoeing time, and the children were all well. But as the children grew stronger and became able to take care of themselves, I gave way more to my feelings, and once I let myself slacken my work a little, I realized how worn out I was. I was hardly able to be out of bed more than half the time, and the weaker I got, the more I seemed to worry and study about Frank. I looked back over our long hard life together, handicapped by his bad health and the death of our first children. I thought about how his life had been surrounded by mystery, and I wondered if I had been fair to my children or wronged them when I let him take his secret to the grave with him. I saw that if I lived much longer I would be a burden on them instead of a help, and now that they could get along without me I welcomed the thought of death.

In June of that year I thought sure death had come, and I was glad. A spider bit me on the back of my neck and blood poisoning set in. Our doctor told the children he couldn't save me, and I couldn't live to get to a hospital. I heard him, and I was glad. I would soon be with Frank. I was sitting in a chair with my forehead on a pillow on the table when he told them. I wasn't sorry for them or for myself. We would all be better off. But the children were crying, and I heard the doctor say, "I will wire Dr. Harrison of Tutwiler to come down on the early train. If your mother is living by daylight, let me know."

Dr. Harrison came. I heard them talking, far away like in a dream. He said, "Yesterday she had one chance in a thousand to live. Today she has none. There is no use to add to her suffering by operating. Her heart is so bad we couldn't give her anything to deaden the pain. It will soon be over."

Frank dropped down on his knees by my side, put his arm around me and said, "Mama, could you hear the doctor?"

My jaws were so stiff I could hardly speak, but I said, "Yes, son. Let me go in peace. You don't need me now."

He cried out, "Mama, Mama, don't say that. We need you more than we ever did in our lives. We can't let you go so soon after Father. Tell the doctor you will live."

Their love was pulling me back, forcing me to live on to the time when a mother wasn't needed. I told the doctor I was ready, and that I wasn't going to die. And I didn't. The children's love saved me, and I didn't know whether I was glad or sorry. But a few days later when Frank came to me, I was glad. He looked down at me and said, "Mama, this has made me see your hard work is over forever. If us boys can't do the field work and make a living we are pretty sorry sons. Ever since I was a little boy I could see how hard you were working, doing the work of one good man in the field and garden and the work of two women in the house. I tried then to figure out a way to stop it, and when you came so near death, I swore if you got well, it would be stopped, and it is stopped. You will never work in the field again."

His blue eyes were shining with love and determination, and I thought of another time long ago when he was a chubby little four-year-old boy out in the field with me. He was too small to work but thought it helped me for him to trot up and down the rows with me while I hoed. We stopped under a tree to rest his little legs, so tired from following me up and down. He dropped his chin in his hands, looked up at me with those same blue eyes, full of wonder, and as though he had just solved a problem, he said, "Mama, I been studyin' out a way to make your work easier when I get to be a man."

"Well, tell me, son," I said. "It rests me to know you are thinking of me."

"Mama, I fink of you all the time. And when I get to be a man I am going to dwess you in wed silk all the time, all the time. I fink you would look so sweet. And I am going to get you a big wed bicycle to wide to the field on."

How could I feel tired any longer? I grabbed him, hugged him tight, and said, "Son, I am rested now. I can hardly wait till you are a man—I love red silk so well."

When he spoke this time with the same love shining on his face, he didn't add the bicycle, as I was too feeble to need it, neither the red silk to make me look sweet in his eyes. But I knew now that I would stay with them as long as they needed me. And I think I have.

It was weeks before I could walk around the house even, and months before I could leave the bandages off my head. Leslie took full charge of me and of all household affairs; Frank took charge of all outside work. The little boys had long since had to stop school, and Leslie was tending to their lessons as well as her own studying. So time went on. We were getting along fine, but I was finding out every day that life for a widow was very different from life for a wife. What happened one day early that fall was just one example of the way widows and orphans are treated.

Cotton was just ready to pick. I was still wearing bandages around my head but could do my housework and sew some. Leslie was out nursing a sick neighbor. It was the children's first day picking cotton, and this was always a big event for them. They always raced to see who could pick the most. They all had their sacks that morning but Frank, and I still had his to make. He put my machine out on the front porch where it was cool and light and told the others to go ahead.

"I'll take my harpoon down to the lake," he said "while Mama makes my sack. And then I'll be in the field and beat you all by noon."

So they started their different ways. The lake was not more than a hundred feet from the house, and when I got the sack about done, I called Frank. He came on and set his gun down, still loaded with powder and the harpoon still in it ready to shoot. I was sewing up the last seam of his sack when he went in the house to change clothes, and he hadn't been in there but a minute when he came running out on the porch, looking scared to death, with nothing on but his overalls and just one strap of them over his shoulder. He jerked up his gun and rushed past me. I was sitting just at the top of the steps with my back to the road, and I turned to look. Right at the foot of the steps I saw a half-naked convict with an upraised club in his hand. Just as I turned, he saw Frank and whirled to run, Frank right after him. Neither of them had made a sound, and in spite of knowing how near I had just come to being killed, I had to laugh at that pretty race.

Frank didn't want to shoot him with the harpoon, for he knew it would go clear through his body. He had no shells. They ran a couple of hundred yards before the Negro stopped and threw up his hands. But Frank, not expecting him to stop, couldn't stop quick enough; he ran over the Negro and knocked him down; but he stepped back, still held the gun on him, and spoke for the first time, "Keep quiet, old nigger, for if I have to shoot you with this harpoon it will go clean through you."

I had called the children from the field, and now Frank hollered to Bob to bring him some shells and to Bruce to hitch up the team. "Hitch up quick as you can," he hollered. "We'll take this fellow home."

Just as they got the Negro in the wagon, their uncle, Charlie Lawlor, came along. He told Frank he had been hunting that convict all night with a crowd of other men. "He is a lifer and dangerous. How did you happen to capture him, boy?"

Frank told him, and he said, "Get in the wagon and drive. I'll go with you and guard him."

When they got over to the state farm and turned over the convict, Charlie told Frank he would go and collect the fifty dollars, and Frank could go on back home. Frank came in in such high spirits. He said, "Mama, I'm going to pay forty dollars on your doctor bill, and I'm going to give Uncle Charlie ten dollars for helping me."

But some way I had my doubts about that fifty dollars, for I had learned a lot since Frank died about the helplessness of orphan children in this world. And I knew as soon as I saw Frank's face, when he came back from his uncle Charlie's that night, that I had been right to doubt. He said in the littlest voice, "Uncle Charlie only gave me ten dollars, Mama. He said the rest belonged to him."

I said, "Frank, you will have to get used to that, son. But think how near I came to being killed. If you had been one moment later that convict would have clubbed me to death. So you saved my life, son. Isn't that better?"

His face brightened, and he said, "A thousand times better."

But my heart ached for him then, and for all of them.

Often I wonder how my children's lives would have been changed if Frank had got to make the trip he was planning back to England. As it was, each one of them except Bruce, who has never married, has made a home for himself in this little world of the Mississippi Delta. Frank is married, has two children, and makes a living farming and as an officer of the law. Edris is married to a Mississippi farmer and has one child, a boy sixteen years old. Bob grew to be a normal-sized man and would have been an artist if we had had the means to develop his gift. As it is, he is a carpenter. He, too, is married and has three children; the oldest, Helen, has Frank's faint bluish birthmark across the bridge of her nose and pure, bright, gold-colored hair. Leslie is married, has four little children, lives on a farm and works so hard. Bruce makes a living for him and for me, farming. None of them is rich or brilliant; each of them by hard work year in and year out makes a scanty living for himself and family. But Frank's main hope and mine has been realized; they are each one straight and honest.

But I know by a look in each of their eyes at times, and by a look in Bruce's eyes all the time, that they are misfits, fitted by their father's proud blood, his ideals, and the training he gave them to a life far different from the one that poverty and helplessness made the only way, after he was gone.

I ask for myself no better blessing from God than just to let me keep house for Bruce till I leave this world for a better one, if such can be, and I ask for nothing better to take with me than the memory of my life with Frank and the love of my children and grandchildren.

Postscripts

When the University Press of Mississippi undertook in 1991 to publish the story of Mary Hamilton's life, editor JoAnne Prichard discussed the project with Helen Dick Davis, then ninety-two years old, and her son Nick. Mrs. Davis dictated to Nick the account of the wanderings of Mrs. Hamilton's manuscript, presented in the preface of this book. The process of editing began. Mrs. Davis died in February 1992, but before she died, she had the satisfaction of seeing and going over the copyedited manuscript. After her death, as he put his mother's affairs in order and cleared out her papers, Nick Davis found a manuscript in Mary Hamilton's own hand, including a brief covering letter to Helen Davis and an account of her own early childhood in Missouri (written, as Helen Davis notes in her preface, "on cheap tablet paper"). He also found more pages of his mother's journals written during the same period. The Mary Hamilton holograph, which follows, complete and verbatim, besides containing a startling and vivid account of the 1811 New Madrid earthquake (as told to her by an aged survivor), confirms Mary's claim that she was no speller and had little formal education and Helen's claim that in editing she did not "touch her style nor embellish her material." Also following are several brief excerpts from Helen Davis's journals, written during the difficult days of the Great Depression in Tallahatchie County, Mississippi.

ELLEN DOUGLAS

HOLOGRAPH BY MARY HAMILTON
Verbatim Transcript

I Mary Mann was born in Randolph Co Illinois in 1866. the 4th child and first gurl of my pairants Calvin Mann & Elisabeth Ritching; My father one of 6 children all sittling in homes of thear own around the old home all raised familys there & if any living still there. all but

Father whither it was my coming in the world that brought him bad luck and caused him to be a wander over the country the rest of his life or whither it was his temper, for when I was 3 weeks old he had some trouble at a political meeting with a neighbor he only struck one lick with his fist. but that was enough to cause him to sell out start moving always on the move. never longer than 5 years in the north part of Ill then to Mo. right in the country when the war caused so much trouble. but the dearest country on earth to us children we were healhy happy education ment nothing to us while we got _____ school education and Father and Mother was bothe good old school presbyterians and tryed to bring us up in that faith but as there were no church of that kind we children formed our own ideas of religion. I found mine in nature. in the trees the hills mountains the flowers birds every living thing of that wild country we lived all over Mossiria until I was 17 then Father heard of the praire land in ark moved there to buy a home & settle down but before we could make a trade he took phneum and died. and there I met and married Frank Hamilton an Englishman in _____ then my work of love toil heardships and pleasure of raising my children and living for him still wandering from plase to plase searching for helth and last he found it. after 12 years in the wilderness of the Delta of Miss after loosing my first 3 children but here I felt like I have overcame all my troubles in my old age & can go in pease when life is done surrounded by my children and friends. my husband died 1914. I was left to struggle on with my 5 children to rais them accordin to his as well as my one idea of honesty truthe love to get all the good out of life they can by being good to others to live by the golden rule and leave the rest with God.

Dear Helen

Can you make head or tail of this my hands is weak but my brain is weaker but maby you can make something of it you see my life has been such a roving one it wold be hard to give dates of all plases I lived it would be like a Chinese puzzle.

I love you

Hamplton

Coming sometime in may if I get able

60 years ago Father moved to suthern Missouri on the Ark and Mo line in what was then called the sunk lands. We lived on a butiful Lake that was called little river. Fathers object was to raise cotton we had never seen cotton growing but had heard so much about it. Father thought it the quickest & easest way to get rich farming. as it was supposed to call for little capital and less work. but from the start my parrant see it wasnt going to be the grand sucess they heard it was but was used to failures so determined to get all the pleasure we could out of our stay in that plase as the whole country was a courisaty. we lived on the bank of the Lake it was all the way from a mile wide too three miles wide but shallow not over 4 feet deap from the bank to the channel where small steam boats traveled came out of the Mississippi river and could go to a town about 10 miles above our plase they were trading boats carried all kind of merchantdise they had no regulor landing for they couldnt run only in the narrow chanel but people could here it for miles puffing & blowing if they wanted to buy any thing all one had to do was to get in a John boat paddle out to the Chanal wave a white clothe the boat would stop eaven for a pound of tabacco up to a barrel of flour which was the biggest artical they sold. Whiskey was the plentifulest as there was a few half Indians scattered along the river but lots of white men got whiskey off the boat but whiskey didnot bother us as Father and Mother both looked on it as a dedly poison & sin they did not think it could ever bother us in any shape. but I'll tell of the tragidy that befel a poore little 14 yeare old girl and came so near claiming another little 8 year old girl & I the same age. but why talk of that till we get to it. This lake surfas was covered with green moss and broad leafed Yonkpins cattle all along the river kept fat on them they would wade out as far as they could eating the moss that seemed floating on the waters then swim eating as they went. to us children they seemed to be walking on there hind leggs but the most wonderful of all was the fish of all sizes from small perch to large cat & buffelow weighing 40 & 50 pounds they was caught with gigs. all good for food except turtles & gars there was soft shell and hard shell turtles I have seen them so large they looked like wash tubs walking upside down they would come out of the lake nights craul out in the sandy fields make there nest in the ground and lay there eggs they would be never less than 24 eggs and as many as 40 it was fun for my sister and I to hunt them eggs digg them out and break them in a crock

mix sand with them for play cakes. Father leased a peice of land for
cotton for the rent when ready to pick the first rowe was the landlords
then two for Father we only picked our own the landlord picked his
every one picked in baskets whither it was because clothe was to scarse
to have seaecs or because they didnot know any better and they sold
the cotton in the seed the nearest cotton market was 40 miles. but us
children loved the country and neighbors above all I never could get
our wandering about that strange land it was black sandy soil smothe
and level but broken with spots of pure white sand white as salt. that
part of the country would average about 4 to the acre some not more
than 12 feet across but some was 50 & 60 feet across and in the sumer
so that not a blade of grass would grow in them and a child could not
run across not even a small one barefooted they was called sand Blows.
in my childish mind I thought they were holes leading to the torment
and was afraid to put my foot even in the edge of one for fear I would
sink into the badplase. but an old Indian woman told us the true story
of the sunk land she was a frendly Indian about 95 years old she said
she was only a small child when the great Earthquake came 5 are 6
familys of whites and Indians living on the Mississippi river what was
now little river all at once it came with a rumble and roare like a storm
the earth began to shake and quiver it kept up for days the waters
powered over the bank soon overflowed all the country every family
had a canoe but began building raffs to save there familys and what
household goods they could all stock was drownded they were lucky to
save there selves the white people was so sure it was the end of the
world and the Indians and whites all joined in prayer of thanksgiving
that they were the chosen ones of the world that stood a chance to be
saved. they kept there rafts as clost togather as pasable and was pre-
paired to stand any hardships to be saved on all sides of them they
could here that rumble and shake there rafts would rock from side to
side then it seemed the earth would open water and mud would boil up
then with a roar muddy water would shoot up high as the tops of trees
it would some times blow great trees out by root and suck them back in
the ground out of site never to be seen again. but when the waters
went down that was the sand blows (but as I still thought satens suck
hole) she said one of the sand blows caught her fathers raft blowed the
tree up that there raft was tied to broke some of the logs loose sent it
sailing off they lost nearly all ther provisous all there meat of curse that

made all the kids cry for meat the one thing they couldnt get but one day some geese flew low over there raft and her dad shot one and it fell wounded on the raft she said her & her brothers & sisters fought over it tore it to peases ate it raw and it was the best meat she ever tasted but when the waters went down they could tell by the trees that they went more than a mile from there old house sites and the bank of the Miss river but there wernt no bank no river all gone nothing left but that ugly lake and that spotted ground but we soon found the river had left us lots of fish and that black sand soon made plenty of course soon deer & Bair was plentiful. that was the story the old Indian told us how much was so I cant tell but from the looks of the country I think it was. there were severel familys living in the sunk land along the lake some good some not so good all had from 1 to 2 children of school age but no school no church so my father told some of the men after crops was layed by he would teach a 3 months free school if they would all go in together and build some kind of a house or shed as the wether was warm so they put up a shed and Father taught school he ask no pay there was from 15 to 20 kids of all sizes atended 4 of his own. Father thought a school would bring the people closer togethers and in a way it did we were all well liked but as Father wouldnt join in any as the drinking bouts of the country some of them took afence but when they found he could hold his own but minded his own buisness they all respected him and before that 3 months school was out he had many friends but we was given to understand there were two things they would not have one was law and preachers was anothers and soon we was to found out how true it was one thing Father taught in his school was singing and us children could all sing pretty good. it was near the midde of November the weather was still plesant. Crops was all gathered and Father & Mother was thinking of staying another year. When it happened our closest and best neighbor lived less than half a mile of us they had two kids Sid 10 and Nellie 8 just my age my brother John was not 11 yet. so we make a pretty good team we had another neighbor Chamber a young couple with a small child. Mrs Chambers had a sister a pretty girl 14 years old she had came on to visit to her sisters they too lived on the lake bank Mr. Chamers had gone on the boat to the town 10 miles away with 3 of his neighbor men. Mrs Chambers came over to our house to see if Mother would let John and I as well as Nellie and Sid go stay till Mr. Chambers got home we all

four went after supper, we with the new girl was having a good time
playing all kinds of games with Mrs C joing in the baby laughing and
clapping her little hands. we were in the midest of our play all singing
when in came Mr C. looking half scared to death but the other 3 so
close behind. drunk one a big readheaded and red bearded fearce
looking giant of a man and the loudest one of the lot he had a jug he
layed it down on the floor and all 3 caught our hands jerked us over
the jug saying now sing ring aroud a jug damn you and gallop get some
life in you all. Mrs C. had picked up her baby who was screaming she
turned to her husband and said John what do you mean bringing these
drunk bruts home he tryed to reason with them tryed to make them
leave this big red bawled at him you know damned well what we cam
for so you just hand that gal over. Mrs C screamed and ran to her sister
with her baby in one arm put her other around the girl to protect her.
things was hapning so fast we were all crying the poor girl begging as
one of the other men jerked her away from her sister. old red had
knocked Mr. C down tyed him up and other shoved the little boys in
the kitchen and locked them in us two little girls ran for the door but
that big giant caught us shoved us in chairs told us to sing or you get
the same treatment. my brother hollered sing on you and Nellie for
gods sake. old red said that good if you sing you wont be hurt as we are
going to have some real fun and we want some musick. we began
crying & singing at the top of our voices. I want to be an angle. we
were to young to know what they were doing but thought they were
killing her tourching her to death and her sister to. she put the baby in
my lap saying hold my baby and save it if you can one of them brutes
grabed her threw her across the bed but just then her sister got the
front door opened managed to get under the house and all 3 brutes
after her I tiptoed to the door unlocked it John came out with a
butcher knife cut Chambers cords and we four children ran far home
Chambers told his wife to take the baby and go the save youre self &
that baby. I will get help that is all I can do we all burst in the house
out of breath crying so we couldn't hardly talk but among us made
them understand and for the first time in my life I heard the word
rape. Father took his muskit started out to rais a crowd. but when the
people found out who was leading the ourcry every one was afraid they
told Father if he valued his life and his wifes & childrens he wouldn't
interfear and only 3 or 4 picked up courag to go hunt them. What an

awful night for that poore sisters and for us all knowing she was suffering the worst torchers & nothing but death to releive her. about 3 the next morning we herd a moaning at the door mother unbarde the door there was that poore child crawling up the steps. her sisters cry of oh my _____ silver rings in my ears yet _____ 60 years it all comes back as vived as horable as that awful black night. she was brused and bleading her clothes almost all tore off begging her sisters to kill her to end it all. Father come home about sunup sick & tired discouraged Chambers begged Father to take his broken wife & sister _____ home to her Father & Mother they loaded up 2 wagons with what they could hoal of that broken home Father took them home the poore girl was still alive when he left them but died in less than a week the first thing Father done when he got home was load up his family with our household goods and get as far away as possible to a country _____ where law was _____ alowed. a sturdy hardy people not fearing man or the devel yet when I look back I wonder what saved us little girls it must of been they feared our Fathers when we got away from there Father wrote a full account to the St Louis papers but we never heard any more about it.

The Journal of Helen Dick Davis
Excerpts from 1931–1933

January 28, 1931
Sunny, hot January Day. Doors and windows open and sun streaming in. It lies in great blocks on the green and gray linoleum, and our son is standing tiptoe in his walker trying hard to fall on his face in order to devour the great warm sun on the floor. As a birthday present to our daughter on her third birthday we had brought the victrola here into the nursery and put it on a low stool in the corner by my desk so she can play it herself. Precisely speaking, it is a phonograph, with a lovely carved, flaring wooden horn. It came from my family's attic along with most of the other furniture in the room—the cot, the low table to hold the baby's basket and bath things, the small clothes bars. The table where we eat we bought for 50¢ at a junk store and painted green. The chairs we painted black, leaving the cane seats yellow. The stove we bought with my husband's last month's eight dollar check

from the government, which he draws from being a disabled veteran of World War I. The stove with its six little isinglass windows in the door makes me think of my grandmother, whom I loved. Yesterday Rube [my husband] stretched some coarse screen around it to protect our son's curious fingers.

Today Rube has gone to the County seat, on some committee to try and get help from the Red Cross. He has little hope of getting it. For some reason none of the returned World War I soldiers have any good to say for the Red Cross. The Salvation Army and the Jewish Relief Agency they praise, but mention of the Red Cross brings a rude guffaw, nine times out of ten.

Conditions here in the delta are very bad. An old Negro man came to the back door yesterday and said he and his wife have had nothing to eat but one rabbit in two weeks. They have made shoes of inner tubes. Actually the Negroes are better off than the class of white tenant farmers who, since the Negro migration to the north, has become a roaming class of ne'erdowells. Known as "poor white trash," "buckreys" and avoided alike by whites and blacks, their numbers have increased enormously since the shortage of Negro labor. This year, with banks breaking everywhere, most of the big delta land owners have no way of getting "furnish money" to feed their labor, and the road is full of Negroes and whites looking for homes. The few farmers able to feed their labor have no trouble getting all they want. The floating class of whites is suffering. Everyone turns them away. No one wants them unless he can't get Negro labor. So their present plight is terrible.

Yesterday Rube, driving to Charleston, passed a woman and four children on the highway. The littlest girl, about four years old, flagged him down. He stopped and when they asked for a ride to Charleston told them to get in. The woman said they had been walking since the day before, early in the morning. Had had nothing to eat and had slept in an empty cabin up the road. Had left the baby, too young to walk, with a neighbor. Rube bought them milk when they got to Charleston, but had no more to give them. Our own cow is without food and the taxes—on the eighty acres of land we purchased with rash optimism with our first check for $1600 for four stories sold the first year of our marriage—are due the first of the month.

April 1931

I wrote until midnight last night—Rube and the children asleep. And then when I did go to bed I couldn't sleep. Lay awake listening to the sounds outside. The moon made everything as bright as day. Two mocking birds singing their throats out, and now and then I heard the long sweet shrill cry of a kildeer passing overhead.

May 1931

I must try and make some starch and wash Rube's only pair of wash pants. It has turned suddenly so hot that woolen pants are unthinkable. I never made any starch. I am wildly impatient about all things except writing. With that I have unlimited patience, even on a day like this with the mercury at 102 on the front gallery in the shade. Dust rolls in from the road in front of the house. My patience with writing and my wild impatience with everything else is what makes me believe I can write. I'd go crazy if I had to live in the house with me rushing in and out, darting here and there trying to get the day's routine going of its own momentum, so I can sit down at my typewriter and write. I feel as if writing, successful writing, is going to burst in my mind like a forgotten word on the tip of my tongue, and suddenly blossoms. Until then there is little use crowding it. Or is that merely procrastination? I told Rube today that I thought when the word finally came to me, I bet I'd be able to write stories as easily as letters. He said, "There'll always be a difference—the difference between irrigated land and rain." I'm sure he's right. Just before coming to bed I had helped Rube skin three squirrels he had shot hunting that afternoon. I held the heads while he skinned them—but only after he took out the eyes. The brains were a great delicacy. I now know why butchers aren't allowed to serve on murder juries.

August 1932

Today and all these days of furious writing are too short. If only one could go back and take eternities off the days that have been so unendurably long in one's past and piece out these days of joy and creativeness that are so short. My brain is like a scrap bag—here a piece of a story, there a fragment of a character—silks and woolens, hot and cold, lace and ticking, velvets and calicos, and I don't even remember what the scraps are from. My brain is ugly like a yo-yo- quilt that women in small towns make and raffle off—endless little puffy round things, circles with the edges gathered tight, and sewed together in rows without respect to material or color—two thousand or more for one yo-yo quilt. Tasteless—what is taste anyhow? If they admire and get aesthetic pleasure from a yo-yo quilt—isn't it the same aesthetic pleasure *I* get with a beautifully pieced old quilt? Why is mine "good taste" and theirs "terrible taste"? In fact, *is* it?

October 1932

Townes Duncan, a planter near here, three days ago died of a heart attack. Yesterday I went to express, by my presence, my respect for him and sympathy for his wife, Lucy. Lucy and her husband's mother were sitting in the family room when I arrived. They greeted me cordially and went on with their sewing. "What are you sewing so industriously?" I asked, as no other words came to me. Lucy and the older woman exchanged blank glances, and looked down at their sewing. Lucy said nothing but Townes's mother said, "Why, you see, we're just keeping busy. I don't really know what we're sewing. Tea towels, I guess. This is a piece of old curtain. I'm just hemming. We've got to be doing something, you see. We hoed in the garden all morning."

I felt as if they were apt at any second to fly into a million pieces, as if every word she uttered was uttered to break an unbearable silence; as if their eyes were on the clock wondering how many more seconds they could count on my staying to be a flimsy distraction between them and the abyss of loss on the edge of which they trembled.

I understood for the first time why bereaved people rush around dyeing stockings and clothes black. The anguish of bereavement has to find some activity, and dyeing things black is activity connected with the dead loved one, the only activity that does not look forward to a future without them, but somehow honors the past with them.

Intense depression stayed with me all day and I was still lying thinking of Lucy and the tension in that room after I went to bed. As if the tension had suddenly become articulate, a sound shattered the dark outside, that brought me bolt upright. Rube, beside me, caught my arm and steadying me, held it. Shrill screaming, inarticulate words poured out into the darkness, then suddenly were muffled. "Somebody's got her inside the house," Rube said. "Some damn fool killed another one. I heard the shot. Did you?" I hadn't. "How do you know?" I said. "You can't mistake that death wail once you've heard it," he said.

He went to sleep long before I did. I lay wondering if articulate grief is easier to bear than numb, silent grief, and if it is healthier. Is it like physical pain—when it is not mortal, not deep, one cries out; but when a terrible thing happens like a leg being cut off, or a mortal wound, crying out is impossible. Was the bereaved Negro woman screaming in the quarters suffering as much as the silent Lucy and Townes's mother?

This morning when Lillie Belle came she told me old big Syl had killed Ace Lucas's boy. Ace's boy had married Syl's wife's daughter. She had left him and come home to her mamma and last night the boy came to beg her to come back to him. Big Syl shot and killed him. He left two children—just Nick's and Louvica's ages.

January 28, 1933

I am typing about four hours a day and working from two to three every night on this book which must be in by March first. God, if we can just win the prize. Mrs. Hamilton is still here.